CRANSWICK ON
PORSCHE

A modern interpretation of the Porsche story

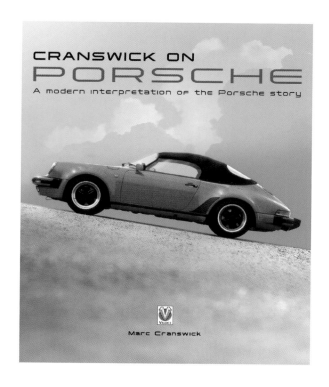

Marc Cranswick

CRANSWICK ON
PORSCHE
A modern interpretation of the Porsche story

VELOCE PUBLISHING
THE PUBLISHER OF FINE AUTOMOTIVE BOOKS

Contents

Introduction

Porsche – Established 1931

Ferry Porsche always insisted that Porsche was founded in 1931. This was the year his father, Dr Ferdinand Porsche, started the Porsche design bureau. Both before and after World War II, Porsche's design expertise was sought inside and outside Germany's car industry. Such wisdom gave rise to a textbook-definition sports car: the 356 (so called because it was Porsche's 356th work assignment).

What's so special about Porsche?

Porsches are fast, expensive and exclusive, but so too are rival sports cars from Ferrari, Maserati, Lamborghini and Jaguar. However, there are qualities that set Porsche apart from such illustrious competitors: for a start, radical design.

Dr Porsche was behind the most popular car of all time – the VW Beetle – and after WWII, the design was offered to automakers around the world, including Ford. They all passed, but Porsche's creation had the audacity to sell over 21 million examples, and stayed in continuous production for 65 years.

Even more audacious was Porsche taking this unlikely family-car hero and making it the basis for its first sports car – the revered 356. Using a layout others said was plain wrong, Porsche continued its thinking with the 911, a sports car acknowledged as a triumph of development over design.

Not content with achieving the impossible, after 27 years of confounding the critics, Porsche socked it to 'em again! Famous for air-cooled, rear-engined cars, Zuffenhausen tried its hand at water-cooled, front-engined cars. Porsche, a small automaker at the time, developed its front- and rear-engined sports cars, side by side for 20 years. Both kinds of Porsche were considered to be at the top of the sports car field. After proving it could play both games, Porsche concentrated its efforts on its traditional mid- and rear-engined sports cars.

Then there was the winning. Toyota spent an amount equal to third-world debt to win Le Mans in 2018. Other companies have won Le Mans too, but none as many times as Porsche: 19 and counting at the time of writing. In contrast to Lamborghini, which steered clear of factory-backed racing, Porsche's motorsport diversity is unequaled in the sports car world, winning the final 1973 Targa Florio with a 911 Carrera RSR; SCCA D-Production with a 924; the Monte Carlo Rally; and Formula One as a constructor and engine supplier. Even the humble 914 was no stranger to La Sarthe, and the giant 928 successfully tried its hand at record breaking; from production cars to specialized pure racers, Porsche has done it all!

To win, first you must finish, and Porsche's quality and reliability are legendary. The sturdy, autobahn-conquering design of Dr Porsche's Beetle continued with the cars that bore his name; it's something Italian and English rivals can't match – nor the UAW nightmare that is Corvette. It's a quality even 21st century, bean-counter-loving Mercedes can't claim. From winning on the racetrack to modern resale value, Porsche quality can be trusted, and is by many. Indeed, Porsche carried its reputation for durability (once associated with its air-cooled VWs) into the modern post-Beetle era.

Porsche was expert in the business of keeping going when it came to road and race. This longevity was matched by a commercial performance rivals like TVR could only dream of. The air-cooled 911 was one of those rare volume-produced cars that didn't need advertising – good times and bad, it got around. With over 250,000 914/924s sold, chances are you know them as well. For the era under consideration, Porsche AG was an independent company. This was maintained for so long, because Porsches sold well.

When so maany cars are sold all over the world, you are going to reach and influence lots of people. Porsches have been featured in all kinds of media, and many have been inspired to express Porsche's sporty and quirky character in art. So what's so special about Porsche? Nothing Ferrari, Aston Martin, Corvette and Jaguar don't already know … and wish they had themselves!

Marc Cranswick

Wide white Continental tires were appropriate, since '51 MY represented the Porsche 356's North American debut. The 356 cost the same as a Cadillac, and just 32 were sold that year. (Courtesy Porsche)

In the '70s, the 911 was brown but never down! (Marc Cranswick)

For high-flyers in the '80s, the 911 Carrera 3.2 was a dream car par excellence. (Courtesy Porsche Cars GB)

The original 1977 240bhp Porsche 928 evolved into the 350 horsepower 928GTS. The V8 coupe also bequeathed its Weissach-axle thinking to the 993. (Courtesy Chuck Zachman)

Foreword

By Mr Alois Ruf Jr

I was infected by the Porsche bug in my early years. I was just 13 when my father, Alois Sr, and I were unexpectedly introduced to a Porsche 356 that a gentleman had crashed at the side of the road. Luckily, the man was fine, but the machine was damaged. We ended up buying this 356 and my father and I started a project to repair it. Working night and day, the car was reborn to perfection.

After enjoying the car for almost a year, we sold the 356 to a man tapping on our window during a short stop – this encounter made us realize the scale of enthusiasm for these cars, and turned out to be the start of RUF Automobile and of a lifelong love story with Porsche.

In the early '70s, we settled our focus on the modification and improvement of the 911. In 1987, we came up with the CTR/Yellowbird concept, which propelled us into the limelight and into modern pop culture.

In 2017, we made the decision to present an all-new carbon monocoque CTR/Yellowbird as a true technical evolution of the original CTR. This purist CTR/Yellowbird concept showcased all of RUF's technical and emotional know-how, creativity and experience: it represents our ongoing love affair!

My passion for the history of Porsche has inspired my own personal philosophy and the philosophy of RUF Automobile. Today, my lovely wife and business partner, Estonia Ruf, shares this passion, and she is my greatest support.

So, I hope all readers and petrolheads thoroughly enjoy reading *Cranswick on Porsche*.

Mr Alois Ruf Jr
RUF Automobile CEO

1987 CTR Yellowbird

The CTR received its certification for normal road use. This incredible car, a 469bhp, twin-turbo coupe, exceeded the top speed world record for production cars on the Nardo Racetrack at a rate of 342kmh/213mph!

Foreword

By Joe Ligo

I will never forget the first time I drove a Porsche on a racetrack. I am not a professional driver, and (unlike many people who love cars) I have no delusions regarding my ability. I have driven a few hot laps in various cars over the years, but all my seat time in Porsches has been on public roads with clearly posted speed limits.

So, one day in February, when I wheeled out of the pits in a turquoise Porsche 911 GT3 RS, I was determined to find out why so many people loved these cars so much. Was there really 'no substitute' as Porsche advertising claimed?

By the time I reached the second turn, I understood. The car felt absolutely magnificent. It stayed locked to the pavement and reacted instantly to my slightest whim. The highly bolstered seats held me perfectly in place, yet were completely comfortable. Every part of the car felt as if it had been sharpened, dialed-in, and tested to perfection. Years of ecstatic articles in auto magazines finally made sense: now I understood the Porsche phenomenon.

When I got out, a co-worker with much more experience than me asked how I liked it. I told him it was amazing. He said with a grin, "Yeah, anybody can look like a hero in that car."

And right there is the secret to Porsche. For decades they have been building cars that give their drivers an experience they cannot get anywhere else. This book captures that phenomenon as it evolved through the years, and explains how, after all this time, there really is no substitute.

Joe Ligo
Automotive historian and creator of AutoMoments

Ferry Porsche with the revised '60 MY 356B. The 356B restyle was largely the work of his son Butzi Porsche, who would go on to do the 911. (Courtesy Porsche)

Dr Ferdinand Porsche – the man behind the name

Many know the name and brand, but relatively few know that at the age of 17 Ferdinand Porsche surprised his father by wiring the family home for lights, chimes and even intercom! Born in Austria in 1875, the good doctor had an interest in electricity and propulsion, and he learnt a metal working trade from his tinsmith father. At trade school he exhibited the lowest grades in class. However, his obsessive manner combined with many light bulb moments would result in a prolific design legacy with patents aplenty.[1]

Ferdinand Porsche wasn't limited to trade school in his home town of Reichenberg. A man of great vision, doctorates could wait. The title was in fact honorary, bestowed by the Technical University of Austria in 1916. And why not? The Austrian Emperor had just given Dr Porsche a medal for aero engine work, and when working at Lohner in 1900, Porsche created the only front-drive Porsche to date. It was a vehicle with his 'Mixtdrive' concept: a gasoline engine generated electricity via a dynamo, powering electric motors in the front hubs. In other words, a hybrid!

At the time (and since), Dr Porsche was proclaimed as one of the greatest automotive engineers, albeit including the likes of Adolf Hitler, stating that Ferdinand Porsche was Germany's greatest.[2] It's also true that Dr Porsche worked for a number of companies before setting up shop himself – Austro-Daimler being just one. A major reason for this was Porsche's hot headedness and outspoken nature. At one Austro-Daimler board meeting, many obscenities were spoken to management.

Porsche design bureau 1931

Ultimately, an unsuccessful design streak and a merger of Daimler and Benz saw Dr Ferdinand Porsche move on and form his own design consultancy. However, not before he delivered a few expletives during his resignation from what was now Mercedes! Dr Porsche was like Sir Alec Issigonis, a great big-picture man, and to bring his ideas to engineering fruition, the new 1931 design bureau had a talented staff.

The staff at Porsche's Stuttgart-based bureau included ex-Steyr man Josef Kales, gearbox specialist Karl Frolich, and Karl Rabe. Rabe was an old associate (going all the way back to 1913[3]) and protégé of Dr Porsche with an aviation background. Prior

A 1955 oval rear window version of Doctor Porsche's immortal Beetle. As Ferry Porsche said in 1985, the post war mobility of the West German public was greatly aided by his father's work. (Courtesy Syme Magazines)

This is the first Porsche 356 completed at the Stuttgart works on April 6, 1950. Gmünd-made 356s were aluminum paneled. Steel cars were heavier at 785kg. (Courtesy Porsche)

Far left: Dr Porsche with the Porsche 356. He realized his dream of making a sports car that bore his name. (Courtesy Porsche)

Left: Dr Porsche and Ferry, with the 356's T369 flat-four of 1950-51. From the early '50s to the early '90s, Ferry Porsche had a guiding hand over Porsche's operation. (Courtesy Porsche)

The Dannenhauer & Strauss coachbuilt 356 cabrio of Jurgen Grendel shows that, early on, buyers went to specialists for that custom touch. (Courtesy Volkswagen AG)

Above: Privateer racer Gilberte Thirion, with her 1951 Porsche 356SL. Pictured in 1952, there were four 356SLs out of the 50 aluminum-bodied Gmünd coupés. (Courtesy Porsche)

Below: Thieu Hezemans at Zandvoort (Holland), putting his lightweight 356SL through its paces, in a Dutch Grand Prix support race. (Courtesy Porsche)

to spending the rest of his working life at Porsche, he had been the chief engineer at Austro-Daimler. Retiring in 1966, he went on to become a senator.

Another member of staff was Josef Mickl, who was Porsche's aerodynamicist; this was an important new area, given how streamlining had come to the fore by the 1930s.

The final main member of the design bureau was Dr Porsche's own son: 21-year-old Ferdinand Porsche II, also known as Ferry Porsche. Ferry needed no encouragement to enter the family business. The design and construction of motor cars was something he wished to devote his whole life to, and it came to pass. Ferry was actively involved in Porsche design, and Dr Porsche had encouraged drawing board proficiency. However, Ferry was also good in the field, testing Porsche creations.

Ferry Porsche tested the 1930s mid-engined Auto-Union racing car, an example of the Porsche bureau's pioneering in the mid-engined competition field. During a Nürburgring evaluation, Ferry came up with the LSD (limited-slip differential) that helped the handling of the Auto-Union racer. Later, Ferry and some Porsche technicians were photographed assembling and fitting the T369 motor during late 1940s development; this power plant would power the 356s of 1950-51, the first production car to bear the Porsche name. To emphasize the Germanic importance of function, Ferry opined that even the most beautiful watch is useless if it doesn't work.

Dr Porsche didn't want Ferry to race cars: he reasoned that he had only one son, but many people willing to drive his cars. One such individual was Herbert Linge, a former Porsche apprentice and the first man hired in 1947, with respect to the imminent start of 356 production. Linge was famous for always bringing his toolbox and racing helmet to a circuit. Porsche even hired out Linge to other automakers concerned with racing, with Linge returning with useful rival information.

In the post-war era, the Porsche design consultancy did the Type 113 small diesel tractor for Piero Dusio. It was productionized by Allgaier Tractors in the '50s. (Courtesy Porsche Cars GB)

Herbert Linge devised a quick fix to save Hans Herrmann's Mille Miglia class victory. A multi-tasker, Linge even drove the new 911 into sixth place on the 1965 Monte Carlo Rally. He also drove the camera car for Steve McQueen's *Le Mans* movie. Linge came ninth overall, despite having to stop several times to reload the film camera! Herbert Linge was truly a fast racing driver. The future would see a move away from custom coachbuilt bodies placed on a supplied chassis and driveline. With this trend and the eventual Porsche brand cars in mind, it's good that Porsche had an in-house body designer. This was 27-year-old Erwin Komenda, someone who was part of the era when jello-mold curved bodies and faired-in headlamps came to prominence. The form also served to conceal a rear air-cooled motor.

Wartime work

It couldn't have been easy working for Dr Porsche, who forcefully directed his team to carry out his ideas, just so. However, being quite the P T Barnum showman, he had a knack for attracting work for his consultancy. Between the first and second world wars Porsche was into helicopters, patented the use of torsion bar springs for cars, and even designed farm tractors.

Top right: Marshall S Green with his new 1952 Silver Fish Gray 356 1500S coupe at the top of Mount Equinox, Vermont. (Courtesy http://quantumrun356.com)

Centre: By 1954 model year, US importer extraordinaire Max Hoffman was taking one third of 356s produced! (Courtesy Cornell Publishing)

Below: This 1952 Porsche 356 belonged to racer Betty Haig. It subsequently became part of UK Porsche importer AFN's collection. (Courtesy Porsche Cars GB)

There was that common thread of propulsion, and with Hitler becoming German chancellor in 1933 what happened next was inevitable. Dr Porsche's Mixtdrive concept had been used in WWI. It permitted electric carriages to cross weak bridges over the Alps, where trains couldn't go. One such carriage even moved the largest road-transported artillery piece – a Škoda mortar. The 26-ton barrel fired a 1-ton shell! In WWII, Mixtdrive also featured on Porsche's version of the Tiger tank. Dr Porsche was also behind the Daimler-Benz DB 600-piston engine that powered the Messerschmitt 109.

However, the best known creation of the Porsche design bureau was the VW Beetle. Hitler wanted a people's car for workers of the Third Reich, a vehicle to go with Germany's new autobahn network. One could purchase a KdF Wagen (KdF standing for *Kraft durch Freude*, meaning 'strength through joy'), using a book of coupons. The color was black, which would have pleased Henry Ford – the concept of people in a worker's paradise, aka totalitarian state, where everyone saved up to drive the same kind of car, painted the same color. "The State will decide and provide."

The Trabant thought wouldn't have occurred to Angela Merkel alone. However, the Beetle was no Trabant, and perhaps folks would like to drive their neighbour's car, if it was a Porsche? The Führer had some definite ideas concerning the people's car. He informed Dr Porsche about these at the Kaiserhof Hotel in Berlin in May 1934.[4]

Hitler intimated an air-cooled car capable of carrying two adults and three children at 100kph (62mph). The fuel consumption (six liters per 100km) and the price (1000 Reichmarks) were both rather miserly. However, if anyone could get the job done, it was Dr Porsche. Hitler, upon seeing the Porsche design bureau's Type 60, insisted on a lower bonnet line and the importance of the aerodynamics.

Hitler was no automotive visionary. The requirements he outlined were auto fashion, or hope, at the time. In any case, the Porsche bureau completed technical drawings of the people's car by 1937. The KdF Wagen initially had a 985cc flat-four,

Prince Metternich and Baron Treffe's 356 1500S convertible, finished 11th in this 1952 edition of the Carrera Panamericana. (Courtesy Porsche)

and all independent suspension. The motor was enlarged to the pre '54 Beetle's 1131cc in 1942 for the amphibious Schwimmwagen.

This larger motor was then passed on to later military Beetles called Kubelwagens.[5] The KdF Stadt was renamed Wolfsburg after the war, and the Kubelwagen became Herbie the Love Bug. Herbie finished his days in Mexico in 2003, with 21,529,464 copies made! Sales peaked at almost 400,000 units per annum in America with 1968 model year. Each one of those Beetles was imported from what became West Germany, and VW became the number three automaker in the world.

The engineering brilliance of the Beetle came courtesy of Porsche. No wonder VW reached an agreement that Porsche wouldn't design an economy car for a rival until 1973. It has been alleged that Porsche got one Deutschmark for every Bug built. In addition, VW's managing director Heinz Nordhoff employed Dr Porsche as a consultant from September 1948. Nordhoff went on to have a great working relationship with Ferry. Indeed, Porsche itself re-established ties to the thriving VW after the war, specifically with regards to parts supply and project consultation. However, Porsche would enter the 21st century as an independent sports car maker, as it had been since 1948.

Credit for the VW, and the early Porsche flat-four motor, should go to a young Austrian engineer named Franz Reimspiess. The Bug's 1930s 948cc 'E-Motor' had some advanced alloys, and ingenuity was needed to make the Bug's 990RM price a reality. The OHV E-Motor did this and more. The Bug's design origins came from both in and outside

One-armed racer Otto Mathé, taking his 356/2 1100 Gmünd coupe to victory in the 1953 International Austrian Alpine Tour. (Courtesy Porsche)

A 1956 356A at Shoshone Valley, Wyoming. *Auto Motor und Sport's* Uli Wieselmann said the 356A's handling was safe enough, even for dear granny! (Courtesy Eric Green)

The Porsche 356 Cabrio was a style icon from day one. No wonder Princess Grace of Monaco had one! A 1957 356A is present. (Courtesy Porsche)

Porsche. The central backbone chassis concept was courtesy of Rover and French firm Simplicia, early in the 20th century.

Within Porsche's own consultancy, there was the luxury Wanderer, an Auto-Union member. Then there were small car prototypes created for motorcycle company Zündapp: the early '30s Type 12, and the 1934 Type 32 for NSU. The latter featured the Beetle's eventual torsion bar suspension. After the war, VW bought Auto-Union (DKW) and NSU, making the Bug a very voracious insect! Even earlier, in 1926, Viennese engineering student Béla Barényi completed his auto design thesis on a car like the Beetle. Barényi showed his work to Dr Porsche in 1931. Then there was the contemporary Tatra Type 97. The Type 97 was a small, rugged flat twin air-cooled ride from Czechoslovakia; a Czech people's car and Bug rival, squashed by the Germans when Hitler's troops occupied Czechoslovakia. A mere 500 Type 97s were made before the Tatra assembly line was turned over to weapons manufacture for the Third Reich's war effort.

Type 97 had something in common with Porsche's own Type 12 and Type 32: they were all rather pricey to produce. All with nary a hope of meeting Hitler's 990RM edict. The 1937 Tatra Type 87 also certainly cleared the price tag high jump.

This large, luxury '30s dream car was made, and had a 95mph streamlined 2.9-liter air-cooled V8.

A bigger Bug there never was, for this limo's V8 lived in the tail of its backbone chassis. Said motor was behind the rear axle line, like the Beetle, and contributed to Tatra's legendary tail happy handling reputation.

The great Hans Ledwinka

On the subject of '30s streamlining, the cutting edge work of Viennese duo Edmund Rumpler and Paul Jaray should be noted. The basic Beetle ideas were not unique to the Porsche design house. However, there is one important engineer, a contemporary of Dr Porsche, whose work many, including Dr Porsche, referenced. His name was Hans Ledwinka.

Ledwinka's story is interesting due to its parallels to Porsche's. And yet, there are great differences between him and the good doctor of Stuttgart.[6]

Born in 1878, Hans Ledwinka picked up his trade knowledge from a locksmith uncle. Like Porsche, he entered a fledgling European auto industry, and after the reorganisation caused by World War I he called Czechoslovakia his home. Unlike Porsche, however, Ledwinka was a Slavonic lateral thinker able to put his engineering ideas into practice under his own steam. Not a hothead, he was respected and was always asked to return to companies he had previously worked for.

Indeed, Hans Ledwinka was a problem solver. He corrected the work of others, in addition to displaying his own personal creativity. Matching Dr Porsche, Ledwinka had also worked at Steyr, and in light of his successful tenure there he was invited back to Nesselsdorf. The company he returned to was the newly named Tatra of 1922. It was here that Ledwinka left his mark with the Type 87 and 97. Tatra was a pioneer of independent rear suspension, and Hans Ledwinka was involved with the scary, oversteer-seeking, swing-axled backbone chassis of the Type 87 V8.

Long before Porsche started refining their Gmünd coupés, Dr Porsche himself mentioned occasionally looking over Ledwinka's shoulder. It seemed luck wasn't on Ledwinka's side either. Like Porsche, he was jailed for alleged war work, but with no one on the outside to pull strings he remained imprisoned for six years.

After the war, Tatra filed an intellectual property lawsuit against VW. It was contended that ten patents had been infringed. The court agreed that Tatra and Ledwinka's work had originated earlier. Plus, by the dawn of the '60s many folks were driving a 'Wagen' embodying Ledwinka's touch – ie the Bug! In 1961, VW made a financial settlement but Hans Ledwinka didn't receive a cent. In 1967, he died in obscurity and relatively poor.

The doctor goes to jail

Dr Porsche also endured troubled times after the war. During the conflict, the Porsche team designed

Below: North American importer Max Hoffman's first try to create the ideal American 356, the 1953 Type 540 America Roadster. (Courtesy Porsche)

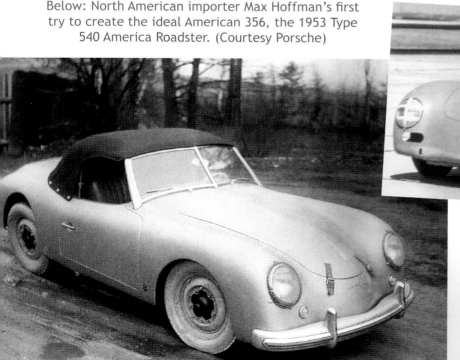

Above: All 14 of the Type 540 America Roadsters that landed in America wound up racing, just like this example piloted by Jack McAfee at the 1953 Moffett Airfield race. (Courtesy Porsche)

– amongst other things – a tank called Maus. Complying with Hitler's needs, this vehicle could cope with 10ft of water and turn within its own 33ft length. The Maus was, in fact, the world's largest tank! So it was only natural that the good doctor got caught up in subsequent war reparations.[7]

The Porsche design bureau had moved to Gmünd in Austria by 1944 to carry out war work in security. After the war a Porsche delegation, including Dr Porsche and Ferry, was invited to the French-controlled sector of Baden-Baden. The purpose was to discuss the creation of a French people's car. A rival party came to power and promptly placed the Porsche party in jail for work done under the Third Reich. It seemed the design invitation was a trap.

Political and commercial interests were afoot. During the war, Dr Porsche kept Pierre Peugeot from being jailed by the Nazis quite a few times, but then Monsieur Peugeot filed false claims against Dr Porsche to get him imprisoned. The French just didn't want Herbie breathing down their small car necks. The Bug might even have stormed the Bastille, by being built on French soil![8] Given the number of countries the VW ended up being assembled in, the French fears were justified. Credence was lent to the theory that France didn't want a small car rival, and the invitation was a trap due to this, when Renault consulted Dr Porsche (at the time incarcerated) concerning development of the crucial Renault 4CV!

Porsche was no fan of Hitler; he was apolitical on the subject of the Nazis. Louise Piëch, Dr Porsche's daughter and elder sister of Ferry,

organised the release of her father, brother and husband, Anton Piëch. Louise Piëch was a successful racer, and would go on to manage the many business interests of the Porsche clan for many years.

Organising the release was one thing, finding bail money was another. Here, Karlo Abarth was of indirect assistance. Viennese born, Abarth was married to Anton Piëch's secretary, and introduced Italian industrialist Piero Dusio to Ferry. Dusio supplied boots to the Italian army, and was linked to sports cars that utilised Fiat hardware. Dusio wanted a grand prix racer, and the Porsche design staff could help. The 1948 Cisitalia Porsche 360 GP car, was a mid-engined, flat twelve-cylinder project, with driver-selectable all-wheel drive.

Porsche had the pedigree of its '30s Auto Union racer to draw upon, but the Cisitalia never came to grand prix fruition because Mr Dusio ran out of cash. Fortunately, there was enough from the design fee to spring Ferry from jail after six months. Dr Porsche was released in 1947, and his health did suffer from the experience.

A 356A Speedster mit hardtop! Ferry wasn't too happy about the low rent, low profit margin Speedster. He felt a Porsche should be more luxurious and refined. (Courtesy Porsche)

Above & opposite: With the Speedster's upscale 1959 356D (Drauz) replacement, and Scandinavian Airlines, one would be flying first class. A discerning lady would prefer the quality of coachbuilder Drauz. (Courtesy Porsche)

However, if there was one thing that kept him going, it was the dream of a sports car; it had been Dr Porsche's lifelong ambition to make his own sports car, and that dream was about to come true!

Type 356 – The First Porsche

While in his mid-30s, Dr Porsche designed and drove a sports car with a low drag, tulip-shaped body. This racer, with its small frontal area, was driven by Dr Porsche at the Prinz Heinrich Trials of 1910. In his years of Austro-Daimler tenure, Dr Porsche designed a one-liter racer for investor Count Sascha Kolowrat. Predictably called the Sascha, this mini marvel won its class in the 1922 Targa Florio. In spite of this background, interest was muted. Austro-Daimler bosses didn't want this sports car, nor a people's car.

This indifference was part of the reason Dr Porsche resigned and departed the company. The sports car concept was taken over to Porsche's own consultancy but the Third Reich saw no purpose in a sports car based on the people's car, so Porsche designed the mid-engined V10 water-cooled Type 114 sports car, though it never went into production. Then there was the Type 64, a Bug-based sports car that resembled the Type 114. Getting warmer,

the Type 64 had a tuned Bug flat-four in the tail. This sports car was ready for the September 1939 Berlin–Rome–Berlin road race. Three Type 64s were constructed. Unfortunately, the outbreak of WWII put the kybosh on the road race, and the road racer.[9]

Dr Porsche wasn't alone in being bitten by the sports car Bug: Ferry was into the species as a hobby before the war. He drove a supercharged Beetle ragtop. The realisation soon came that a vehicle with this kind of power, but less weight, could be a genuine mover and shaker. Once bailed out of jail, Ferry started turning the dream into reality. It was at Gmünd in June 1947 that he and Karl Rabe commenced work on the Porsche bureau's 356th project: Type 356! The body for this bolide was done by Erwin Komenda, and it seemed all roads came from Porsche's racing past.

In form and in substance the first 356 prototype took inspiration from the '30s Auto Union racer, the 1.5-liter Cisitalia and the Type 64 Bug sportster, closely resembling the latter two vehicles. Indeed, there was much in common with the subsequent Speedster. That is, a low windshield, disappearing top, and no side windows. The Gmünd coupe gave rise to the Porsche 'upside down bathtub' calling

card – an iconic look that continues to define the marque in the 21st century. In substance, the 356 prototype adhered to cutting edge racer practice, with its midship layout.

The first 356 ran around in chassis form in March 1948. The chassis followed the previously mentioned racers by featuring a space frame. The body itself had aluminum panels. However, pretty quickly, Ferry had a change of heart, and took it closer to Dr Porsche's Beetle. The suspension, steering, brakes, motor and gearbox were already VW Beetle stuff on the prototype, except the flat-four was turned the wrong way around! It soon became clear a mid-engined mobile, wouldn't have much space for folks or their luggage.

It seemed practicality determined the Porsche 356's rear engine placement. In a 75th birthday interview with journalist Steve Cropley, Ferry said customers wouldn't have liked a mid-engined 356. Ferry Porsche believed in an all-purpose sports car; a car with enough accommodation, durability and ability to cope with all weathers and road conditions. It was the Porsche way to have all this and be able to drive flat out anywhere.

There was a proving ground – the road that goes up Austria's highest mountain, called the Gross Glockner Pass – that was used to see if a car measured up to the Porsche ideals. As Ferry said, "… not every modern car still has its brakes at the bottom. But a Porsche does."[10] He was happy with the way the mid-engined 356 handled Gmünd's mountain roads. Later in 1948, the Type 356/2 resembled the car that would soon be close to the hearts of many a car lover.

The second draft had a punt-type platform chassis, topped with a body that was, at this stage, aluminum. At the front were VW-style independent trailing arms and transverse torsion bars, and at the rear were independent swinging half axles, radius arms and transverse torsion bars. Worm and roller steering and four wheel drum brakes would have been no surprise to the Bug owner. Nor, the infamous placement of the hotted up VW flat-four … aft of the axle line!

In truth, VW didn't make a flat-four like this. Power for the 1086cc motor was a Porsche 35+bhp, not VW's 25bhp. A modest 7:1CR, with modified heads and dual downdraught Solex carbs, delivered an un-Beetle like 80mph top speed. With a 0-62mph time of 23 seconds, the Porsche was in the European style of high cruising speed, but with modest acceleration.

Ferry Porsche likened cars to watches, on the subject of reliability, and the prototype 356 may have been a beautiful timepiece, but it was having trouble keeping good time. When going to the Porsche family estate of Zell-am-See, Austria, the mid-engined Type 356 suffered a buckled frame. The prototype's torsion bar suspension housing nearly collapsed. Fortunately, a resourceful Ferry was able to effect a repair using two pieces of scrap iron borrowed from road workers! Such shenanigans were not disclosed when the 356 made its international debut at the 1949 Geneva Auto Show.

A coupe and a ragtop were on display, and interest was great. This continued when the new sports car was shown to a gathering of major VW dealers and overseas importers: 37 cars were promptly ordered. Of course, the first Porsche patron was a Swiss gentleman called Herr von Sunger. He allowed the journal *Automobil Revue* to test his 356. A positive revue generated further orders for the new sports car. The demand was there, but what of the supply?

Initial series production took place in a makeshift garage like Gmünd. The 356 was produced in sporadic fashion during 1949, but the signs were positive. That year, in terms of parts supply and other regards, Porsche rebuilt links with the now-booming Volkswagen. Porsche also needed new works. The firm had been in Zuffenhausen before the war, but the old facility was now occupied by the US motor pool. Porsche was supposed to be moving out soon.

Porsche's interim home was a rented Stuttgart workshop, care of the Reutter Coachworks. This concern had secured the tender to build 500 Porsche 356 bodies. Indeed, given the delayed American departure due to the Korean War, Ferry and co would be at the Reutter workshop during 1950-51.

The first Stuttgart-built 356 came to be in Easter 1950. The Reutter-bodied cars were quite different to the Gmünd editions. The latest Porsche 356s were easier to make, steel-bodied cars.

Fifty of Komenda's alloy-bodied Gmünd coupés were retained for racing. The 356 was already showing the Porsche credo of evolution and 'polishing the diamond.' Erwin Komenda worked up a smoother body, with a higher waistline. Then there was the iconic V-shaped roof, which accompanied a split screen. These latest 356s still used VW parts, but better VW parts.

With all the progress came the sadness of Dr Ferdinand Porsche's passing in January 1951, at the age of 75.[11] In March 1951, the 500th Porsche 356 was built. Work stopped for one hour, and workers gathered around car number 500. On this car, a wreath and placard were placed. Dr Albert Prinzing, an instrumental figure in helping to restart Porsche's production, said a few words.

Along with the changes in production venue, there were improvements to the 356 – like more power! In 1951, a 1286cc car was announced. This '52 MY 1300 took the 1100's 40 to 44 horses. Torque rose from 51lb/ft to 59lb/ft, enough to drop the 0-62mph time by 1.5 seconds to 22 seconds, and increase top speed from 87mph to 90mph. The 1100 would continue through the 1954 model year, and the 1300 was quickly followed by the 60bhp 1500, with 75 pounds of twist.

The 1488cc motor was a complicated solution to a Porsche power problem. The 1300's bore was at the limit, so Porsche used a roller bearing crankshaft (RBC) to increase the stroke within a VW crankcase. The RBC was an intricate 13-part affair made by Hirth. It involved more frequent engine overhauls for the VW/Porsche OHV flat-four.

Along such lines, the 1953-54 RBC 1300 Super had 60bhp and 64lb/ft, 0-62mph dropped to 17 seconds, and top speed rose to 99mph. The 1951-52 1500 trumped these readings with 15.5 seconds and 105mph respectively; it was the first production Porsche to break the 100mph barrier.[12] It would take the all-wheel drive Gruppe B 959 to break 200mph!

With a desire for more, not less, demand for 1100s and 1300s gradually diminished. Porsche needed a regular 1500, so along came the 55bhp plain bearing 1500 with 55bhp for 1954 and 1955 MYs. However, with Hirth having invested so much loot in the RBC version, and this unit now being

a reliable race motor, the 70 horse 1500S (Super) continued to the close of 1955. Porsche 356s after 1952 featured a Porsche four-speed gearbox. To cope with the escalating power of Porsche powerplants, Zuffenhausen introduced its all-synchro four-speed box for all flat-fours in 1952. The gearbox was based on a rejected VW design. Herbie wouldn't get a fully synchro four-speed until 1961! Well, there was a reason one paid more for a Porsche. In 1950, the 356, at 10,000 DM, was already double the price of a VW Beetle, but sold well as buyers were willing to pay for Porsche's engineering refinements.

That four-speed worked a transaxle through an indirect shift linkage. For many, this air-cooled VW and Porsche mainstay has felt vague enough for Luke Skywalker to call on The Force for guidance. However, Porsche wisdom was seldom questioned.

Porsche synchromesh was designed by Leopold Schmidt for the Cisitalia GP car. It was so good that the design was taken up by many companies, and proved a sound royalty source. The world paid Dr Porsche for designing a better mousetrap!

The winter of 1951/52 saw a one-piece windshield accompany the 1500's introduction. Zuffenhausen was achieving sufficient production volume for such niceties. So auf wiedersehen split screen, and hello new bumpers. These were mounted higher and further forward than before. Rectangular taillights also saw former round units deep-sixed, and the 1500 motor became the first unit with an Alfinger crank.

However, this all paled next to Porsche's next big step … the 356A. 🐎

A 1958 356A Carrera GS is displayed. The 356
Carrera was the first road-going Porsche to
attain 100 horsepower. Its four-cam engine was
the brainchild of Porsche's future managing
director, Dr Ernst Fuhrmann. (Courtesy Porsche)

356A – Polishing the diamond

The Porsche 356A made its debut at the Frankfurt auto show of September 1955. The regular 1500 was toast, and in came the new 1582cc 1600. It would be MY 1971 before the Beetle got a 1600! There was the regular 60bhp, 81lb/ft Type 616/1 1600, and the 75 horse Type 616/2 1600 Super edition with 86 pounds of twist. The latter could reach 108mph and did 0-62mph in 14.5 seconds. The increased displacement allowed Porsche to increase compression ratios and take advantage of the new mid-'50s higher octane gas.

The FIA had also introduced a new 1600cc class limit for touring and grand touring cars. Naturally, Porsche was interested in this for 'win on Sunday, sell on Monday.' With the devil in the details, the 1300S and 1600 now sported cast, not fabricated, intake manifolds. Solex 32 PBIC carbs allowed better idling, and low-speed torque came via improved intake passage design. However, some 1300S cars were still supplied with 40 PICB Solex units.[13]

General 356A refinements ran to improved sealing rings – observe the joint between the oil cooler and crankcase. The Solex fuel pump now had an integrated fuel filter. As a mid-MY upgrade (December 1955) the 1300 and 1600 were recipients of Alfinger forged crankshafts. There was also a new mounting for the forward end of the gearbox. The former weak single rubber sandwich was replaced by two separate circular rubber mounts on either side of the transaxle's front, the latter being attached by short arms from a newly cast front cover.

The clutch throwout bearing and associated crosshaft mounting were improved. Replacing former 5.00x16in tires was new 5.60x15in footwear. Stronger steering tie rods/balljoints joined a steering linkage adjusted to produce a roll understeer effect, and the caster angle was doubled. This new setup would invite harsher steering wheel kickback. Solving this was a small hydraulic steering damper between the pitman arm and lower torsion bar tube.

Well, you could do all the above or just redo the sheetmetal and rework the tailfins, but that wasn't Dr Porsche's bag. The 356 may have looked little different to casual observers, but general Beetle looks aside, this Porsche was now mechanically far removed from Wolfsburg. Even the 356A's modest visual changes weren't readily discerned. Porsche

Only five right-hand drive Speedsters were sent to Australia. This 1956 356A Speedster was one of them. (Courtesy Porsche)

Here, Gunther Molter is pushing his '59 356A Convertible D, on the Carousel section of the 1961 Nürburgring 1000. The upscale Drauz coachbuilt ragtop was a true gentleman's racer. (Courtesy Porsche)

had merely retouched earlier sales brochures. Why waste money on tire kickers and something so superficial?

The 356A did have wider tires, rubber-faced rubstrips below the doors, and that new constant radius curve windshield, rather than the old central vee screen. The floorpan was lowered 1.4in – so no more false floorboards – and the handbrake was moved from the driver's right side, under the dash, to the left side, out of the way.

The new 356A dashboard carried three large gauges within the steering wheel circumference. Readouts ran to speedo, center tach and fuel/oil temp combo gauge. Oil temp was a very European sports car practice, and passive safety involved foam rubber padding under the dash cap upholstery.[14]

The 356A was a safe car for experts and novices alike. *Auto Motor und Sport* editor Uli Wieselmann said, "Even dear Granny can take a turn faster with a Porsche than with an average car." Even as early as 1955/56, Porsche was reducing tail end wag.

However, Porsche wasn't the only one making refined, VW-related, rear-engined sports cars. There were rivals on both sides of the Atlantic: in America, the VW and Porsche-engined Devin and in Europe, the Denzel. Coming into 1954, the Denzel was Austria's only listed car maker. So Porsche like, and Dr Porsche and Ferry came from Austria too! The Denzel was the work of Wolfgang Denzel of Vienna, Austria, and was also derived from VW hardware, similar in appearance to the 356, with a little more concession to looks than function perhaps. Notable features were unusually good low-speed torque from the diminutive 8:1 CR motor – courtesy of Denzel's own head designer – and an extra rigid welded tubular frame.

The unstressed aluminum body was handbuilt by Denzel. The body sat three, so Denzel was pleasing French mistresses long before Matra did with its Bagheera! Denzel had a FIA international racing compliant model, and had done well in the Alpine Rally since 1949. Speedcraft Enterprises of Exton, PA was Denzel's US agent. It all sounds good, so why was it that by 1959 Denzel was wound up with only 300 cars sold?

Chalk it up to another expensive flat-four Euro import with 6-volt electrics, and a price tag equal to the also glacial selling $3500 Chevy Corvette. So why did Ferry's 356 do so well, and Wolfgang's Denzel bite the dust? Perhaps it was the company Porsche kept.

A man called Max – importer extraordinaire

Pretty soon after WWII, sports car makers cast an eye around the globe. They worked out that the only place where people had the money to buy their cars was America – MG certainly did – so it was handy to know the right 'go to' guy Stateside, and Porsche did. His name was Max Hoffman. Hoffman was also originally from Austria but lived in America, and had introduced Americans to classy European imports, from Mercedes to Rover. He met Ferry Porsche at the Paris Auto Salon in October 1950. It was an encounter facilitated by Porsche business manager Dr Albert Prinzing. Max was very interested in selling Porsches in America. A virtual 1951 unknown in the United States, 32 Porsche 356s were sold that year.[15] However, that import tally grew to almost 150 cars

in 1952, 450 in 1953, and by 1954 Max was taking one third of Porsche's output! Porsche was well on its way in the USA, but it wasn't that easy. In the fall of 1950, Max Hoffman took delivery of three Porsche 356 1100s. One was for himself, the other two were for racer Briggs Cunningham. The 1951 Porsche 356 was the same price as a Caddy! How does one sell an unknown sports car for that much money? The Porsche was literally given a badge.

It was at a lunch in 1952 that Hoffman insisted that Ferry add a badge to the Porsche, so Ferry sketched one on a napkin. It was a combination of the crest of Baden-Wurttemburg, with its six stag horns and the Stuttgart coat of arms. The latter provided that black prancing horse.[16] There was also a question of value for money and the kind of car US buyers would like. The value came courtesy of the 1954 Type 356 America, in coupe and convertible forms. It had a 55 horse 1500, with max power at a tractable 4400rpm. This somewhat budget-priced 356 had a VW cam for that flexibility and babbit-type conrod bearings to keep price down. It would still do over 90mph – not bad for '50s America.

The road to 356 Speedster

You could order the 75bhp 1500 Super, but that cost a lot more than the regular 1500. By 1954, Max Hoffman was only importing 1500-powered 356s.

Racer Bill Proctor having a February 1955 Sebring test run in a new Porsche Type 550. (Courtesy Porsche)

The 550 was Porsche's first car specifically designed for racing. Here, on August 28 1955, Ernst Lautenschlager was racing the Spyder at the Nürburgring 500. (Courtesy Porsche)

DOCTOR'S P

"The P...
joy to ...
cruise a...
per hou...
35 mpg...
excellen...
superch...
But the...
about!"...
Story b...
photog...

ROCTOR

'58 COUPE REBORN

VINTAGE CAR
012

This 1958 Proctor Coupe, was a fiberglass-bodied VW special built by Sydney's Ted Proctor. It originally had a Porsche 1300, with Roots supercharger from a WWII Spitfire fighter plane. This is summed up nicely in the quote from the article:

"The Proctor is an absolute joy to drive and will happily cruise all day at 55-60 miles per hour, whilst returning 35 mpg. The handling is excellent, although the supercharger is a bit noisy. But then, that's what it's all about!" (Courtesy Syme Magazines)

s an absolute
d will happily
t 55-60 miles
t returning
andling is
ugh the
s a bit noisy.
s what it's all

Noble,
y Mark Bean

The car you see here is the second of four Proctor Coupes built in Sydney by Ted Proctor. The Proctors were probably the first Australian-designed and built Volkswagen-based fibreglass specials and, as far as I know, my car is the last surviving example of this pioneering marque.

Originally built in June, 1958, for Doctor Vince Adcock of Newcastle, the car was used as daily transport for his medical practice and for competition use in hillclimbs and sprints on the weekends! The Proctor competed in the first-ever hillclimb held at the famous Silverdale Hillclimb in western Sydney.

It was fitted with a 1300 Porsche motor and supercharged with a Roots cabin blower from a Spitfire fighter's V-12 Merlin engine. The transmission was modified with close-ratio gears by Jack Bona, the VW guru. Doctor Adcock sold the Proctor in 1960 and the history gets a bit hazy after that.

I bought the car in 1981, after it had been dragged from a tractor shed on a farm at Dungog, in the Hunter Valley. The car was a total mess, with about four inches of rat droppings in the interior. Most of the major parts were intact, but the engine was

This suited the US desire for more displacement. As Max Hoffman did later with the BMW Bavaria, the 1500 America was a stripper with a larger, formerly optional engine. Everything on the 1500 America was optional. It sparked buyer interest with a relatively low bait price. However, something more special was in the background.

Right from the start there was a market for something fancier, more upscale and further removed from the Bug. Such a car appeared as early as 1950, for young enthusiast Heinrich Sauter. Being based on the 356, Sauter's custom car had a Porsche front fascia, bob tail, low-cut doors and alloy body panels.

Upon becoming the 356's US importer in 1950, Max Hoffman felt the Porsche was underpowered and overweight … ouch! To fancy up the 356, Hoffman took Ferry to visit American commercial artist and car guy Coby Whitmore.

Whitmore produced 356 sketches with more flowing lines and a door dip. The latter styling item was familiar to Americans from British sports cars, and had a functional hop-over benefit! Concerning

this American Roadster, Ferry thought of producing and selling maybe 5 cars per year. Max was more 5 per week The inspiration for this kind of Porsche had existed even earlier. Of course, that very first May 1948 356 prototype was very minimalist, very Speedster-like with its scant glass. Two convertibles were made at Gmünd, and a further six came from Swiss firm Beutler. Now, Hoffman's desires had led to the Type 540 'America.'[17]

Porsche told journalists this Type 540 was an 'export only' model. It employed the biggest Alfin drum brakes Porsche had and the first use of the Type 528 RBC 1488cc motor, plus non-synchro four-speed. This 'America' was badged Glaser of Weiden, but was actually made by the coachbuilder's postwar reincarnation Heuer.

The 16 cars had typical 356 torsion bars/parallel trailing arms at the front, and swing axle suspension at the rear. The 2.5 turns lock-to-lock steering was handy, in light of Porsche's ultimate oversteer. The 356 floorpan was reinforced, due to the absence of a roof, and the two-piece windshield was more solidly made than the normal cabrio.

That windshield could be removed courtesy of two wing nuts and one bolt, for 'bugs in the teeth' racing! Answering Max's concerns that the model was overweight, the Type 540 lacked hubcaps, trunk lining and even a tire iron! The 110+lb weight saving and tuned 1500 equaled a better power-to-weight ratio than a Jaguar XK120. It managed 0-60 in 9.3 seconds and a top speed of 110mph. The 75bhp at 5500rpm was triple that of a VW, and the modified alloy heads were topped by dual Solex P40 carbs with special intakes.

Briggs Cunningham bought two, and they were raced in 1952-53. Indeed, 14 of the 16 Type 540s produced wound up racing; that is all US cars delivered! One car stayed in West Germany, and one was lost. One of the US imports was used at the first race on the new Connecticut Thompson racing circuit in 1952.

The Type 540s came in Modegrau (Modern Gray), with standard rolling stock having uber-rare 3.25in-wide rims wearing Metzeler 5.00x16in bias belted tires.

Jacky Ickx and Chopard Co-President KF Scheufele in a Porsche Type 550 during the Mille Miglia vintage car race. Swiss watchmaker Chopard started sponsoring the event from 1988. (Courtesy Chopard www.chopard.com)

This 'America' wasn't the commercial winner Max Hoffman wanted. A mass production price of three grand would have been okay, but at $4600 the Type 540 was too pricey. To add insult to injury, Heuer was out of business in 1953 as there wasn't enough

production or investment to make it viable. However, Max would triumph with the Type 540's Speedster successor.

The September 1954 Porsche 356 Speedster was the $2995 special Hoffman was looking for. Aimed to compete with Austin-Healey 100s and

The delightful interior of this '62 356B coupe, is as apparent as the abundant footwell space afforded by the Porsche's rear transaxle. (Courtesy Porsche)

The 1956 Carrera coupe offered 100 DIN horses at 6200rpm, or 200kph (124mph) from its 1498cc four-cam flat-four. (Courtesy Porsche)

For '62 MY, the 356B got a larger rear window, and bigger engine lid with dual air intakes. A power sunroof became optional at this time also. (Courtesy Porsche)

Baron Huschke von Hanstein was Porsche's Competition Dept boss, and this is his custom orange '62 356B coupe outside Porsche Werk 1. (Courtesy Porsche)

Proudly flying the local flag, the Stuttgart Baden-Wurttemberg autobahn police chose the 356B convertible. Overkill for hot pursuit of a Beetle 1200! (Courtesy Stuttgart Baden-Wurttemberg autobahn police)

Triumph TR2s, it was a back to basics lightweight 1500 stripped of the usual European finery. This did not please Ferry's or Porsche's family pride. Ferry felt that it degraded the marque, not being consistent with Porsche's luxo nature and real ragtops. In America, folks owned several cars for various purposes. However, in Europe a gentleman's express would have to offer sports, luxury and ride comfort all in one car … and yet here was Porsche's 'upside down bathtub,' as many called it!

The Speedster's shallow side openings were intended to keep the rain out. The wide doors eased entry, and the high placed shifter plus comfy seats made it functional. The weight saving even knocked two seconds off the 0-60 sprint. Less was more: in America, the Speedster was, much to Porsche's chagrin, its best seller! Those hollow doors carried no sound deadening, and that plain interior made poor Ferry wince. However, the car was loved, especially in California. James Dean owned one, you know?[18]

For the normal convertible and Speedster, Porsche had a factory hardtop option for $170. From MY 1955, the Californian company Glasspar did a hardtop for the Speedster. It was available from Porsche dealers for $285 (1957 price). The purists may have decried that hardtop's use. However, by the late '50s Ferry's own 356 had one. Porsche refinement has no substitute.

The Speedster had no seatbelts, but the 70 horse 1500 Super motor meant it lived up to its nameplate. Sales were speedy too. 4822 Speedsters were made between 1954 and 1958. Of the 26 right-hand drive cars, three went to Britain, five to Australia and 18 to South Africa, and refinements were included.

During 1955, the ride was softened thanks to new spec laminated torsion bars. A swaybar had been introduced at the front in 1954. In the words of *Thoroughbred & Classic Cars*' Ian Young: "The ride is as smooth as an Eskimo selling ice cream to Pavarotti." Things certainly got smoother for '56 MY as the Speedster received the 356A's upgrades. This included a ZF steering box that improved handling.

With the 356A came a choice of 1600, 1600 Super or GS Carrera. The plain bearing crank 1600 was less troublesome than the previous RBC motors. By the end of '54 model year, all Hirth three-piece crankcases for regular 356s were phased out. Up to this point, Porsche had been using a modified VW crankcase.

In Speedster production, 1900 units had been 356s, with 2922 being 356A era cars. 1958's dual Zenith NDIX carbs made for a tractable upgrade. The final '58 Speedsters built carried a small round badge on the passenger side dash, with a laurel wreath and words concerning Zuffenhausen's continued racing success: "1950-57 Deutsche Sportwagen Meister Schaften."

The Speedster was a great seller but the stripped nature meant low profit per sale. Its replacement rectified the situation. From 1959 model year, the upscale 356SD fitted in with Ferry's ideals. The SD had a higher windshield, reclining seats, a nicely finished ragtop and a $700 price hike! Ferry thought that US buyers who were already paying Caddy prices for the 356 were good for a few dollars more. The 'D' in SD stood for the car's coachbuilder, Drauz. Californians missed their Speedster. To mentally placate them, Porsche renamed the SD the D-Type Roadster for '60 MY. A very Jaguar-like sports car moniker!

Porsche's design consultancy tradition continued after the war, specifically with small diesel tractors and the Type 113 for Piero Dusio. The design was first taken on by Allgaier Tractors, which made 25,000 copies between 1949 and 1957. Porsche was also involved with Studebaker, working together to design an affordable American family car. The proposal was a four-door sedan with 3.1-liter V6. Ferry Porsche, Karl Rabe and Erwin Komenda took a trip to America for the project. Sadly, the collaboration ground to a halt when Studebaker ran out of greenbacks. The design contract was terminated at the close of 1954.[19]

Racing improves the breed

Baby tractors and a natty sedan for Kermit & Fozzie, aren't very Porsche! Unfortunately, in the early days Porsche had its hands full making the 356 a viable production concern, so the task of trackside glory fell to privateers. Herbert Kaes, a nephew of the good doctor, was an engineer who drove the first ever race in a car called Porsche. That car was 356 number one, the venue was the Austrian Innsbruck city circuit, and the date was July 11, 1948. Kaes upheld Porsche family honor by winning! This class victory was followed by an 1100 coupe's win in the 1950 Swedish Midnight Sun Rally. Prince Joachim zu Fürstenberg and Count Konstantin Berckheim were at the wheel. Then there was the successful one-armed circuit racer Otto Mathe, from Austria, who was an 1100 coupe Alpine Rally victor. The first factory Porsche effort happened at Le Mans. It all started with an invitation from French journalist

Charles Faroux, and early signs weren't good. Both 356 entrants were destroyed in pre-race accidents.

A third 1951 Le Mans Porsche 356 was speedily prepared. It carried French Porsche concessionaires Auguste Veuillet and co-driver Edmond Mouche to a class win, and 20th overall. That's where the Porsche Le Mans legend started! The cars used for that Le Mans were lightweight, alloy-bodied Gmünd coupés with tuned motors and enclosed wheels. They were 200lb lighter than the steel-bodied Stuttgart 356s and lapped the Le Mans circuit at an average speed of 100mph.

This was all well and good, with the racing 356s generating good publicity for Porsche. However, in sports car racing the 356 was quickly outclassed by specialized designs intended just for racing. An example came from the Frankfurt VW dealer Walter Glockler. From 1950, he successfully campaigned mid-engined 'VW Specials.' Such racers were similar to Ferry's 356 prototype. Porsche backed Glockler's racing exploits, and his racer, which Glockler called a Spyder, inspired Porsche's first specially designed racing car: the Type 550 Spyder. It was fitting that Walter Glockler gave the Type 550 its debut win at the Nürburgring in May 1953.

Porsche had started work on the 550 in 1952. The sports car had an alloy body by Erwin Komenda, which could be opened or closed. There was the tubular, ladder-type frame, underslung at the rear. Of the six crossmembers, pairs carried the torsion bars for the front and rear suspension. In keeping with Porsche evolution, not all the goodies came at once. An early 1954 'Buckelwagen' or 'hunchback' body 550 initiated the later used underslung frame.[20]

The familiar Porsche swing axle rear suspension was specially designed to resist jacking up. The 550's trailing arm rear suspension didn't appear on the prototypes, the first two cars made. The Type 550's hinged rear body and engine cover panel opened to permit lifting out of the engine/gearbox/ZF LSD from above as one unit. At the heart of the Spyder was the first entirely Porsche motor: the famous four-cam Type 547. This motor was designed by Dr Ernst Fuhrmann.

In the early '50s Fuhrmann was a young Viennese designer. He would eventually leave Porsche to head Goetze, before returning to Zuffenhausen to replace Ferdinand Piëch as the technical director. Between 1972 and 1980, Dr Fuhrmann was Porsche's managing director. His Type 547 motor was a complex flat-four with a twin-cam arrangement per bank, that utilized a space saving kingshaft camdrive.

It was very oversquare for the '50s, had hemi combustion chambers, two spark plugs per cylinder, big valves, and its 1498cc produced 114bhp at 6800rpm. The dry sump oil cooler lived in the 550's nose.[21]

The Porsche Spyder gave respected Belgian engineer and eventual Le Mans winner Paul Frère his first race at the La Sarthe circuit.[22] Porsche built two 550s for the 1953 Le Mans race. Both had the OHV 1500s in 78bhp guise. It was enough for first and second in class, positions claimed, respectively, by the driver pairings of Richard von Frankenberg/Paul Frère, and Huschke von Hanstein/Wilhelm Hild. The third 550 built was the first car with the dry sump, twin coil, four-cam motor. Car number one was third at the August 1953 Freiburg Hillclimb. It was driven by Hans Stuck.

The Porsche factory also did two 78 horse 550s for the Guatemalan team, led by Jaroslav Juhan, in the Carrera Panamericana. Juhan's car was fastest on four of the eight five-day stages but had to retire. Teammate Jose Herrarte got a class win, with the 356 coupe of Fernando Segura second in class. However, the big news was Hans Herrmann's 1500cc class win in the 1954 Carrera Panamericana. He was driving the Type 550 with four-cam motor. Celebrating this triumph, Porsche put the four-cam motor in the road-going 356. The result was the '56 MY 100bhp 356A 1500GS Carrera!

Le Mans 1954 was another seminal Porsche outing to the famous French circuit. There were four Type 550s from the factory, distinguished by different color rear fender tops in red, blue, green and yellow. Erwin Komenda had ended the rear fenders in taillights to keep them visible. Of the four cars, three had the four-cam motor and one had an 1100cc unit. Paul Stasse and Johnny Claes in chassis 550-12, the No 39 car, were first in class and 12th overall. The 1100-powered 550 was also first in class and 14th outright.

Unfortunately, the two other 550s didn't see the checkered flag at the Club de L'Ouest. That said, Porsche went on to dominate with a 1-2-3-4 result at the Nürburgring.

The 550-12 chassis racer was shipped to Jaroslav Juhan for the 1954 Panamericana. In Juhan's hands the Spyder came second in class and fourth overall. He got the same results at the Buenos Aires 1000. This 1954 Le Mans class winner then spent the next 30 years in South America, doing some club racing. It then made its way back to Europe in the late 1980s. The fact that this 550 still had its original motor was a testimony to Porsche durability. It's not known how many Le Mans Type 550s were built in 1954. Mystery also surrounds the whereabouts of the Type 550 owned by actor James Dean. It was in 1955 that a car accident claimed Dean's life while he was driving his Porsche Spyder. The car was rebuilt as a wreck by George Barris, to tour as a traffic safety exhibit. In 1960, it was stolen, and has never been seen since.

The rebuilt wreck of James Dean's Spyder wasn't quite what it seemed. Barris Kustom folded a sheet of aluminum over the ripped-open driver's side. The customizing firm then welded what they created to a stripped shell obtained from a Porsche racer. Barris' employees beat the aluminum bodywork with 2x4s to simulate accident damage.

So, this exhibit car that toured various venues for three years had some secrets. In one case a sign placed above the exhibit car said: "The Greater Los Angeles Safety Council Presents James Dean's Last Sports Car." Over the years, George Barris maintained this vehicle was taken from a sealed truck, or secured railroad car. Last publicly seen in 1960, it's possible one or more of Dean's fans didn't like this ghoulish display, and destroyed the exhibit to stop further show tours.[22a]

1956 was a significant year for Porsche. It was the silver jubilee of the formation of the Porsche Design Bureau, considered by Ferry to be the true start of the company. 1956 also marked the return to Porsche's old factory, and the production of its 10,000th car – a 356A. In 1950, they made 335 Porsche 356s; now Zuffenhausen was around the 5000 unit per annum level, and rising. According to a Porsche sales brochure at the time, "One won one's spurs on the sedate 44-hp Damen." The 356 Damen 1300 was the least powerful Porsche, and, as the name and era suggested, it was directed at lady buyers.[23]

With the increased scale of production, parts were ordered in bigger batches, which made it harder to do frequent model revisions. However, 1956 saw an improved gearbox casing, and the 1957 Carrera Deluxe came with a heater, a 10bhp power drop, and was easier and more refined to drive. Porsche saved up quite a few upgrades for the 1958 T-2 series, a 356A MkII. This iteration made its debut at the Frankfurt International Auto Show. On the face of it, 12,700 DM got one a 100mph drum-braked 1600, with the 1600S on 109mph, but the details went deeper.

The T-2s used the Zenith NDIX carbs, a 356 first. Porsche could now utilize the same basic carbs on the 1600 and 1600 Super. The former used a

24mm venturi, with black fan shroud and 60bhp at 5000rpm. The latter was on 28mm, with silver fan shroud and 75bhp at the same rpm. It was easier living with a plain bearing crank, and the new Haussermann clutch was smoother and easier to pop. Previously, 356s employed a Fichtel & Sachs clutch. The shifter had been moved back for easier reach, and a more compact shift pattern introduced. It all allowed the heater's temperature control knob to live in front of the shifter.

All 1300s had ended in 1957, and 1958 was the final year for the four-cam 1500GS Carrera. More practical were the 356A's redesigned door handles and latches. The floorboards were reinforced so seatbelt mountings could be fitted, and the larger 16.75in Carrera tiller became standard across the range. There was a new steering box from ZF, with 16:1 ratio and 2.26 turns lock-to-lock. This unit had replaced a VW worm and nut system with 14.15:1 ratio and 2.4 turns lock-to-lock. It had dated from the 1930s Bug!

On the outside, Porsche emblem hubcaps were standard on the 1600S, unless optional Rudge knock offs were purchased. For all cars the dual exhaust outlets were now in the lower part of the bumper guards. For '58s, a front quarter vent window was standard on cabrio but optional on the coupe. Plus, there was now a larger rear window on cabrio and Speedster tops. For all the volume production, the 356 was still a very traditional coachbuilt car. At the Porsche works, parts were custom adjusted to fit individual cars as they were built. So NOS and secondhand panels won't necessarily fit a given car, even if the year and model are correct. Some fettling is needed.

Indeed, the constructional properties of 356s, make the term 'mass production' seem inappropriate: it was just lots of busy artisans putting together complex cars.[24] It was a platform chassis like the Beetle, with a very rigid bulkhead aft of the gas tank, and heavy box section sills. The area below the doors involved a hollow box through which heated air from the boxer motor reaches the interior, via heat and defroster vents. The box section makes for a rigid chassis, but is also a trap for condensation and corrosion.

Rust on the 356's lower door edge is common, due to poor drainage design. The area in front of the doors sees the metal outer skin folded over 180 degrees on itself. This sandwiches another piece of metal in between. The three layers of metal were then spot welded. The inner metal wasn't coated or painted, so was rust prone. The central hollow box has the lower part of its inside wall used to support the outside of the floor. The outside and bottom of the box are made from a single curved panel. It's a longitudinal member to which jacking receptacles are welded.

The box section has front and rear closing panels. The rear of the box section chassis has the torsion bar housing attached. Making rear closing panels, which are at the back of the longitudinal, from patterns is difficult, due to their complex curved shape. The luggage compartment floor, under the gas tank, is long discontinued. However, it's rarely a rust problem. There is a hole in this panel, and a fuel cock protrudes into the passenger compartment. This somewhat compromises safety between the firewall separating the interior from the luggage compartment/gas tank location.[25]

Torsion bar suspension was something the Bug, '30s Auto Union racer, and 356 all had in common, thanks to Dr Porsche. The forward placed gas tank was also Beetle-like, but all the time the 356 was evolving beyond Bug. In September 1959 ('60 MY), the 356B brought more improvements. Although the higher headlamps and bumpers were motivated by North America. Brakes were improved and the floorpan was modified to create more rear space.

With one exception, all 356Bs were 1600s, starting with the base 60bhp model, then the 75 horse 1600S and the new 90bhp 1600 Super called Super 90. These were all 1582cc rides, with the 1600GS Carrera GT on 1588cc. The GT brought 115bhp and 99 lb/ft, 124mph (200 kph) top speed, and 0-62mph in 10.5 seconds. This last version ran to the end of the 1961 model year. Most Carreras were now bought by privateers for racing, and the 1600S got the Super 90's uprated valvegear.

During the whole 1955-65 era, the Carrera was a four-cam version of the 356's OHV motor, with the unenviable complexity of 14 bevel gears! Well, for '63 MY this four-cam got more potent, with displacement increased to two-liters. The 1966cc 9.5:1 dual carb flat-four was the pinnacle of 356 performance, boasting 155 ponies! The Carrera 2 was directed at GT homologation, and weighed 890 kilos. It had 144 lb/ft and could sprint from 0-62mph in 9 seconds. Top speed was also 124mph, but with greater in-gear go than the Carrera 1600s.

For the final 356 iteration, the 356C of July 1963 pruned variants to two 1582cc models of 75bhp and 95bhp. They were the 1600C and 1600SC respectively, and marked the first appearance of the famous "SC" suffix. Performance for the two was 0-60mph in 14 seconds, and 109mph top speed; and 0-60mph in 13 seconds, and a top speed of 116mph respectively. The 935kg 2-liter 2000GS had 130bhp at 6200rpm, with its four-cam delivering the same factory performance figures as the Carrera 2.

For the 356C the Super 90's clutch was given to lesser 1600 models, and flat hubcaps indicated the presence of four-wheel disk brakes. This Ate system was like Dunlop's set up, but contained a 'Porsche Patent' rear drum brake for better handbrake action. It should be noted that the Carrera 2 and 2000GS ended at the close of '64 MY. This left just the 75 and 95 horse 1600s to see out 1965, alongside the new Porsche 911.

356 – A legend in its own lifetime
Fifteen years after it all began, Porsche wasn't primitive, but the American sporting car market was. In *Popular Mechanics'* 1964 annual, BMW was introduced as an honorable Austrian company. The Bavarians probably enjoy *The Sound Of Music*, but don't call 'em Austrians!

The Corvette could be optioned with a Fuelie 375 horse 327 V8, but only four-wheel drums. True sports car choices, if one regarded the MGB and Jaguar as more grand touring (GT), were few. With a production run of 76,302 cars, the 1948-65 Porsche 356, was perhaps the only real, volume-produced sports car available on an international basis. Next to Ferrari and Maserati, Dr Porsche was the Colonel Sanders of sports car![26]

Fortunately, it was increasingly difficult to lay an egg when handling a Porsche 356. Speaking about the 356B in its 1960 April 15 issue, journal *Autocar* had this to say: "Over the years, various modifications to the suspension and steering have given the car progressively more orthodox handling characteristics …" As a 1600cc coupe capable of 0-90mph in well under 30 seconds, the near 110mph 356 was judged as a sports car of rare efficiency and distinction.

Long familiar with Zuffenhausen's wares, *Autocar's* 'Greatest Sports Cars Of All Time' piece, at the end of the 20th century, highlighted many Porsches. Of the seminal 356 it offered its opinion: "To be blunt, it was little more than a souped-up Beetle …" However, quality was noted as being top drawer from the start. By 1964, the British market Super 90 cost £2277 and recorded 0-60mph in 13.2 seconds, on its way to a 115mph top speed. It was ten seconds and nearly 30mph better than that first Gmünd 1100.

Between the humble Beetle and glamorous Porsche 356, there was the Karmann Ghia. Some owners have fitted Porsche 356 and 911 motors. A 1964 coupe is shown. (Courtesy Syme Magazines)

Autocar judged the early 40 horse 356s as sluggards, with swing axle rear suspension that was treacherous in the wet. However, by the '60s, Princess Grace of Monaco had a Porsche 356, and Autocar praised the final 356 1600SC for its predictable handling. They acknowledged much had been done to cure rear end weight bias, including a spring to reduce rear weight transfer when braking or going off throttle.[27] One was more in control, and so was Porsche. With the 356C's introduction,

Porsche had taken charge of coachbuilder Reutter.

With the rise of a legend comes a rise in value. In the movie Harper, Paul Newman played a low rent gumshoe with a weathered T-1 Speedster. Car guy Jay Leno admitted he came to Porsches late in life. During the late '60s to early '70s, he could see little appeal. Compared to Corvettes, Porsches had little horsepower and cost so much. In the mid-'70s, however, he observed one could pick up a used 911 for a small sum. Slowly, over time, values for all

A 1963 356B Cabrio, pictured in the scenic location of Kirchberg. The 356 was the coachbuilt coupe, that turned high volume seller. (Courtesy Porsche)

air-cooled Porsches have risen. In March 1985, a UK dealer advertised a 1954 356 vee screen, as the last of its type in the world, in fine fettle, which was quite a claim, and the price was £9250. The dealer also sold Beetles, and said their 356 had been carefully repainted in their workshop, and carried a one year warranty on engine and gearbox.[28] Fast forward to 1996 and journalist Howard Walker visiting the biggest classic car auction in the world: the 25th Barrett-Jackson event held in Scottsdale, Arizona in January. A blue Speedster made $42,000, and a Chevy V8-powered 911 reached 25 grand.[29] It didn't stop there: in 2008 a barn find 1956 Speedster with 1600 Super motor, sold for $115,000 at a Russo & Steele auction. The car needed a full restoration. Dinky Toys used to make a scale diecast model of the 1959 Porsche 356A coupe, catalog no 182. With prices for the real thing reaching heavenwards, this could be a viable avenue for future Porsche collectors!

Porsches have always been pricey, but they have also held their value, which cuts down on depreciation. A major reason for such low depreciation, is high reliability and sound build quality. They used to say a Fiat X1/9 was built to last an Italian summer, while a Porsche, at least in the air-cooled era, was a car for life. On the eve of the July 1993 Coys auction of the 1954 Le Mans 1500cc class-winning No 39 Type 550, Malcolm McKay noted the Spyder, still with its original motor, was well put together and looked capable of another 24 Hours of Le Mans!

Then there was the owner experience of *Thoroughbred & Classic Car*'s international editor Robert Coucher. His 1964 356 coupe had a balanced and blueprinted 9.5:1 motor with Shasta aluminum pistons, sports cams and Weber carbs. All this and more was built by Barry Curtis. This 286,000-mile white 356C was a London daily driver, that Coucher took on the 1999 June Liége-Rome rally.[30] No 109 beat out all 356 entrants, and only suffered an exhaust manifold bolt that worked loose. The problem produced a nice crackle and pop on the overrun, according to Coucher. A wipe of the windshield and oil check then preceded a drive to Viareggio, where a back street exhaust shop fixed the loose bolt. After 2500 miles of use it was back home to London.

The oil and filter were changed, valve clearances adjusted, the car waxed, and it was back to ambling around town! Such reliability came in handy when racing. Before one finishes first, first one must finish! Speaking of number one, Porsche believes the first 356 built was road registered on June 9, 1948. To celebrate the 70th birthday of this icon, Porsche built a replica. Modern 3-D scanning and computer-assisted milling helped to recreate the bodywork of 356 No 1. The car, without engine or gearbox, went on a world tour in 2018!

From a Mickey Mouse 550 to Formula One

In the trial and error cauldron of pre-CAD race car development, Porsche hit a snag with its 550 'Mickey Mouse' RS. This lightweight 550RS had a low frontal area aero body, and a suspect rear suspension design, hence the nickname. Richard von Frankenberg wrote off this 135bhp mouse at the Avus test track in 1956. The next evolutionary step was the also lowered and lightweight 550RSK. The 'K' referred to the front suspension frame shape.

Even with small, downforce-inviting fins added to the RSK bodywork, control problems were still apparent in early 1957. Still more design fettling added to the 1954 Mille Miglia class win by Hans Herrmann. In the 1958 Sports Car Championship, Porsche was second only to another automaker, which also started in the late '40s … Ferrari: all

Top: By the time of this 1964 356C, the 356 was being sold alongside the 901 (Zero) series 911. The 356C's arrival coincided with Porsche taking control of coachbuilder Reutter. (Courtesy Porsche)

Lacking the power gadgets of US cars, European cars up to the late '60s got by on six-volt electrics. So, having the ignition between the seats, like Saab, helped with cold winter starts, through a shorter current path. (Courtesy Porsche)

According to Zuffenhausen, the 356C 1600 made 75 or 95bhp, at a respective 5200rpm and 5800rpm. These motors supplied respective factory-claimed top speeds of 175 and 185kph. (Courtesy Porsche)

The fashion icon that was the 1964 356C Cabrio. However, changing customer tastes and safety regs led to a cooling off of soft tops for 20 years. (Courtesy Porsche)

The 356C was spacious for its size, but fitting that much luggage *and* Fido suggested artistic license! (Courtesy Porsche)

As a final 356 incarnation, this 356C Spyder is revered. However, feared federal law meant no more ragtops until 1982. (Courtesy Edito-Service SA)

from developments of James Dean's racer of choice, the 550.

1959 saw Zagato beat out Wendler to supply lightweight bodies for the new '59 Abarth Carrera. Karlo Abarth, from Vienna, had his stylist Franco Scaglione reduce the Carrera coupe's front fascia by five inches. With 15 per cent less drag and 100lb less weight, the Abarth Carrera used its four-cam motor to be a dominant class winner in 1961-62.

Back in 1959, it was also a Spyder victory for Jürgen Barth and Wolfgang Seidel in the Targa Florio. In sports car racing, Porsche had the improved RS60 Spyder in 1960. That year, it was victory for Jo Bonnier and Hans Herrmann in the Targa Florio. Herrmann won in a RS60 Spyder at Sebring, while partnered with Olivier Gendebien.

There was also success for Zuffenhausen with 550 descendants in Formula 2.[31] For 1957, the new 1.5-liter category was a winning place to be

for Porsche and its RSK related racers. There was simultaneous development of the Formula 2 and Spyder sports cars. Porsche loaned one F2 machine to Stirling Moss' sponsor Rob Walker for the 1960 racing season. However, a crash in a Lotus sidelined Moss, and he was unable to utilize the Porsche much. Even so, Bonnier and von Trips came first and second respectively in the Porsche F2 car at the 1960 German Grand Prix. The Porsche F2 car in 1956 and 1957, was basically a stripped RSK Spyder.

There followed a center seat RSK and open wheeler Type 718. The latter made its debut at the 1959 Monaco GP, where it unfortunately crashed on lap 2. Porsche was developing its sports car, F2 and planned F1 car through 1960! Porsche was the last works team to run a four-wheel drum braked car in Grand Prix racing.

Its first disk-braked machine was the Type 787 at the 1961 German Grand Prix. With an eye to F1,

and trying new developments for the better, Porsche was working on a flat eight 1.5-liter motor and six-speed manual transmission. This motor wasn't ready for the 1961 racing season. Plus, the six-speed box proved too tricky for F2 drivers to master. In the works, too, was an all-wishbone/coil chassis for F1.

In 1961, at the German Grand Prix, Dan Gurney and Jo Bonnier came second and third respectively in Type 718s, achieving those final standings on the last lap! Innes Ireland won the race held at the Solitudering circuit, in a Lotus 21. This racing venue also provided the final Type 804 GP victory, when Gurney and Bonnier bagged a respective 1-2 finish!

Rulebook changes and a return to mid-engined racers from front-engined cars, opened the door to a refinement of Porsche's Formula 2 car. So it was that Porsche entered F1 as a constructor during the 1962 racing season. The car was the Type 804, powered by a four-cam 1494cc flat-eight with bore and stroke dimensions of 66x54mm. It had 10:1 CR, four carbs and made 180bhp at 9200rpm. This motor worked through a six-speeder.

Front independent suspension was via wishbones and longitudinal torsion bars; the rear saw independent wishbone and longitudinal torsion bars, too. No planned coils. Porsche four-

wheel disk brakes stopped the 170mph racer. The drivers were Dan Gurney and Jo Bonnier. It all looked good, but success didn't really come. Gurney managed one championship win at the French Grand Prix, when faster cars dropped out.

Dan Gurney came fifth in the 1962 F1 World Championship, Bonnier was 15th. The development period for the flat-eight was too long, and rivals had caught up on power. Then, as now, finding the perfect

1. Some famous Porsche racers, at the 1959 Nürburgring 1000. The 718RSK at the top, 356A 1500GS Carrera GT in the middle, and 1600 version further down.
2. Paul Ernst Strähle and Herbert Linge, in their No 225 356A Carrera, on the 1957 Mille Miglia.
3. Herbert Linge and Antonio Pucci in the No 24 356 Carrera Coupe 2000, at the June 7 1959 Nürburgring 1000.
4/5. Herbert Linge in the No 72 356B 1600GS Carrera GTL Abarth, at the Achum airfield race held on 14-15 September 1963.
(All images courtesy Porsche)

The 1962 356B 2000GS Carrera 2 motor on display. Porsche had considered the two-liter Carrera motor for the 911, but cost and complexity ruled it out. (Courtesy Porsche)

At the 1963 Nürburgring 1000, Hans Joachim Walter and Sepp Greger's 'Triangle Scraper' bodied 356B 2000GS Carrera GT won the two-liter GT class. The Linge/Barth Porsche entry expired. (Courtesy Porsche)

A great historical Porsche racing identity, Erwin Kremer pushes his 356B 1600 GS Carrera GT in Neuss, at the fourth annual RWAC slalom in 1964. (Courtesy Porsche)

4. RWAC Autoslalom 1964 in Neuß

The class-dominant 356B 1600GS Carrera GTL Abarth had aero styling courtesy of Franco Scaglione. (Courtesy Porsche)

F1 combo was a tough task. Porsche could see they would have to spend even more money, to get on even terms with Ferrari, BRM and Lotus. Discretion being the better part of valor, Porsche decided that being a sports car constructor was a better bet.

The decision did Porsche's sporting image no harm. Le Mans and Paul Newman inserting a 356 motor in his Beetle were testimony to that. The line between Porsche road and race was indiscernible. In the 1971 Dario Argento movie thriller *Cat o' Nine Tails*, Catherine Spaak's character scared James Franciscus' journalist to death, as she heeled and toed his silver 1960 Porsche 356B through Rome at breakneck speeds. Hang in there Mr. Novak! 🐎

Right: Porsche racers at the 1962 Solitude F1 Grand Prix. Here, Jo Bonnier's Type 804 qualified 11th and finished second. Count Carel Godin de Beaufort's Type 718/2 qualified 18th and came fifth. (Courtesy Porsche)

On August 5 1962, Jo Bonnier scored a seventh place at the Nürburgring Grand Prix. With a competitive F1 car needing a lot more investment, Porsche decided to concentrate on sports car racing. (Courtesy Porsche)

Later, Catherine Spaak's character Anna Terzi raced around Rome in a Porsche 356, in the 1971 movie *Cat o' Nine Tails*. (Courtesy Porsche)

Thora Hornung, shows the 1963 901's early distinctions: no door moldings, plus a round gas cap. This became oval on the 911. (Courtesy Porsche)

The third generation Porsche

The all-new Porsche 911, the 356's successor, was completely expected. A rear-wheel drive, rear-engined coupe of tear drop shape, with evolved styling and air-cooled boxer motor. It all seemed a foregone conclusion. The Porsche story of 1948-63 predicted it. Modern fans of Porsche's mystique would judge the first 911 as a natural good fit. That the car would drive well, be well assembled from quality materials and be praised internationally would also come as little surprise. After all, it was a Porsche! However, on launch and behind the scenes, things weren't set in stone.

When *Popular Mechanics* reviewed the Porsche range for '64 MY, it showed a well-sized picture of a coupe of modern appearance and larger than the 356C. This car carried the license plate TYP901, and the publication didn't comment on this mysterious coupe at all. The photo was taken at the 1963 Frankfurt International Auto Show. The coupe was the new Porsche 911 on its international debut. However, at this time it was called Porsche 901.

As per the 356 and Porsche practice, the new model moniker simply represented the job number of the Porsche design consultancy. It was the 901st new project Porsche had embarked on since the Porsche

The 911 on debut at the 1963 Frankfurt International Auto Show, as the Type 901. Type 901 prototypes had no door moldings, and tailpipes exiting the rear valence. (Courtesy Porsche)

Design Bureau started in 1931. When the coupe was formally launched a year later, as a '65 MY machine, it became the Porsche 911. Once again, Monsieur Peugeot had made an impression on Dr Porsche's timeline: the French firm had registered all three-digit serials with zero in the middle, so Porsche had to change the numberplate.[32]

There was also some difference of opinion within the Porsche clan and company, concerning the new 911's form. Ferry Porsche gave little impression the 911 could have been anything, other than what it

An early 0 series Porsche 911 at the Australian sports car specialist dealer Geoghegans in 1966. Ian and Leo Geoghegan were successful touring car racers in the '60s and '70s. (Courtesy Nanette Geoghegan)

was. According to Porsche's guiding force, the 356's replacement needed more space and refinement. For the caddyshack crowd, mention was also made of a need to fit a set of golf clubs in the trunk. Just the one set – obviously the mistress doesn't play golf! No doubt Porsche set a sports car design precedent in providing for golf clubs.

Ferry said the company had considered a mid-engine layout for 911, but there just wasn't enough interior wiggle room. The sentiment was echoed by *CAR* magazine. In January 1988's 'Porsche 911 Carrera' article, the journal said that compared to mid-engined cars, the 911 was easier to get into. The big doors were a boon and overall there was "good headroom and better than exotic visibility. And the layout allows a token pair of rear seats." It wouldn't have been possible in a mid or front-engined car of such abbreviated length. Looking back on the decision to go rear-engined, in 1984 Ferry said, "We have not regretted it."

A difference of opinion – Butzi Porsche
It's certainly true that the 911 offers more interior space and comfort than a 356. For spaciousness, the convertible versions of the latter were a necessity, not a luxury! However, some were looking for more. Early on, Californian coachbuilder Troutman-Barnes, who had made the first Chaparral sports cars, created a four-door Porsche 911. The car was for William J Dick Jr, graced the cover of *Road & Track* magazine, and possessed a 21in wheelbase stretch.

Pininfarina was of the same mind with its 1969 B17. This 911 was still a two-door car, but with a 7.5in wheelbase increase. A light green example resides in the Porsche museum. Great minds think alike because the 911's creator, Ferdinand Porsche III (or Butzi to family and friends), was also looking for more space and power. In design proposals a full four-seater and sports wagon were considered, but business realities dictated otherwise. Either concept would have needed a bigger motor, and as Butzi said, West Germany's and Europe's tax structure made a large engine difficult.

Two liters was the fiscal cut-off point in Italy and Spain, 2.8 liters in France. Beyond this and one had a very rich man's plaything and small sales volume. Enough for Ferrari, not enough for Porsche, which didn't wish to know all its customers by name.

It was the start of great things, the 130 horse air-cooled SOHC flat-six 1964 911 motor. The concept would continue until 1998, when European Union noise regulations, smog law, etc moved Porsche from luft to wasser boxers. (Courtesy Porsche)

The 911's two-liter flat-six in 1965. For reliability Porsche moved from Solex to Weber carbs in mid 1966. However, the later had bore spacing that required offset manifolds. The Webers also lacked chokes, and ran dry in hard cornering. (Courtesy Porsche)

A sport wagon would have needed more living room. In the end, Butzi admitted, "We're a sports car firm." The statement was made, with a hint of regret, to journalist Jerry Sloniger: Butzi Porsche wasn't one for compromise.[33]

The only Porsche that Butzi had owned at that point was a Speedster. He had a love for wagons, and his personal transport at the time was a Pontiac Tempest compact wagon; so very practical, as he confessed to CAR's Jerry Sloniger in September 1966: "You can't drive fast today anyway …" In the article 'The third Mr Porsche,' Butzi said he was personally against the '+2' concept of token rear seats. He said when you give a man a chair he expects comfort. In his opinion it was much better to do a pure mid-engined two-seater. Alternatively, a real grand tourer should have the engine up front and luggage in the rear, Butzi felt.

Porsche was five years away from its 928, but various new directions were being discussed. In the 1960s the VW Beetle, Renault 8 and 10, plus the Fiat 600/850 ranges were strong sellers, but few new rear-engined cars were coming along. Exceptions were the new 911, Hillman Imp and Škoda 1000MB.

The world was moving to front-wheel drive and Butzi said, "I'd have to see if the Toronado works before talking about front-wheel drive." He thought front-wheel drive worked better with a heavier car but that hill and snow traction still favored cars like the Beetle and Porsche 911.[34]

By the mid-60s, the Corvette was getting well established, and Butzi said Porsche might do a fiberglass car one day. The stumbling block was exterior finish quality. Customers in West Germany and Europe expected better, especially at Porsche prices. Of course, Porsche had been the first German company to do a series of fiberglass cars. This started with its work on the Formula One machine. The 911 shape went back to 1959/60 and used ideas from even earlier.

Porsche had a lot of time to come up with the 911. It expected to get at least ten years out of a car. Opinions on the 911 were sought, even from beyond the Porsche styling studio, as there had been internal conflict over the car's development. Ferry gave the nod to Butzi over the work of long-time Porsche body man Erwin Komenda. Butzi's work covered the 356B and 904 racing car, along with the 911/912. That all

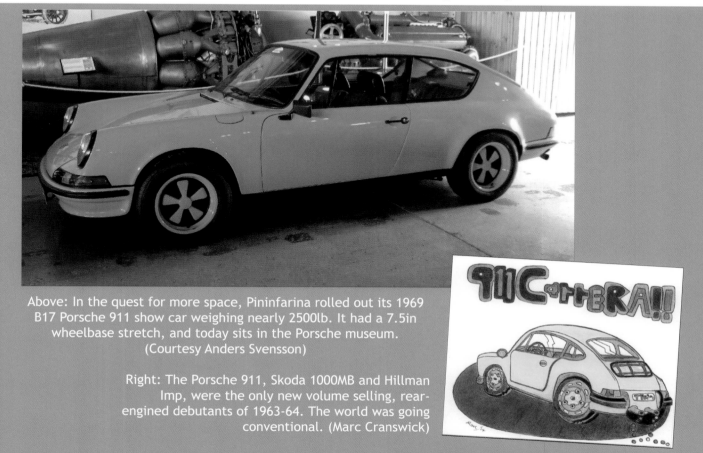

Above: In the quest for more space, Pininfarina rolled out its 1969 B17 Porsche 911 show car weighing nearly 2500lb. It had a 7.5in wheelbase stretch, and today sits in the Porsche museum. (Courtesy Anders Svensson)

Right: The Porsche 911, Skoda 1000MB and Hillman Imp, were the only new volume selling, rear-engined debutants of 1963-64. The world was going conventional. (Marc Cranswick)

The new flat-six Porsche 911 (901) was going to be 25 per cent more expensive, than the already pricey 356C. Solution? A flat-four 911, called 912! (Courtesy Barwaut Verhoeven www.912registry.org)

makes for quite a resume! However, as in modern design times, success has many fathers.

The admission was made that in the 356's era, Ferry Porsche had a very big input concerning Porsche's first production car. However, the 911 was more of a team effort. Indeed, times had changed between the first Dr Porsche and the third Mr Porsche. Professor Ferdinand Porsche was an instinctive engineer, stylist and winning Alpine trial racer – a hands-on all-rounder. However, Butzi's chief concern was the 911's shape, testing comfort, and internal packaging that came from his styling. Things had also changed from the usual form following function.

The 911 was clearly more of a styled and – subjectively – attractive coupe than the 356. The older car's visual charm wasn't exactly a design intention in

the manner the 911 was. As Butzi explained, previously there had been no need. In America, especially after the war, the choices of automobile were legion. Styling and advertising were very important things to help differentiate products in the market place, and help them stand out from the madding crowd. Such rampant consumerism didn't exist in immediate post-war West Germany. Over there, difficult economic conditions made owning any new car the stuff of dreams. Styling departments would come later.

By the 911's era, styling and marketing mattered. The 911's instrument surrounds were originally matt black, but the sales department thought chrome looked more upscale. So chrome it was, and dazzling reflections go hang! Half of Porsche's production was now exported: in the new international climate, styling had become less nationalistic. In addition, Butzi added, "Our cars must be Porsches first, not just German." Many of those global buyers were American men seeking a young, sporty image.

In spite of the 911 being the doyen of the Playboy set, the spirit of the Porsche design bureau still held sway. Half of Porsche's work was still design consultancy: companies asked Dr Porsche to design a better mousetrap, because they knew Zuffenhausen could. One such firm was West Germany's biggest automaker, VW. Dr Porsche had come up with the globe-conquering Beetle, and now Wolfsburg had Porsche under contract to create Herbie II. It was to be a small, mid-engined family sedan, where the water-cooled motor resided under the rear seat.[35]

Porsche was a company of conviction. The attacks of Ralph 'No Defense' Nader had sullied the poor Chevy Corvair, and helped kill off new rear-engined cars. Unperturbed by incorrectly inflated tire pressures, and with owners unfamiliar with the handling properties of rear-engined cars, Porsche, Hillman and Škoda battled on. Funnily enough, the Škoda 130S Rapide would go on to be known as the poor man's 911!

The monocoque-bodied 911's chassis helped pack more room for luggage and people than the 356. Space efficient torsion bars ran parallel with the body at the front lower wishbones, and MacPherson struts for wheel location made carrying a golf bag at the front possible. Bringing up the rear it was transverse torsion bars, trailing arms and a low mount bracket. That last item helped create space for the rear '+2' seats. There were 15x4.5in rims wearing 165/70 HR-15s, swaybars at both ends and all around tube shocks. Your sports car is ready Mr Nader![36]

As part of the up-to-date Euro sports car practice, all independent suspension was joined by four-wheel disk brakes, and twin universally jointed rack and pinion steering. To move the 2381lb coupe, the two-liter four-cam motor had been considered. However, refinement and a need to cut cost and complexity swayed Ferry to an all-new flat-six of 1991cc. Bore and stroke were 80x66mm, and dry sump lubrication kept the center of gravity low – got that Cayenne?!

The motor had part spherical combustion chambers and single overhead cam (SOHC) layout. It made 130bhp at 6100rpm and 128lb/ft at 4200rpm. The air-cooled Porsche flat-six high-revving nature ruled out hydraulic tappets. It added valve clearance adjustment to the maintenance schedule. There was 9:1 CR and carburetion came courtesy of two Solex 40 PICB carbs. Performance figures were 0-60mph

Left: It looks like a 911, but is, in fact, a 1967 912. Porsche's entry level four-cylinder coupe, married the 911 shell to the 356C Super 90 motor. (Courtesy Barwaut Verhoeven www.912registry.org)

The Porsche 912 had one quality that the 911 could only dream of ... neutral handling! Two fewer cylinders rearwards, meant no tail wagging. (Courtesy Barwaut Verhoeven www.912registry.org)

in 8.3 seconds, 0-100mph
in 22.7 seconds, a 16.1 second
quarter mile and 131mph top speed,
all according to conservative Porsche.

The 911's drag coefficient was only 0.385.
This was good for the era, and accorded with Porsche
thinking that a rear-engined car with small frontal area
would produce a high top-speed on modest power.
The 911's lightness and small size, like Beetle, was a
boon for maneuverability and agility. The wheelbase
was a mere 87in, length was 163.9in, width was
63.4in and height was 52in – over 10in shorter than
a Corvette, but with two more seats and a trunk lid! A
type 901 five-speed transaxle was worked by a remote
shift linkage.

Porsche 912, 911 Targa & 'S'

Between September 1964 and March 1965, the new
911 wasn't alone. The new Porsche was 25 per cent
more expensive than previous Porsches. For sales
security, the trusty 356 1600SC was retained for
another year. From April 1965, the iconic 356 was
replaced by an entry level '0' series car, called the
912. This starter Porsche was basically a 911 with
the 356SC's 90bhp OHV flat-four. The 912 also
came standard with a four-speed and plain interior.
Porsche's decision was vindicated; early on, the
cheaper 912 outsold its 911 big brother. When all
was said and done, over 30,000 912s were built by

Zuffenhausen during 1965-69.[37] Who said old wine in
a new bottle doesn't work?!

In spite of some commercial success, many look
upon the 912 as a poor cousin. It is spartan and
the lower power means one has to keep the power
on through corners to maintain momentum, rather
than to ward off traditional Porsche oversteer. *Car
and Driver* got acquainted with the 911 and 912 by
mid-1966. It felt the latter was comparable to the
contemporary BMW 2000CS coupe. The BMW did
offer more genuine four-seater comfort, but at the time,
the 912 was cheaper at $4690, with close-ratio five-
speed included.

The BMW was $4985, and had compromised the
front fascia styling due to US lighting laws. *Car and
Driver*'s 0-60mph, quarter mile and top speeds for
both cars were 11.7 seconds, 18.1 seconds at 77mph,
and 115mph respectively, versus the Bavarian's
10.6 seconds, 17.7 seconds at 79mph and identical
115mph top speed. *Car and Driver*'s 911 stats were
7 seconds, 15.6 seconds at 90mph and 130mph. All
that flat-six energy cost $6200.

In this era, *Car and Driver* kept making

On the mechanical side, Sportomatic involved a shifter micro switch, solenoid, pneumatic valve and modified Type 905 gearbox with torque converter. (Courtesy Porsche)

You could even have Sportomatic on the 1967 911S! Two pedals, with the clutch done via electromechanical action. (Courtesy Porsche)

As Butzi Porsche said, Porsche was working on an automatic transmission, and would only release it when it was right. The result, was 1967's four-speed Sportomatic semi-auto. (Courtesy Porsche)

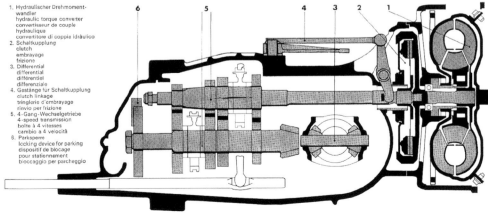

PORSCHE   SPORTOMATIC

1. Hydraulischer Drehmoment-
    wandler
    hydraulic torque converter
    convertisseur de couple
    hydraulique
    convertitore di coppia idràulico
2. Schaltkupplung
    clutch
    embrayage
    frizione
3. Differential
    differential
    différentiel
    differenziale
4. Gestänge für Schaltkupplung
    clutch linkage
    tringlerie d'embrayage
    rinvio per frizione
5. 4-Gang-Wechselgetriebe
    4-speed transmission
    boîte à 4 vitesses
    cambio a 4 velocità
6. Parksperre
    locking device for parking
    dispositif de blocage
    pour stationnement
    bloccaggio per parcheggio

W 141 Dr.-Ing. h. c. F. Porsche KG · Printed in Germany · Änderungen vorbehalten · Juli 1967 · M

comparisons between Stuttgart and Bavaria. Later, they even said that the BMW 2800CS could outpace 911Ts and Ls. However, bare figure and value comparisons only scratched the surface. By this stage, the North American import market was already becoming distinct between brands. It's unlikely the Porsche devotee would have considered the BMW. It's improbable either brand's faithfuls would have looked at the Mercedes 230SL. Similarly the 912's charms needed closer inspection to be discerned.

The experience of Danish 912 owner Rodney Pope, was instructive. The boss of a cleaning company, he had owned over 110 cars to that point. The list included the Porsche 924 Turbo and 911 Turbo, before he joyfully discovered the 912. He did so when meeting famous Danish Porsche restorer Bent Clausen. Clausen had been restoring Porsches for over 35 years by this point, since the early '50s, and owned a 912. Mr Pope thought this was a strange choice, given Clausen could have his pick of any Porsche. Pope asked Clausen why a 912? Clausen didn't answer, he just took Pope for a ride.

Very quickly Rodney Pope became a 912 convert. He noticed the excellent handling and noises, courtesy of the 356 1600SC, and 35mpg fuel economy. And as Butzi Porsche said himself, with increasing road congestion where could

Left: As the higher performance 911 version, the dual carb 160bhp 911S arrived in July 1966, as a '67 MY debutante. (Courtesy Edito-Service SA)

The 1968 911L 2.0 was the luxury grand tourer for a couple and a moderate amount of luggage. An A series 911 is present. (Courtesy Porsche)

Above: The somewhat spartan interior of the entry level 1968 911T. Under the hood, penny-pinching cast iron cylinders kept the 911T's price down. (Courtesy Porsche)

• Dean Smith was a regular at Carroll Speedway in L.A. during the Troy Ruttman/Walt Faulkner era. He has read *C/D, Road & Track, Sports Car Graphic* and *Autoweek* since they were first published.

He's a construction superintendent who, in the Fifties, worked for Tony Parravano, an L.A. home builder known in racing as "The Golden Screwdriver." Stirling Moss, Masten Gregory, Ken Miles and Carroll Shelby all drove for Parravano who kept a stable of up to 21 Ferraris and Maseratis. Dean Smith worked on the team after hours and used to tow the cars to Bakersfield and Pebble Beach.

"Those," he says, "were the greatest days in the world."

Parravano vanished in 1956, after the IRS caught up with him. He is very likely in Mexico.

Dean Smith drifted away from racing. He kept to Porsches, and rarely missed a race at Riverside, but he wasn't involved.

He is now recovering from a California divorce, but with his new wife, Georgia, who is 27, he is getting back into his old stride. They both autocross his 911S, desert ride Kawasaki scramblers and water-ski. This year he was an organizing official in the annual Porsche Club of America parade, which was held at Anaheim.

During the spring he built a swimming pool behind the house and gave Georgia a '69 Torino station wagon as a surprise birthday present. Today, he's thinking about getting a new 911S and wishing that his 17-year-old son, Steve, would get his hair cut.

Dean Smith: Life begins again at 40

Above: Car and Driver's September 1969 cross section study of its readers, the first and third generations of Dr Porsche's work are on display. (Courtesy *Car and Driver*)

one drive fast anyway? The superb gas mileage, and VW and Porsche air-cooled quality, really meant something in fuel-excise, tax-ridden Europe. Plus, the 912 really did handle well. Compared to a 911 there was less weight behind the transaxle. The 912 was more neutral than the Swiss!

Pope said one needn't fear rain, like in his 911 Turbo, and his 912 five-speed attracted positive reactions. At car shows, his white '66 912 five-speed with red PVC plastic interior and lots of chrome turned more heads than the latest 964 chassis 911! The car was purchased in 1990 after a three-year restoration, and Rodney Pope had been using the 912 as a daily driver for a couple of years, even during the Danish winter.[38] Today, the idea of picking up a 912 for 30 per cent less than an equivalent 911 is an appealing one.

The 911/912 is seen as the archetypal Porsche, and yet for 20 years it lacked what the 356 had made a traditional Porsche quality: a real ragtop. Fears of pending federal rollover and roof strength tests hung over automakers like the sword of Damacles, so Porsche devised something different for the 911. In its 1967 sales brochure Porsche claimed, "Four-in-one" concerning its 911 Targa. The moniker was taken from the Targa Florio road race, which Porsche won 11 times, including its final running in 1973. The targa car involved a folded roof that could be stowed in the

In 1969, the 911E's two-liter injected flat-six made 140bhp at 6500rpm. However, the same sized 1969 911S motor produced 170bhp at 6800rpm. (Courtesy Porsche)

front luggage compartment. A zip up and out rear plastic window went in the rear parcel shelf.

Not a full convertible, but legal and very popular. Porsche seemed to use the term cabriolet interchangeably with targa top and a normal convertible. Announced in September 1965, targa joined the Porsche lexicon. The brushed stainless steel rollover hoop became a fashion icon. The use of targa tops and, in turn, T-tops, was popularized by Zuffenhausen, and soon appeared on sporty cars across the world, and into the 1990s. It would soon become available on all 911/912 variants for '67 MY.

The 911 Targa was the work of Butzi Porsche. He had some thoughts and misgivings concerning cabriolets in general, and the 911 Targa in particular: "There has never been a successful rear-engined cabriolet. This is a major factor here and the failing in my targa. Still, I think it looks better than one first thinks – and could be better still."

Jaguar's aerodynamicist Malcolm Sayer (he didn't like being called a stylist) came up with the E-Type. Enzo Ferrari said that Jaguar was the most beautiful car in the world. Perhaps partly because he was trying to wrangle a discount from Pininfarina! During the classic era, it seemed modest men were able to single-handedly come up with works of art very quickly. Cars like the XKE and 911 have become design icons.

Any visual shortcomings with the 911 Targa were due to having to minimize tooling cost. Porsche had a number of new 911 developments for 1967. They came under the umbrella of the 911 Zero series' replacement: the 911 A series. In 1966, Butzi had said, "We are trying automatic gearboxes, but they won't come until we are entirely happy."[39] That day had come, and for the next decade Porsche's Sportomatic was the 911's … automatic choice.

Sportomatic involved a four-speed box where gear changes were accomplished through an electro-mechanical clutch. There was no clutch pedal, just like the good doctor's Beetle from 1968. It was a semi-automatic affair. However, the VW Type 1 Beetle's automatic 'Stick Shift' device was a three-speed box. Whether Porsche or VW, so close were the two concerns, merely touching the shifter was enough to pop the clutch. In the case of the 911, one then guided the stick through the usual H pattern of first through fourth.

There was a torque converter, so effectively one wasn't missing a gear, versus a 911 five-speeder.

Whether 'S' (above) or 'T' (left), the 2.0L was road tax handy, for Italy and Spain. (Courtesy Porsche)

One thing to be careful with in both VWs and Porsches, was the subconscious habit of resting a hand on the shifter while driving. To do so would bring the embarrassment of disengaging the clutch and ending up in neutral! There was very little loss of mechanical efficiency with Sportomatic when comparing three-liter 911s. *Autocar's* January 24, 1976 Test Extra brought 0-60mph, top speed, and fuel economy figures of 7.3 seconds, 141mph, and 21mpg respectively, for the high comp 200bhp 911 Carrera 3.0 Sportomatic. The same journal's December 17 Autotest of a low comp 180 horse 911 SC 3.0 five-speed manual brought equivalent figures

of 6.5 seconds, 141mph, and 17.9mpg. For further comparison, *Autocar's* May 28, 1977 road test of the 285bhp Jag XJ-S V12 auto yielded 7.5 seconds, 142mph, and 14mpg. All of which showed the efficiency of Porsche and the Sportomatic.

As soon as pressure was placed on the Sportomatic's stick, a micro switch opened a pneumatic valve via a solenoid. Then a vacuum cylinder popped the clutch, which reconnected post shift when the stick was released. Sportomatic worked on a modified Type 905 gearbox. The torque converter avoided the problem of stalling when one pulled up to the lights with the 911 in gear. The H pattern saw L, D, D3, D4, in place of first through to fourth. L was like first,

The road-legal Porsche 906 as shown at the DAMC05 Oldtimer Festival, held at the Nürburgring in 2008. (Original image courtesy Lothar Spurzen)

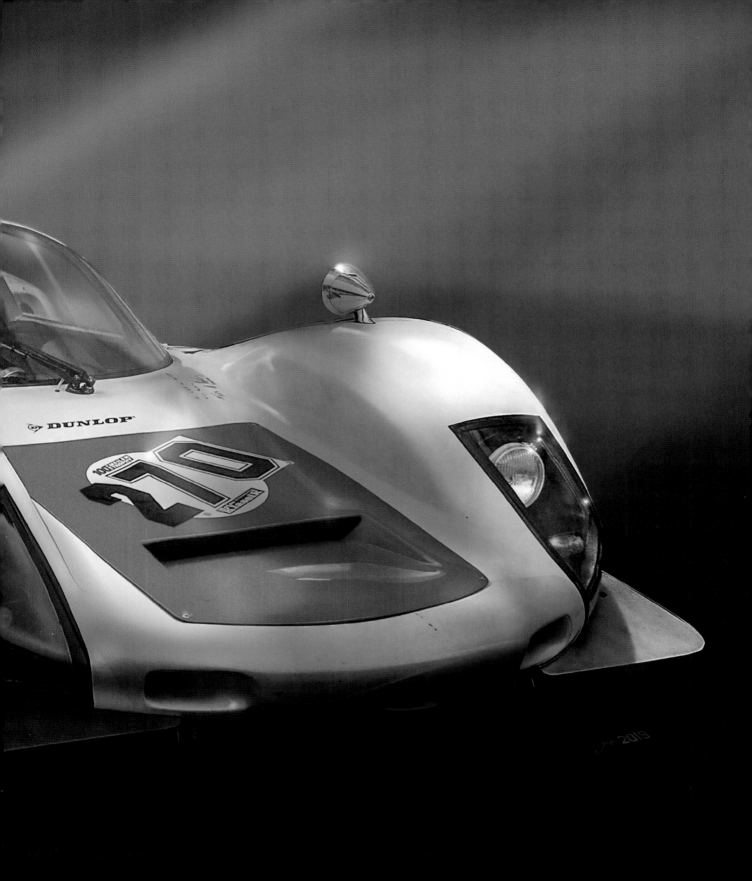

but Porsche recommended taking off in D (second) whenever possible. D and D3 were shorter than the five-speed's second and third. D4 was an overdrive ratio, with the torque converter masking ratio gaps versus the 911's five-speed box. A park mode locked the layshaft when the 911 Sportomatic was parked.

TV's *Dream Car Garage* host Peter Klutt talked about Sportomatic when driving the 2.7-liter 1973 911 Carrera RS. He said racer Peter Gregg considered automatics a natural choice for powerful cars like the 911RS, and that the Sportomatic's micro switch was a boon, because it stopped drivers resting their hands on the shifter – keep two hands on the wheel! At the movies, Sportomatic and the targa top were both seen on one yellow 911E 2.4 in the 1974 flick *The Destructors*. There was a playful road flirt between Michael Caine's Alfa Montreal V8 and Maureen Kerwin's 911.

Sportomatic could be specified across the 911 range, including on the new July 1966 911S. As with past 'S' versions, this was a performance flagship for the regular road cars. At its heart was an upgraded two-liter flat-six. The compression ratio had jumped from nine to 9.8:1, with new carburetion being two Weber 40 IDS units. A more aggressive cam profile, bigger valves and oil cooler came along for the ride too.

The figures were now 160bhp at 6600rpm, with torque of 132 lb/ft at an also high 5200rpm. 0-60 was eight seconds, the quarter mile took 15.8 seconds, with 0-100mph 2.7 seconds swifter at 20 seconds flat. Top speed for the $7074 '67 911S was 137mph.

Rims were up from 15x4.5in, to 15x5.5in for the A series 911. And the two-piston caliper four-wheel disk brakes were still sized 11.1in (282mm) at the front and 11.22in (285mm) at the rear. However, compared to the normal 911, the 911S had ventilated disks at each corner. The handsome cast magnesium alloy Fuchs were also introduced, and became a regular up to the late '70s.

The expanding 911 alphabet – T, L & E

In the UK not all players were present. At the Earls Court Motor Show, looking at the coming '67 MY, only the 912, 911 and 911S were at hand. The 1967 911S had a projected price of £3500. The left-hand drive only targa was yet to arrive.[40] However, soon there would be something for everyone: after the entry level 912, came the new '68 MY 911T, still with the two-liter flat-six, but utilizing the cheaper 912 interior fixings, and cast iron cylinders for 110bhp. Twenty horses stronger still was the 911L, with L standing for Lux.

The 911L also benefitted from the 911S vented brake rotors. 1968 brought a glass backlight replacement for the targa's former plastic window. The targa style had been available on 912s from 1966. The 912/911T/911L/911S carried on to mid-'68 model year on the 911's original 2211mm wheelbase. These are now known as the short wheelbase (swb) cars. With the B series 911, Porsche sought to address the 911's traditional rear end waywardness.

1980 Formula One World Champion Alan Jones said you knew who had come to a dinner party in an early Porsche 911. Their hands were still going up and down while holding the cutlery, even when not eating! This was from mile after mile of steering corrections, as the squirrely 911 followed every road camber change– a steering wheel can be too alive. So Porsche extended the 911 wheelbase by 57mm; it was now 2268mm or 89.3in.

In moving the rear wheels 2.25in backwards the engine/transmission remained in situ. The increased angle of the driveshafts needed new CV joints. The revised 911 body had slightly flared rear arches also. These accommodated the now 6in wide rims. A magnesium casting for the flat-six block reduced weight, and further helped mitigate final oversteer. Changes to the fuel delivery system were also afoot.

The replacement of the Porsche 356B with the 356C had seen a transition from dual Zenith 32 NDIX carbs to the solid shaft Solex 40 P-11. The 912 made use of the split shaft version of the latter carb, and the Solex 40 P-11 was a popular design. The early two-liter 911s utilized the Solex 40 P-1 spill type carburettor. Here, there were effectively six separate carbs sharing a single manifold, with a recirculating pump to supply them.

Solex carbs had the advantage of bore spacing that permitted a direct shot into the 911's intakes. However, Solex reliability problems prompted Porsche to make a hardware switch to Webers. When the 911 was new, the Solex carbs worked fine in daily driver duty. However, by the 4000-mile mark several owners experienced driveability and tuning problems, which motivated Porsche to make a supply company change to Weber.

From mid-'66, Porsche transitioned from Solex to Weber. Porsche 911 owners could return to their dealer for a free retrofit. Many took advantage of the retrofit, but many elected to stay with Solex. In any case, carbs were temporary, fuel-injection was the future: fewer moving, wear-related parts compared to complex carbs, a more accurate fuel mixture and better atomization. You would expect fuel-injection

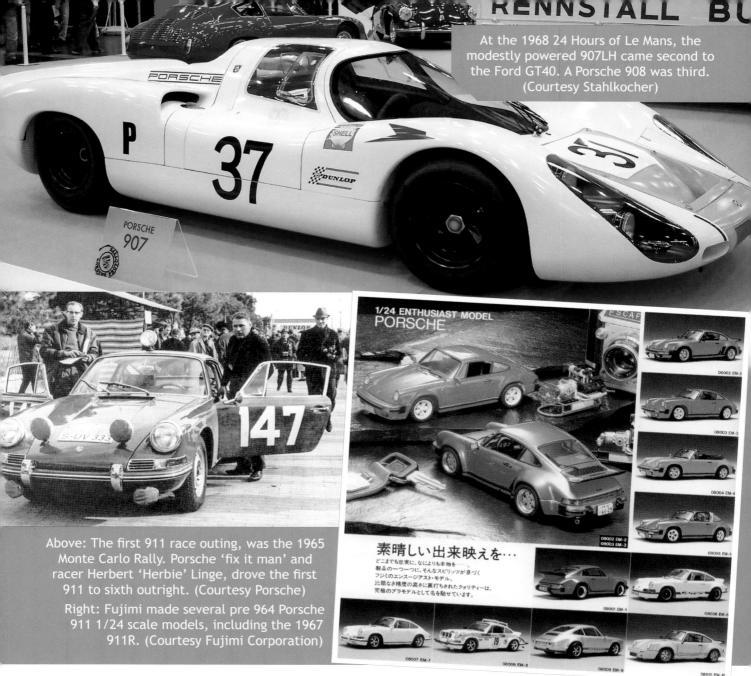

PORSCHE
907

1/24 ENTHUSIAST MODEL
PORSCHE

素晴しい出来映えを…

どこまでも忠実に、なによりも本物を
製品の一つ一つに、そんなスピリッツが息づく
フジミのエンジョイアスト・モデル。
比類ない精度の高さに裏打ちされたクォリティーは、
究極のプラモデルとして名を馳せています。

Above: The first 911 race outing, was the 1965 Monte Carlo Rally. Porsche 'fix it man' and racer Herbert 'Herbie' Linge, drove the first 911 to sixth outright. (Courtesy Porsche)

Right: Fujimi made several pre 964 Porsche 911 1/24 scale models, including the 1967 911R. (Courtesy Fujimi Corporation)

on a German car. For '68 MY US VW Type 3 1600s had Bosch D-Jetronic, but for '69 MY Porsche used high-pressure Bosch mechanical fuel-injection on top Porsche 911s.

On VWs, fuel-injection was for better driveability, economy, pollution control and performance. On Porsches, fuel-injection was more for high performance. There was a high-pressure fuel pump and associated injectors. The 911E replaced the 911L, and the latest 911S took on fuel-injection too. Power and torque for the 911E and 911S came in at 140bhp, 129lb/ft and 170bhp, 135 lb/ft respectively.

The 911S' outright performance was unaffected.[41] The 911S power and torque arrived at 6800rpm and 5500rpm respectively. So, please do make use of that close ratio, dog-leg five-speeder!

During this 1965-69 era the humble 912 was still around, with Porsche keeping the model parallel with 911 development. This included the wheelbase stretch, and replacing the trunk's single battery with two 35amp units. The idea was to achieve more even weight distribution, and to pin down the front end of the 911/912. The car got light in the front end at speed and started to wander. Unfortunately, the 912's price had been wandering northwards too.

The final '65 Porsche 1600SC was $4577, the 912 replaced this model at $4690 with the 911 at $6490. By 1969, with the revaluation of the Deutschmark, availability of the 911T and cheaper rivals with equal or more performance spelt the temporary demise of the 912. The use of the 911 body wasn't helping either: it was expensive. Porsche was making the 912 and had trouble keeping a price gap between 911 and 912. The 912 just wasn't budget enough.[42]

Of all the 911/912 versions, the 911E probably best summarized the Porsche spirit: that blend of upscale sports luxury, where comfort didn't take a back +2 seat. In taking over from the 911L, the 911E came standard with self-leveling hydropneumatic front MacPherson strut suspension. The system was optional on the 911T and 911S. A 'Comfort Kit' was available for the austere 911T. All '69 911s received larger rear brake calipers, with the injected 911S getting bigger front alloy calipers. However, for sports/luxo value for money, the 911E competed well against rivals.

In late '60s America, the 911E didn't have many rivals, and only it and the BMW 2800CS offered +2 seating. The cheapest and swiftest rival was the $6250 Jaguar XKE: from *Road & Track*'s figures it did 0-60mph in eight seconds, the quarter mile in 15.7 seconds with 15.9mpg overall. Next came the $7654 Mercedes 280SL with respective stats of 9.9 seconds,

17.1 seconds, and 17.5mpg. The $7995 911E recorded 8.4 seconds, 16 seconds at 83mph, and 18.4mpg, with the $8107 BMW 2800CS giving 9.3 seconds, 17.4 seconds and 19mpg.

For a blend of handling, performance, comfort, economy and small size, there were no American rivals, or rivals from anywhere else. The 911E was a quality grand tourer with all independent suspension and refinement. To find more car would have necessitated visiting a Ferrari or Lamborghini showroom, at a much greater cost. Fuel economy in 1969 only mattered in terms of driving range and the inconvenience of having to stop and fill up. In this class, only the Porsche and the Jaguar were pure sports cars and the 911E had much more interior

space. The Jaguar's front-mounted gearbox and high rocker panels, meant the driver sat in a trench with a small footwell.

Jaguar entry was via the 'leg feeding method.' In contrast, the front of the 911E around the shifter was quite flat, and there was the bonus of some rear seating. Plus, unlike the XKE, the 911 could have factory a/c in left and right-hand drive versions. The 911E's three rivals were all around the 3000lb weight level. This explained their need for three- and four-liter six-cylinder engines. However, with Porsche, less always seemed to bring more, with the two-liter 911E offering gold medal efficiency!

From Sugar Scoop to 908 & 911R
In 1964, there was a racing car that shared Butzi Porsche's drawing board with the 911; it was the Porsche 904. This mid-engined sports car represented an engineering and styling departure from Porsche practice. Gone were the labor intensive spaceframes, and handmade aluminum bodies. The 904 utilized a sturdy spot welded, box frame chassis, with a fiberglass body bonded to said chassis. The rigid, unified structure was stiffer than a spaceframe, but complex. The fiberglass body was made up of 50 individual parts, which make restoration tricky.

The 904's suspension followed the design of Porsche's 1962 Formula One car. At the front lived double wishbones, with a complex four-link rear suspension. There were two main crossmembers, and fabricated hoops for the front and rear suspension. There were telescopic shocks and springs all round, and front and rear swaybars, but no torsion bars! It had been hoped that the 911's new two-liter flat-six would be placed ahead of the axle line, but it wasn't ready. Technical Director Hans Tomala decided on the trusty four-cam two-liter flat-four. Porsche's engine man Hans Mezger reworked the four-cam to 180bhp at 7200rpm, using bigger valves and revised ignition timing.[43]

The planned Porsche 911 five-speed transaxle also produced awkward shifting, and differential failures, early in the going. A functional need to cool the brakes saw Butzi's stylish rear grilled vents replaced with the sugar scoops that gave the 904 its nickname. Form follows function, perhaps, but Butzi

The 911T's 110 horse motor, could run on 2-star* petrol in the UK, or leaded regular in America. (*See page 78). An unusual trait for an exotic sports car. (Courtesy Porsche)

Porsche brought aesthetic charm to the Porsche line. When it came to product design he received training at the top institute in Ulm. With limited fiberglass experience, Porsche sought help from aircraft manufacturer Heinkel.

Heinkel made the body and chassis complex, and *Car and Driver* tested the 904 in 1964. The journal got 0-60mph in 5.3 seconds and 0-100mph in 12.2 seconds. The factory estimated top speed at nearly 160mph. All up, slightly better figures than a late '60s big block 'Vette, but with a much smaller engine. The 904 was a good looking car and Butzi's favorite. The tight time constraints with the project meant "there was no time for anyone to interfere." Porsche had manufactured enough Carrera GTs to qualify for GT racing.

The 904 made its debut at Sebring in 1964, and won its second race, which was the 1964 Targa Florio. Here, the 904 was aided by the expiration of the front line '63 Spyders, which led driver pairings Colin Davis/Antonio Pucci and Linge/Balzarini to a respective Porsche 904 1-2 finish! The 904 was very reliable and dominated its two-liter class in endurance racing. That was certainly the case at Le Mans in 1964. The 904 wasn't disadvantaged by its big 15in rims.

Unfortunately for the Porsche 904, there were big changes in the offing: FIA rulebook changes for 1966 and Ferdinand Piëch taking over racing car development meant the end for the 904. From this

point the 904/6 was mainly for privateers. Interest in the 904 continued, in spite of the Piëch racers, and 5 or 6 years later a second production run was considered. Journalist Karl Ludvigsen saw one at Zuffenhausen, painted orange, fully trimmed and with a 911S engine. Sadly, that's as far as it went. The 904 was an instant classic, so much so its short steering column saddles indicator and main beam lights paddles resembled those on the Beetle![44]

New FIA Group 4 rules paved the way for Porsche's next racer, announced in January 1966: the 906. With this and subsequent designs, Ferdinand Piëch ignored cousin Butzi and went clean sheet. Piëch was into light weight and aerodynamics. Instead of the body being part of the rigid structure, as per the 904, the 906 had a tubular spaceframe and unstressed fiberglass body. It also had gullwing doors and was much lighter than the 904, at just 1280lb. The body's fiberglass was laid up by hand, not sprayed like the 904, so production results were more consistent.

Oftentimes powered by the 901/20 flat-six, the 906 was also known as the Carrera 6. A two-liter class car, rather than an outright contender. However, the car's lightness meant it usually punched above its weight. Piëch's weight-saving strategy ran to beryllium brake disks, and the use of titanium and magnesium. Although it wasn't until the 908 that Porsche switched from steel to aluminum for its tubular spaceframes.

A one owner from new 1970 911E. The coupe still wears its original paint! (Courtesy William)

The 906 became a test bed for the use of fuel-injection. Fitted with Porsche's flat-eight motor, the 906 was used by privateers in the big car Group 6 category.

The 906 was Porsche's first racer to be tested in a wind tunnel, but to save money it used suspension components made in advance for the 904 Series II that never was. Like the 904, the 906 used 15in rims with a pitstop-unfriendly five-bolt pattern. However, its 910 successor was developed to utilize the lighter and smaller F1 style wheels/tires. The 910 did hillclimbs, with such reduced unsprung weight being a boon for handling.

The 906 certainly accumulated the results. It was sixth overall at the 1966 24 Hours of Daytona, and fourth at that year's 12 Hours of Sebring, the latter with drivers Hans Herrmann

It would take the optional 'Comfort Kit' to lift the base 911T to this level of plushness. However, even the 911E exemplified Germanic spartan luxury. (Courtesy William)

The tractable 911E's good torque delivery made it faster accelerating to 100mph, than the 911S! (Courtesy William)

Porsche bored out its flat-six to 2.2 liters for 1970. This placed the latest 911E on 155bhp. (Courtesy William)

and Herbert Müller. The 906 achieved class wins at these races, and at the Monza 1000, Spa 1000 and Nürburgring 1000 also. Privateers Willy Mairesse and Gerhard Muller got an outright victory at the 1966 Targa Florio.[45] Then there was the 906s' 4-5-6-7 1966 Le Mans finish behind the 7-liter GT40s' 1-2-3. It would be an understatement to say the 906 had done well in 1966.

Porsche's next move was the 907 sports car prototype racer, an intermediate step on its road to the big car class. Built during 1967 and 1968, the driver now sat on the right. Ferdinand Piëch thought it would be advantageous on the clockwise running racetracks. The 907 made its debut at the 1967 Le Mans endurance race, with an enduro-suited two-liter flat-six and vented disk brakes. It secured fifth behind the big boy Fords and Ferraris, using a Mulsanne Straight compatible long tail.

Porsche got really serious with the 907 at the 24 Hours of Daytona. A team of 20 mechanics and engineers yielded a 1-2-3 result. Porsche anticipated the car pooling of the fuel crisis years, with the lead car being shared by five drivers. The racers included Vic Elford and Jochen Neerpasch.

This was followed up by a 1-2 triumph at the 12 Hours of Sebring, achieved by the respective pairings of Jo Siffert/Hans Herrmann and Vic Elford/Jochen Neerpasch. Elford's partner went on to run BMW Motorsport. Neerpasch came up with the idea of making M cars as a side business while racing e9 BMW 3.0 CSLs, which he had helped make competitive.[46]

In 1968, Vic Elford and Umberto Maglioli won the Targa Florio after a disastrous start. Initially, Elford lost 18 minutes due to tire failure. Cars like the small engined 904, 906 and 907 were great on tight, twisty circuits. Here, the big, powerful cars just didn't fit. Their reliability also meant enduro race surprises when the powerful cars didn't deliver, like at *Le Mans* in 1968. That year, Porsche's 907 successor, the 908, didn't do too well at the French circuit. The 908 won the Nürburgring 1000, but alternator problems and misinterpretation of the pit repair rules, led to a Ford GT40 winning the race. Gianrico Steinemann and Spoerry came second in the two-liter flat-six 907. Rolf Stommelen and Jochen Neerpasch came third in the 908/02 Spyder.

Porsche had been developing its three-liter flat-eight motor to suit the FIA rule changes that were afoot. This motor was going to be in the 907, but actually made its factory debut in the 908. Not happy with the idea of dominant seven-liter Ford and Ferrari V12 prototype racers, the powers that be banned them in 1968. So, the Group 6 Sports

Prototype class was now with three-liter prototypes (Porsche 908), or five-liter stock blocks (old GT40s). Enzo was a little displeased, but at least he still had Formula One. He might have called the FIA officials a bunch of 'baciagaloops,' but this has never been confirmed!

Thinking ahead, and taking a risk, Porsche went beyond three-liter prototypes and built 25 flat-twelve 917s in advance. In the meantime, the 908 found its feet, and the 907 did the deed in the hands of privateers. They got on the podium at Monza in 1969, and recorded seventh outright at Le Mans in 1971. Originally, the 908 was a long tail high speed track racer, as the 908/01 LH, with the moderately powerful 350bhp three-liter flat-eight. However, it found its calling in 1969, while the 917 was having its own troubles.

To comply with 1969s Group 6 rule changes, Porsche removed the 908's roof and long tail. Aluminum tube frames were now utilized, and the result was the 908/02 Spyder. This newbie beat out Ferrari with a 1-2-3 finish at Brands Hatch in

the 1969 BOAC 500. It also won the Monza 1000, Targa Florio and Spa 1000. Then there was the 1-2-3-4-5 domination at the Nürburgring 1000. With the big powerhouse 917, and little 908 for twisty tracks, Porsche won the International Championship for Makes during 1969 to 1971.

For 1970, the 908 as the 908/03, became even more compact. It was based on the 909 hill climber, and weighed only 1100lb. The 908/03 won the 1970 Nürburgring 1000 and Targa Florio. Porsche then fitted the car with vertical fins, and it didn't do well at the 1971 Targa Florio. Here, Brian Redman got badly injured. However, a 1-2-3 at 1971's Nürburgring 1000 redressed the balance. This was a happy venue for the 908, which won the race from 1968 to 1971, and again in 1980.

The 908 almost triumphed at Le Mans in 1969 and 1980. At the 1969 race Porsche introduced a brake pad wear warning light, but the drivers purposely ignored this. They were trying to stay out longer, and on terms with the big engined GT40. Unfortunately for Porsche, the brakes went south towards the end.

Herrmann and Larrousse's 908 was beaten by just 200 meters! The winning Ford GT40 was the same car that won in 1968. Reinhold Joest's 908 LH came third at Le Mans in 1972, but his 1980 908 that finished second turned out to have a 936 chassis underneath. This was odd, since Porsche didn't sell the 936 to privateers.

The 908 had a similar chassis to the two-liter 907. For 1972, the three-liter class of Group 5 Sports Cars now had a higher weight minimum, so privateers added weight, and subsequently the 934's 2.1-liter turbo flat-six. This lifted the 908/03's 370bhp rating to over 500 horse! Up to the early '70s, Porsche was mainly doing sports car racing under Ferdinand Piëch's direction, but there were some 911 activities too. The 911 made a splash with rallying, specifically the 1965 Monte Carlo Rally. Herbie Linge came sixth here. It was the start of a successful rally program.[47]

In 1967, Vic Elford and David Stone won their class in the Monte Carlo Rally. There were also overall wins in the German Rally, Tulip Rally, Geneva Rally, and Sobiesław Zasada won his home Polish Rally in

The aluminum crankcased 1970-71 911s, shown here in Coupe and Targa forms, had 2.2-liter flat sixes, and sometimes Fuchs rims. (Courtesy Porsche)

Left: By 1972 the relatively affordable 911T was on 2.4 liters and 130bhp in Europe. Porsche 911T 2.4 1972-73 production totaled 9289 units. (Courtesy Porsche)

Butzi Porsche's favorite 911 color choice was orange. He questioned why German racing silver had to always be chosen. A 1972 911T 2.4 is displayed. (Courtesy Porsche)

The fuel injected 1973 911E 2.4 Targa, is shown in US spec. It was the final year for the sports/luxo 'E' version, and the last year for normal bumpers in North America. (Courtesy Porsche)

The torquey mellow yellow sports/luxo '72 911E 2.4L, was no faster than the outgoing 2.2L version, but required less urban shifting. (Courtesy Porsche)

a 911S. Elford and Stone won the 1968 Monte Carlo Rally using a 911T with 911S mechanicals, and second were teammates Paul Toivonen and Marti Tiukkanen. Björn Waldegård took out the Swedish Rally.

The Spa 24-Hour Race was won by Erwin Kremer, Helmut Kelleners and Willi Kauhsen, sharing a Porsche 911R. The 911R was the lightweight 911 vision of Ferdinand Piëch. The 911R weighed a mere 1782lb, so expectedly it had fiberglass panels and plexiglass windows. Power of 210bhp at 9000rpm and 152lb/ft

at 6800rpm came from a Type 901/22 1991cc 10.3:1 flat-six with dual Weber 46 IDA3C carbs. The car was an early swb 911, of 2211mm wheelbase. Porsche reckoned it good for 250kph, so priced 'em at 45,000 Deutschmarks. Apart from four prototypes, only 20 911Rs were constructed. That said, homologation/race specials being the slow sellers they always are, some of the 20 were still gathering dust in 1971![48]

The 911R gained fame through an endurance record breaking attempt, a mere 20,000km jaunt, in a leisurely four days no less. This world record attempt was conducted at Monza in 1967 with sponsors BP and Firestone. Attempting the run was Swiss racer Gianrico Steinemann, but his first try in October 1967 collapsed, literally. After less than ten hours his Porsche 906 broke down. The front suspension gave up the ghost, so Steinemann phoned Ferdinand Piëch for help.

There was a rulebook-stated time window to try again, so two 911Rs were sent forth to conquer Monza. Support staff for the endeavor were Helmuth Bott as overseer, Paul Hensler in charge of engines, Richard Hetmann looking at drivetrains, Peter Falk as competitions boss and Albert Junginger with the experimental section. With these Porsche brains, plus Piëch, how could the 911R lose?

The second 911R was driven to the circuit quickly, and part dismantled on arrival; it was the parts car. The prepared 911Rs had two fifth gears, with fourth three per cent shorter. The drivers were told to alternate between fifth gears, to help preserve the Type 901/53 gearbox and LSD. The second record attempt commenced on Tuesday, October 31, 1967 at 8pm. Fog was bad, so small pocket lamps were put along the circuit at five-meter intervals. Four helpers circulated, changing the batteries every three to four hours! This time, the plan worked, with five world

and 11 international records broken. An average speed of 130.77mph was recorded for the 20,000km, with 90 tires consumed in 96 hours. Firestone used 906 front tires on the rear. Just as well that Porsche designed the 906 with 15in rims.

The record-breaking car had chassis number 118-990-001, and gained fame so fast that Switzerland let the car in after the record was broken. It was displayed in the country's first ever race car exhibition in Zurich. The Swiss have strict anti-noise pollution regulations. The first time around they didn't admit the 911R, but now it was a celebrity! The 911R was Piëch's experimental machine; there was no planned role for it. Aside from one car, Piëch kept the prototypes private.

In 1967 and 1968, Vic Elford used a 911R to win the Marathon de la Route. In 1969, a 911R Sportomatic won this event, in the hands of Glemser and Kauhsen. The 1969 Tour de France and Tour de Course, were won by Gérard Larrousse and Maurice Gélin in a fuel-injected 911R, chassis number 118-990-005. In light of the 911R's slow sales, the Porsche Marketing Director put the kybosh on trying to sell 500 911Rs for GT racing homologation. However, lessons learnt were applied to subsequent racing 911s. 🐎

The UK market has always liked its German prestige cars to be well specified and luxurious. This made the 911E the most popular variant. The 1970 2.2L example shown had 155bhp at 6200rpm, and could reach 136mph. (Courtesy Porsche)

CHAPTER
Four
The 911 enters the RennSport era

It pays to advertise! The '74 911's trunk decal, was similar to the '74 Chevy Camaro's 'Z28' hood decal.
Both cars got attractive impact bumpers that year. (Courtesy Porsche)

914 - The Square Porsche

In the mid-60s, the long-standing and mutually beneficial relationship between VW and Porsche was about to create a new sports car. The car in question was the Porsche 914, Fourteener or Square Porsche, as it has become known. Unlike with the later 924, VW weren't looking to replace the Karmann Ghia. Wolfsburg was still wedded to rear-engined air-cooled cars and was in its product diversification phase. VW wanted to have something for everyone. Such diversity meant going upscale. The Porsche 914 would provide the perfect stepping stone from humble VW to glamorous Porsche.

Porsche had been moving upscale since day one, and now needed an entry-level model to maintain sales volume more than ever. It was becoming clear by the mid-60s that an independent company couldn't be viable on the 911's production alone. Tooling and investment for new designs required money. With a sales projection of 30,000 units per annum, the 914 could help. Especially since it had been normal for Porsche cars to be sold through many VW dealers, and handled by VW's importer network around the world.

The friendship between Ferry Porsche and VW's long-time post war boss – the only boss it had ever known – Professor Heinz Nordhoff, would come into play with the 914. One reason Ferry hadn't gone mid-engined with the 356, as originally intended, was that it was hard to adapt VW parts to a mid-engined design – until now. The starting point for the 914 was the front-engined sports car proposal from German industrial design firm Gugelot. Porsche picked up this proposal in the fall of 1966.

Things seemed very promising. Porsche would design the car, and Karmann would build it. Porsche was running flat out just making the 911 anyway. With a VW version of the new car, Wolfsburg would be ordering so many bodies from Karmann that Porsche would get a good price for the 914 bodies they received. Certainly, using the expensive 911 body for the 912 had made the latter a questionable entry-level coupe.

The four-pot 914 would utilize the 80bhp VW 411E 1679cc OHV flat-four. It had Bosch D-Jetronic fuel-injection, making the 914 ideal for the increasingly smog-law-stricken USA. Then there was the Porsche edition, with the two-liter flat-six from the outgoing 1969 911T. Although Porsche tried to put a price gap between the 914/6 and the 1970 911T, the new Fourteener did have much Porsche hardware. The 914/6 had Porsche five-mount hubs, wheels and brakes. This bolide could do 0-60mph in under nine seconds and steam on to 120mph using its Porsche dogleg five-speeder.

The 914/6 was completed at the Zuffenhausen factory, using bodies supplied from Karmann. Both 914 and 914/6 had Porsche's Sportomatic option, and had suspension almost identical to the 911 layout. One difference was the use of rear coils, to accommodate the space hungry mid-engine layout. That said, the Square Porsche had useful, commodious front and rear trunks. Take that Corvette! Plus, 914 development was mainly done at the Weissach proving ground in Stuttgart … very Porsche.[49]

In October 1969, *CAR*'s Philippe DeBarry covered an introduction to the new 914 in the article *So This IS The People's Porsche*. He tried both the 914 and 914/6 in West Germany, and came away with a good impression of both versions. With a projected price of under £2000, the 914 seemed good value. DeBarry judged the shape not exactly beautiful, but the 914 was reasonably quick, and braked and handled well too. It was a mid-engined sports car with a VW flat-four, just like Ferry's 356 proto of 20 years earlier!

The 914/6 was even more impressive. DeBarry found the newcomer outhandled the 911S provided for comparison on the Hockenheim racetrack. The 911S' front end wandered under heavy braking, but the 914/6 was so forgivingly neutral. The writer even considered that a 914/6 with the 911R motor would have a better power-to-weight ratio than the Mercedes C111 rotary-powered supercar. Butzi Porsche had always favored a pure mid-engined two-seater, and mid-engined sports cars were winning races for Zuffenhausen. Why not make what you race? Was this the new Porsche?

The 914 was certainly going to be sold in a new way. VW dealers had to decide if they wanted to sell VWs or Porsches. If the latter, they had to spend big time. To market and distribute the Fourteener, VW and Porsche came up with the joint venture entity, VW-Porsche VG GmbH, effective from April 1, 1969. In America a Porsche-Audi dealer network was formally established on October 1, 1969. Starting from 1970 model year, Porsche-Audi dealers would showcase the new Audi 100, Porsche 914 and established Porsche 911.[50]

With a central, but not anti-clockwise, tach and four-wheel disk brakes, the 914 landed in America at $3595. The newcomer garnered *Motor Trend*'s 1970 Import Car Of The Year title. Above the 914, the 914/6 retailed at $6099, with the latest 911T costing

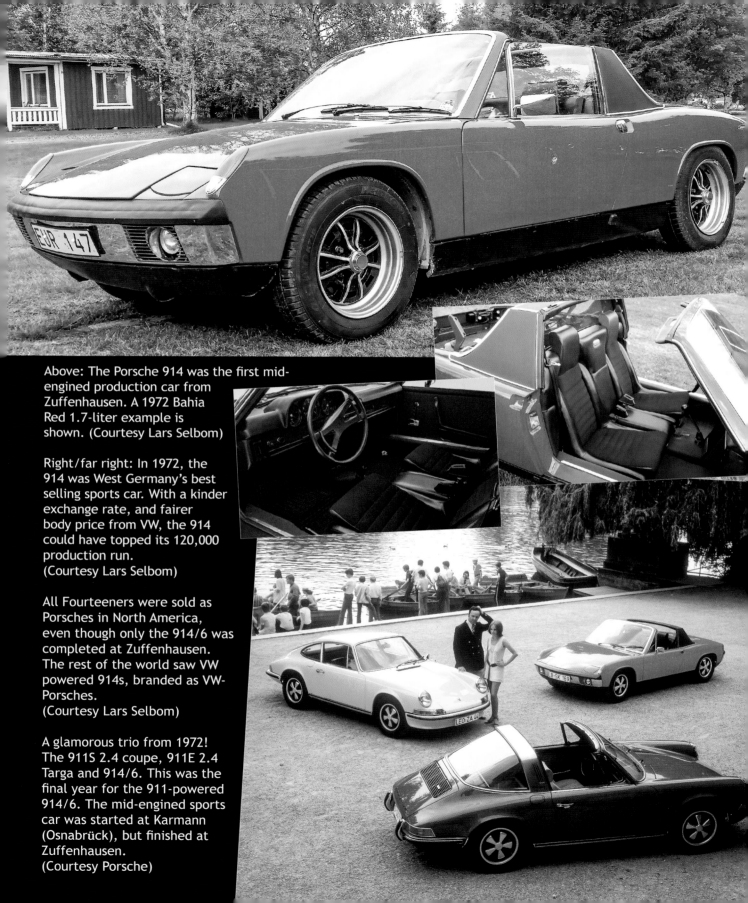

Above: The Porsche 914 was the first mid-engined production car from Zuffenhausen. A 1972 Bahia Red 1.7-liter example is shown. (Courtesy Lars Selbom)

Right/far right: In 1972, the 914 was West Germany's best selling sports car. With a kinder exchange rate, and fairer body price from VW, the 914 could have topped its 120,000 production run.
(Courtesy Lars Selbom)

All Fourteeners were sold as Porsches in North America, even though only the 914/6 was completed at Zuffenhausen. The rest of the world saw VW powered 914s, branded as VW-Porsches.
(Courtesy Lars Selbom)

A glamorous trio from 1972! The 911S 2.4 coupe, 911E 2.4 Targa and 914/6. This was the final year for the 911-powered 914/6. The mid-engined sports car was started at Karmann (Osnabrück), but finished at Zuffenhausen.
(Courtesy Porsche)

$7205. The closeness to the 911 T's price hinted at the 914's first problem: price. The Porsche plan to get a supply of well-priced 914 bodies fell through when Heinz Nordhoff suddenly died on April 12, 1968.

Ferry and Heinz had a gentleman's agreement on the 914 body price. Dr Kurt Lotz had been waiting to take over as VW boss when Nordhoff retired in 1970. However, he was uninformed concerning the gentleman's agreement. VW now wanted the full economic price for 914 body supply. To make matters worse, the bodies Porsche would get for its 914/6, would be fully trimmed. Porsche had originally wanted a plain body, so this placed the 914/6 within the 911 body price range.

Adding insult to injury, the strong Deutschmark and weak dollar made the 914 and all West German imports more price uncompetitive in America. With all the problems going on, a factory right-hand drive 914 wasn't a priority. Indeed, such a RHD version never eventuated. Effectively, this meant LHD inconvenience for the UK and Japan, and an expensive mandatory RHD conversion for Australia. Of course, one could just buy the much cheaper RHD Ford Capri. In spite of early slow sales, the 914 battled on. It achieved success in racing, was developed in the Porsche tradition, and sales did pick up.[51]

The 916 & other upgrades
In 1972, the Fourteener was West Germany's number one selling sports car, and Zuffenhausen was cooking up the ultimate Square Porsche. The 916 was a very special 914/6 with all the goodies

Porsche was working on in 1972. It had the 190 horse 2.4-liter 911S motor, connected to a Porsche 915 gearbox. The coupe had a fixed roof for rigidity and a super plush interior. Porsche built 11 prototypes – some had front-mounted oil coolers, and one even had air-conditioning!

Sadly, the bean counters ruled out the 916. You could see their point. Only 3318 914/6s were sold by the time the model ended at the close of '72 MY. The M471 appearance and rim pack, celebrating the 914/6 GT's racetrack success, had not been popular. It seemed that price did matter with the 914. The four-cylinder cars sold well enough at 115,600. However, if it cost more, folks wanted a 911. The 911 had only been going for a relatively short time, but it had already struck a mighty chord with the Porsche faithful.

There was room for a cheaper Porsche, and the revised 1973 914 range showed this. That year sales rose to 27,000, the Fourteener's best showing. To aid the traditionally awkward VW/Porsche gear change, the shift forks were moved from the tail to the side. Slightly better, but the real news for '73 was the 914 2.0. This replacement for the 914/6, used a hi po two-liter VW Type 4 motor. It made 100bhp and 115lb/ft net. These were very good figures for 1973 America. The new car was nearly as quick as the outgoing 914/6, and a helluva lot cheaper.

In 1973, the 914 1.7 cost $4499, the 914 2.0 was $5049 and the 911T Targa retailed at $8760. There was a 914 2.0 appearance pack: Fuchs, center console/aux gauges, quartz driving lights, dual swaybars and an armrest! 1973 was a very good North American auto industry sales year. Unfortunately, things took a dive in 1974 in the wake of the fuel crisis and ensuing recession. The base 914 now had the Type 4 1800. In Europe it was dual Webers, in America it was the 412E sourced 50-state motor with Bosch L-Jetronic injection. This 8.6:1 1800 made 76 SAE net horses.

The 1974 914 2.0 was still on 100bhp, with Bosch D-Jetronic. In the UK, this variant was looking like reasonable value. In 1974 prices the LHD 914 2.0 was £3096, and went by the name 914SC 2.0. All '74 UK 911s were 2.7-liter cars, starting at £5244, with the 911S and Carrera Targa priced respectively at £5869 and £7536. The Chevy Corvette Stingray 454 automatic and Jaguar XKE V12 automatic retailed for £4150 and £3365 respectively.[52]

The 914 was looking sharp too in 1974. To celebrate the Porsche-Audi Sunoco-Penske team's Porsche 917 1972-73 Can-Am racing season

Below: Built by Karmann of Osnabrück, the 914/4 had four-bolt hubs. It also used the 1970 VW 411E's electronic injected Type 4 1700. (Courtesy Lars Selbom)

Kelly Pretorius did a photoshoot with the Porsche 911WRS (Weekend Racer Sport) for *SXdrv magazine*. The car was created by South African tuner Dutchmann, starting with a 1971 911. (Courtesy sxdrv.com)

triumphs, there was a Can-Am '74 914 2.0 in three color combos: black with yellow trim, white with green trim, and white with orange trim. Sports and luxury equipment were in the mix also. However, the VW-Porsche VG joint venture was on the skids, and, at VW's request, the partnership was dissolved on May 8, 1974. VW had its own problems trying to get the Rabbit ready, and transitioning away from being a rear-engined, air-cooled company. Plus, the sporty new Scirocco was waiting in the wings. Indeed, the winds of change were truly blowing.

Porsche sales people moved into the VW-Porsche VG HQ located in Ludwigsburg. The 1975 914 1.8 and 2.0s got air injection and EGR, and Golden

State 914s even received a cat. 1975 was the crunch year for pollution laws. With things winding down and the 924 having made its Frankfurt Show debut, 1976 would be the final year for the 914. It was now down to a single version, the 914 2.0, and was sold in America only.

Almost 120,000 Fourteeners rolled off the Karmann and Porsche assembly lines. A bit of luck would have boosted that tally to 180,000. Even so, it had become a popular sight on the American scene. It appeared in the 1973 movie *The Mad Bomber;* here, Chuck Connors' crazy urban vigilante confronted a 914 driver who he felt had transgressed road traffic laws. In the popular TV series *The Rockford Files,*

The 911WRS by Dutchmann, represents a restomodded Porsche. An improved 250bhp Carrera 2.7 flat-six, OEM parts and '80s 911 Carrera vented disks were part of the build. The 911WRS rolls, very quickly, on Dutchmann Cup alloy wheels. (Courtesy www.YouTube.comwatch?v=1Fg1xYd9OzY)

911 Series C to G - The business of evolution

After five years at two-liters, the 911 received its first displacement increase. The flat-six was bored out from 80 to 84mm, this took capacity to 2195cc. It was the most obvious change for the new 1970 model year C series 911. However, only X-ray vision would have detected that Porsche had changed the crankcase material from magnesium to aluminum. There was also a bigger 225mm clutch, and Sportomatic was not available on the 911S anymore. With a constant eye to improving handling, the 911's front upper strut attachment points were moved forward 14mm.

In spite of all the above, the 911 didn't look any different - little surprise there. The regular road versions continued with 911T, 911E and 911S as the respective 'budget,' luxury and sports variants. Power was up across the board with the 911T, E and S on 125bhp, 155bhp and 180bhp. Outright performance of the 911T and 911E were little changed, but the 911S was one second quicker to 60 at seven seconds flat, and capable of just under 140mph.

No one had been complaining about the 911's lack of scat, so the improvements for 1971 were more directed at practicality. For the 1971 911 D series PVC-coated and galvanized floor sections were introduced. Even in Europe low pollution laws were raising their disruptive head, with West Germany going to low lead gasoline. With emissions in mind, Porsche adjusted ignition and fuel systems on '71 911s. The 911T was still on carbs, with mechanical fuel-injection (MFI) for the 911E and 911S continuing.

Kelly's 911

Chris Doyle and Richard Middleton's *SXdrv magazine*, shows the popularity of restomodding. Plus, Porsche 911s have often been upgraded with later parts. Such has been the case with South African high-performance tuning shop Dutchmann and its 911WRS (Weekend Racer Sport). The starting point was a 1971 Porsche 911, utilizing a worked Carrera 2.7-liter flat-six.

Bored out with 92mm pistons in a line bored casing, with new crank and bearings, with resized conrods going for 250 horses. Milled heads helped the CR rise to 10.3:1, complemented by a sportier than stock dual exhaust system. Connected to this Carrera motor was a rebuilt 915 five-speed with short shift kit. On the outside a bare metal respray in Viper Green is hard to miss. The restoration included new rubber seals, belts, trim pieces and panels. Porsche 911S level trim and '73 Carrera RS 2.7 rocker panels were OEM-sourced parts.

lawyer Beth Davenport drove a 914. This car was sometimes driven by the show's main character, Davenport's friend and private detective, Jim Rockford.

The 914 entered a market full of sports cars. The German Opel GT was a rival, so too was the Datsun 240Z. As Porsche would experience with the 924 and other lower priced models, it's a competitive area. The mainstream, high-volume automakers will match you on performance and throw in a graphic equalizer and reclining buckets with lumbar support at no extra charge. Then, Zuffenhausen has to defend Porsche credibility, and all the time devotees were saying: "911, there's no substitute."

The interior of the 911WRS has new carpets and headliner. The iconic Porsche Tombstone seats have been custom trimmed in matching Napa leather, with special piping, the dashboard too. Retrofitted Porsche parts included a 911 Carrera RS 2.7 steering wheel, 996 chassis 911 brake calipers and 1980s 911 Carrera 3.2 vented brake rotors. Further custom touches involve Dutchmann Cup alloy wheels, with the tuner's logo milled into the rim.

For the *SXdrv* magazine photoshoot with the 911WRS, model Kelly Pretorius (from Pretoria, South Africa) imagined she was James Dean's girlfriend. Certainly James Dean is as legendary as the '50s Porsches he admired. However, in the Dutchmann 911WRS and Kelly Pretorius we have future icons. In modern times, Porsche, and others, have moved away from manual transmissions. However, Kelly prefers them, believing that if you are going to drive a car, you should actually drive it.

Moving the oil tank

Many were the changes Porsche had ready for the 1972 E series 911. To maintain a low center of gravity, the Porsche flat-six made use of dry sump lubrication. The separate oil tank involved was placed behind the right rear wheel on A to D series 911s. To reduce wild oversteer, through improving weight distribution, 1972 911s had said oil tank moved ahead of the right rear wheel. The tank was now within the 911's wheelbase, and Porsche added an oil filler body flap in this new location.

Moving the tank was a great idea, but sadly it seemed too many gas station attendants mistook this flap for the gas tank filler, with less than humorous results. So Porsche moved the tank back to its usual location the following year. On the right rear intake grille, a square '2.4' engine callout badge now lived. Porsche had increased the flat-six's stroke from 66mm to 70.4mm, giving a 2341cc displacement. Technically it was a 2.3-liter, but marketing liked the 2.4 gain over 2.2. There was also a racing 911 to allude to.[53]

The power gains were real. The European spec 911T, E and S were now on a respective 130bhp, 165bhp and 190bhp. North American 911Ts were pumping out 140 horses. Even though the Euro 911T was still using dual carbs, the American 911T used mechanical fuel-injection like the 911E and 911S. A compression ratio drop for the 2.4 engine accorded with Porsche policy of having one engine that could cope with several markets. In this case, the low lead regular of America and two-star* petrol of the UK with the 911T.[54]

The 1972-73 911T was a kind of practical supercar in Europe, where this class of vehicle usually needed 98 octane gas or higher. The total number made was 9289, and 130 horses arrived at 5600rpm with 145lb/ft at four grand – very tractable. Standard

In Europe the 1975 911S 2.7 was 175bhp (DIN) strong, but federal smog law and pollution controls reduced that figure to 157 SAE net horses. A new pink 911S was given to 1975 *Playboy* 'Playmate Of The Year,' Marilyn Lange. (Courtesy Porsche)

gearbox was a four-speed stick, and the vital stats were 0-60mph in eight seconds, 128mph top speeds and 21mpg overall, with a 250-mile cruising range. In the UK, the 1972 price for a new 911T was £4611, and throughout Europe the 911T was considered good value.

By the late '80s it was estimated only 3000 911Ts were left. Their collector value had risen to £15,000, and yet they were being cloned into 911 Carrera RSs. There wasn't as much interest in preserving them in their original spec as there is today. *Thoroughbred & Classic Cars* magazine said that with Carrera RSs worth 150 grand by 1989, the reason for cloning was obvious. They also noted that at this time 911 Targas were worth ten per cent more in America and ten per cent less in Europe. 911 Sportomatics were worth 20 per cent less, since they didn't fit the 911's sporting image.[55]

Legendary Porsche longevity saw front shocks, engine and transmission expected to deliver 40,000, 80,000 and 150,000 miles respectively, before replacement or rebuilding were required. The most desired gearbox was the five-speed manual, and this was a new unit for '72 MY. The conventional shift pattern 915 box was built stronger to cope with the 2.4's torque. It replaced the dogleg 901 five-speed. Most buyers chose the five-speeder, and the most popular UK market version was the 911E. The production total for all 2.2- and 2.4-liter 911s was 67,004 units. 1972 had seen Fuchs rims provided across the 911 range.

The 911 2.4 models continued into 1973 as the F series cars. Halfway through the model year, the North American 911T switched to the new Bosch K-Jetronic injection system due to stricter pollution laws. Worldwide the 911S received a front aero spoiler to cut front end lift and wander at high speed. The downforce aid was available on the 911T and 911E as an option.

By the early '70s the 911 was a decade old and facing a new wave of mid-engined junior supercars from Italy. They were the Ferrari Dino 308 GT4, the Lamborghini Urraco and the Maserati Merak. *CAR* magazine looked at these, and the Jaguar XKE V12 in February 1973, in its £2750 to £6000 Sports cars category. It also considered the Alfa Montreal V8. Only the Jaguar was older than the 911 and, as expected, the British Leyland bruiser offered big speed at a small price. It also matched the Italians regarding quality control and reliability.

The Alfa Montreal was judged lusty but inefficient, whereas the 911S seemed the wisest place to put

one's ill gotten gains. At this hour it was £5675. The 2341cc flat-six made 190bhp at 6500rpm. This took the coupe from 0-50mph in 4.9 seconds and on to 144mph, autobahn permitting. Even so, there was 16mpg economy and *CAR's* wisdom: "Very smooth shape that is still attractive … corners very well without being tail happy." On the slightly negative side: "Choppy ride, well designed, and cosy interior."[56]

CAR's summation was: "… developed to the point that engine placement does not matter in reality." The journal also thought the 911 might better fit the Sporty Saloon & Coupe category. So thorough and practical was the 911, that it fulfilled duties beyond the mere sports car, and did so well. Such intestinal fortitude helped the 911 survive the year of judgement that was 1974. American federal regulations proved the end for a number of European sports cars; the Austin-Healey 3000 MkIII, the Volvo 1800ES and the Saab Sonett were casualties of law, but the 911 soldiered on in style.

In the G series 911 of 1974, Porsche had done what people thought was impossible: created an attractive impact bumper car. While many imports, and some domestics, adopted bumper bars with the width of a park bench, the 911 complied with Uncle Sam unobtrusively. They were aluminum bumpers on steel mountings with hydraulic dampers. The last item was optional at first. They did increase the 911's length from 4127mm to 4291mm, 162.5in to 168.9in, but you really didn't notice. They looked good, updated the 911, and Porsche applied them to all world markets. The look would continue until the 964 911. Volvo did the same thing, applying its US impact bumpers to all countries, with somewhat less attractive cosmetic results.

The 1974 911 got a new dashboard and interior. Comfier seats had built-in head restraints, there were redesigned dash switches, and a quartz electric clock. However, with a fast moving 911, you would never be late! There were three 911s for '74 MY, with the 2.7-liter (2687cc) flat-six the only normal production engine size. The 2.7 motor had a magnesium crankcase and coated Nikasil cylinder bores: lessons learnt from racing. The base 911 had 150bhp, the 911S was on 175 ponies, with the range-topping Carrera galloping with 210 horses. The first two versions had Bosch K-Jetronic, a smog amigo Continuous Injection System (CIS), whereas the Carrera held on to its mechanical MFI high pressure system from 1973.

From 1974 the 911's outer body panels were

galvanized too. The coupe was still the sensible, sporty choice. Early on, the Alpine A110 had been a contemporary rear-engined quasi rival. By the mid-'70s the Alpine Renault A310 V6 was still targeting Zuffenhausen. The base 911 did 0-60mph in 7.8 seconds and around 135mph. Even so, stats were irrelevant with such a big picture ride. *Thoroughbred & Classic Cars'* Paul Walton provided some perspective concerning the 911: "The Porsche 911 isn't just a supercar, it's an everyday machine and a familiar sight all over the world."[57] You couldn't say that about the Alpine A310.

The other entry-level Porsche - 1973 Sports Bug

The 1974 911 and 911S had respective torque levels of 173lb/ft and 188lb/ft, from their 2.7 motors. With their narrow 2.4-liter era rear fenders and the absence of rear spoiler, ducktail, whaletail or otherwise, they had the quaint charm of a '60s 911, that Porsche credo about evolving while appearing the same.

Herbie, Dr Porsche's first car, had been doing the same thing. In 1969, the Beetle got a gas filler door operated by a lever inside the car, just like a Porsche. Similarly, for '71 MY the Bug adopted the 911's basic suspension layout. MacPherson struts at the front and semi trailing arms at the rear. The

A 1969 picture of model Thora Hornung, in a '62 356B Cabrio. Throughout the '60s Hornung had posed with Porsches, and, with Evi Butz, dealt with Porsche PR, customer relations and racing department micro management.
(Courtesy Porsche)

Top right: With MacPherson strut front suspension and semi trailing arm rear suspension, the Super Beetle was following in the 911's tire tracks! Dr Porsche truly believed in engineering evolution.

Above right and main image, opposite: The 1973 VW Sports Bug, was a sporting limited edition Beetle, based on the 1303 Super Beetle.

Left: The Sports Bug's bigger rims and radials, really improved handling but increased susceptibility to sidewinds. Many converted the Type 1 1600, to an 1835 hottie!
(VW images courtesy David Wilson)

Opposite: With 0-100mph in 12.8 seconds, the 1973 911 Carrera RS 2.7 showed 'em how it was done, without a turbo! (Courtesy Porsche)

The 1973 911 Carrera RS 2.7 was an unprecedented car, it was an homologation special, that actually sold well. Porsche surpassed the 500 unit Group 4 rule minimum, and went on to 1580 cars. (Courtesy Porsche)

latter arrived for '68 MY. Like Porsche, VW had been on a quest to rid its rear-engined cars of that feared wild oversteer.[58]

For 1973 it all seemed to come together for the limited edition VW Beetle Sports Bug. This version combined all of the above with the 1303's curved windsheild, flow-through ventilation system, which included dash vents at the outer ends of the new matte black safety dash, and more: sports buckets with non-slip inner fabric sections, short shift kit and Indy style racing wheel with small red VW logo. Outside it was a high gloss Saturn Yellow or Marathon Silver Metallic paint job, and 5.5in eight-slot vented steel sports rims. Those wide rims wore 175/70HR-15 boots.

There was a Corvette-like 2.7 turns lock-to-lock,

and standard aluminum and magnesium alloys for the Type 1 flat-four 1600. Plus, optional body-contrasting racing stripes and flare tips for the exhaust. The only things missing to make it more Porsche were the front disk brakes available on Euro Bugs, the electronic fuel-injection, and the rack and pinion steering that would eventually reach North American Beetles.

Henry Manney usually tested Bugs for *Road & Track*. He tried a Sports Bug and found it peppy, with a powerful heater, secure handling and adequate resistance to sidewinds. He also mentioned the availability of air-conditioning, a port fitted $500 '74 option, and fitting a big bore kit to the flat-four. It was common practice then and now to machine the flat-four's crankcase to accept a 92mm barrel/piston set. The subsequent 1835 hottie could do 0-60mph in ten seconds if one could placate the So Cal smog inspectors at emissions testing time.

Cheaper than a 914 2.0, and with the benefit of a back seat. If the Sports Bug's $2699 base sticker was too steep, one could apply the engine work to a '74 Love Bug. This was yet another special edition Beetle, but based on the plain, non Super Beetle. It still came with the fancy rims and radials, but the absence of the Super Beetle's

engineering refinements made this budget Dr Porsche experience more early 356 than late 911. Even so, ye olde Bug came with a 24/24 warranty that shamed a Caddy. There were many options with modern cars, but the Beetle provided one thing money couldn't buy: integrity.

The 1973 Carrera RS motor was 210 horses strong. A European spec, and the most powerful road-going Porsche powerplant, to that point in time. (Courtesy Porsche)

Tanja Stadnic with a 1973 911 Carrera RS 2.7 in Wuppertal. The RS ducktail rear spoiler is an artistic icon! (Courtesy www. tanjastadnic. com)

Opposite: The 911 Carrera RS 2.7 at the 1972 Paris Auto Salon. The RS 2.7 was an homologation racing special that took lessons from the 1967 911R. (Courtesy Porsche)

It was still 2.7L all the way in '74 MY, with this line-up of 2.7s. Targa in Light Yellow, Coupe in Lime Green and Orange Carrera. However, the magnesium crankcase was a warranty worry. (Courtesy Porsche)

911S/T & 911 Carrera RS

Porsche wasn't going to race the 911. That's the impression Vic Elford got from Porsche's Competition Manager Baron Huschke von Hanstein. Elford was having lunch with the Baron in Cannes, at the Hotel Martinez. Vic Elford had a troubled year with Ford, and was hopeful when he saw privateers in action, rallying the quite new Porsche 911. Huschke von Hanstein simply said Porsche had no rally department, budget or intention in that direction.[59]

Ferdinand Piëch's 911R was a theoretical exercise, with no plan to homologate. The future of sports car racing was mid-engined, and Porsche had cars for that purpose. However, Elford's lunch provided the Baron with food for thought. Huschke von Hanstein got a plan together, and got Elford to Stuttgart to meet Team Porsche. Porsche had Mr Fix-It, mechanic and racer Herbert Linge; it also had two Miss Fix-Its.

Vic Elford was introduced to Thora Hornung and Evi Butz. Both ladies had been in the racing, public relations and customer relations departments at Porsche for years. Evi Butz would eventually marry racing driver Dan Gurney. Thora Hornung was a model and posed in official Porsche car pictures in the 1960s. Elford said both ladies didn't have direct racing experience, but were invaluable as motorsport micro organizers.

History shows Porsche did race its 911. Indeed, Vic Elford's name became

This is the green-nosed 1969 917 longtail, that wowed crowds at the 1969 Geneva Show. It cost 140,000DM, or ten Porsche 911s! (Courtesy Porsche)

The Porsche 911 Carrera RSR 3.0 was very successful in GT racing during 1974-75. It was succeeded by the turbocharged 934. (Courtesy Porsche)

synonymous with both the 911 and the Monte Carlo Rally. However, it didn't stop there; nor with the 911R record breaker. Porsche went forward with the 911S/T. In the early '70s the European racing rulebook said one could increase the bore but not the stroke. This was tricky for Porsche, since its current 911 2.2-liter flat-six had Biral cylinder liners, which restricted boring out.

To get near the 2.5-liter racing class limit, Porsche took a leaf out of the 917's racing book and went with Nikasil-coated bores. This move, plus special Mahle pistons, paved the way to 2466cc and 2492cc racing 911S/Ts, and the 1972 911 2.4-liter family. This larger-engined 911S/T had an 86.7mm bore, and made 270bhp at eight grand. According to Porsche AG subdivision Porsche Classic, 24 911S/Ts were produced. They were mainly sold to privateers for

Group 3 GT racing, and Group 4 Modified GT racing. However, there were two works rally cars within that tally.

The model's official name was 911S 2.5, described as a works modified 911S 2.4 coupe costing an extra 19,000 deutschmarks, or a total of 49,680 deutschmarks. Technically, it was a new 911S with M491 option and Type 911/70 2.5-liter motor. The 911S/T moniker arose from a precedent set by an earlier 911S/T 2.3 racer. Either way, it's a rare machine. One of the 24 cars made its way to American privateer racer Mike Keyser. What he received was a 911 modified in compliance with international sporting regulations.[60]

To create a 911S/T, a 911 body was taken from the regular 911 assembly line. For this reason, there is no special 911S/T chassis series. The racing department

Peter Gregg's 1973 Brumos Racing 911 Carrera RSR 3.0 is shown. Gregg's dealership, Brumos Porsche+Audi, was like a semi-official Porsche North America racing arm. (Courtesy Gregory Moine)

then added black felt to the roof and interior panels, plus two front buckets. Front and rear fenders were widened 50mm for racing rims and rubber. The front bumper and spoiler were a single, integrated fiberglass complex. The 2.5-liter flat-six arrived direct from the test department, where each motor had been prepared and tested.

Mike Keyser, of Chevy Monza IMSA fame, ordered his 911S/T from Porsche's Sports Division, in November 1971. All 911S/Ts were built during 1970-71. To contest the Endurance World Championship, he hired Porsche works driver and Sports Division employee Jurgen Barth. Keyser even hired a small TV film crew to record their 911S/T exploits. They witnessed successful outings at 1972's Daytona 6 Hours, Sebring 12 Hours, Nürburgring 1000 and Targa Florio. Barth's invitation started with Sebring. However, the team's pièce de résistance came at 1972's 24 Hours of Le Mans. Here, Jurgen Barth, Keyser and Swiss racer Sylvain Garant, took out their three-liter GT class and came 13th overall. At Le Mans, the trio's 911S/T raced under the Louis Mezanarie team banner.

Following on from the 911R and 911S/T, more numerous and better known than both, is the 1973 911 Carrera RS. With the FIA rules against big engined sports cars, ie Porsche 917s, Zuffenhausen wanted to get more down to earth. The avenue was Group 4 modified GT cars. Doing this necessitated a minimum 500-unit production run, and the result was the ultimate road-going and race focused 911 to date. The 911 Carrera RS introduced the bored out 2.7-liter flat-six to the 911 range. The RS 2.7 made 210bhp at 6300rpm, with 188lb/ft arriving at

5100rpm. Bosch mechanical fuel-injection and flat top pistons were part of the deal, so too were extra engine cooling fins.

The Carrera RS revived the Carrera moniker for the first time since Porsche 356 days. Visually, this F series '73 MY 911 was easy to spot. There were flared rear arches to accommodate 7in wide Fuchs, and the rear fiberglass Burzel ducktail spoiler with passenger side 'Carrera RS' callout was hard to miss. The ducktail spoiler was new to the 911. There was a tailwide 'PORSCHE' script decal on the rear base, while a 'Carrera' decal profile script lived on the lower body third, between the wheelwells.

In the years to follow, the Carrera name would be oft used and become synonymous with the 911. The wide rear arch look would become iconic too: soon most wanted the wide look on their 911. Of major importance, for speed, was lightness, and the Carrera RS was certainly light. The 2687cc coupe had thin steel panels, polyester bumpers to match the salesman's suit, and light, thin Glaverbell glass.[61] The total weight was 1984lb, versus 2194lb for a regular 911. Porsche technical thoroughness brought larger brakes, and later examples of the first batch of Carrera RSs had modified rear suspension geometry. This helped fit 280mm footprint racing tires.

Compared with a regular 911, the RS was longer, with measurements of 4127mm to 4147mm respectively. Performance was surpassed by few, if any, contemporary road cars. 0-60mph in 5.6 seconds and a 152mph top speed were impressive, but even more so was its 0-125mph in 22 seconds, compared to a stock 911S 2.7's 42 seconds! 0-100mph in 12.8 seconds was handy, so too was

America's 1975 911 lineup covered the Carrera, regular Coupe and Targa. The Carrera wears upscale Fuchs, the regular 911s roll on 'Cookie Cutter' ATS rims. (Courtesy Porsche)

23mpg overall. This naturally aspirated ride defied the laws of physics. The '73 Carrera RS was one of those rare instant classics. *Autocar* put the ride amongst the greatest sports cars of all time. They said of all the 911s since that first two-liter 901, "the 1973 2.7RS Carrera is the one to kill for."[62]

Autocar went beyond this, and opined that the 964 911RS lightweight of the early '90s had an appalling ride. In addition, they said the 993 Carrera 2 was misnamed, since it wasn't an overtly sporting edition. The popularity of that South American road race moniker has led to overuse by Porsche, as an engine and general model designation, Nearly reaching the point of a modern Audi S-lines, Mercedes AMG appearance packs or BMW M-sport options. You can't say Corvette without Stingray, or 911 sans Carrera. The reason stemmed from that amazing performer, the 1973 911 Carrera RS.

The public bought them readily, so Porsche pushed through the 1000-unit requirement for Group 3 unmodified GT machines. Zuffenhausen eventually reached 1580 cars. Aside from the plain RS, the RST (RennSport, Racing Sport Touring) had a better trimmed, comfort option 911S interior. For the Group 4 dedicated racer, the production total included 49 Carrera RSR 2.8s (2808cc) with 300 DIN horses, thin gauge windshield, plastic front buckets and no backseat. The Carrera RSR 3-liter prototypes took a backseat to no one on the 1973 Targa Florio: they came first and third.

Porsche built 109 911 Carrera RSR 3.0s, and these cars were successful in the 1974 and 1975 racing seasons. The regular Carrera RS 2.7 became a friend to racers at all eschelons. *CAR*'s Gavin Green

The 911 Carrera 2.7 switched from ducktail to whaletail for '75 MY. With the mechanicals of the Carrera RS, and comfort of the 911S, the latest Carrera was more gentleman's express than racer. (Courtesy Porsche)

discovered the car's worth in round six of the 1985 UK Giroflex Porsche Production Car Championship, at Wiltshire's Castle Combe circuit. The national race series was sponsored by the maker of office seating. There were four categories based on power, with minor suspension and brake mods permitted.

Putting the 911's ultimate tendency to oversteer to one side, Green found the '73 Carrera RS easier to drive than expected and said, "The car and I were in this together. Never had a car felt more animate."

Above: The Porsche 924 succeeded the 912E. With Audi 100s to the left and Ro80s to the right, the 924 still managed to maintain Porsche quality at Neckarsulm. (Courtesy Porsche)

Indeed, the 911 Carrera RS's sharp, delicate non-power-assisted steering, great handling balance and sharp, responsive non-turbo 2.7 provided an overall experience above other 911s of earlier and later eras.

For absolute top speed there was the 911 Turbo, with a small overall margin. The lap record for a production Carrera RS at Castle Combe, to that point, was a one minute, 13.5 second time. Pole position at the 1985 meet was a one minute, 12.4-second lap set by Nick Faure in his 911 Turbo 3.3. Faure was an AFN Porsche dealer, pro racing driver and friend of *CAR* magazine. He had just missed out on becoming a Porsche works driver earlier in his career. Nick Faure felt that after the Carrera RS, his 911 Turbo felt like a truck and was a tricky handler.

Compared to the Carrera RS, the 911 Turbo had 500lb excess, and mostly rearwards. It had its role on the fast circuits, but was less reliable and only had four speeds.[63] Josh Sadler, long time owner of UK Porsche specialist Autofarm, said Porsche engines and gearboxes were mighty tough: you could safely race a road car. This made the 911 Carrera the ultimate gentleman's weekend racer. In his view, if you liked the '73 Carrera RS, but didn't like the price, then the 1974-

75 G and H series 911 Carreras were the real thing, literally.

The 1974-75 911 Carrera 2.7 had the same power train, brakes, swaybars and suspension geometry as the 1973 Carrera RS. However, the cars are worth half as much. This wolf in impact bumper sheep's clothing

1. The North American 1976 912E, was a stopgap entry level model. It tided Porsche over between the 914's demise and the 924's start. 2. Whereas the '60s 912 used a Porsche 1600 motor (ex 356), the '70s 912E had a VW 2 litre flat-four. Either way, it was all in Dr Porsche's family! 3. The power was 86bhp (SAE net) at 4,900rpm, and according to *Road & Track*, the 912E did zero to sixty in 11.3 seconds, with 115mph top speed. 4. At nearly 11 grand, the 912E delivered the same performance as the earlier Porsche powered 912, but in a torquier manner. 2099 912Es were made. Today a 912E can be hopped up to perform on a par with a 2/2.2-liter 911, courtesy of the VW aftermarket. (All Courtesy David Lovato)

PORSCHE 1976 912E

was a more numerous street sleeper, at 3300 units. It also had the comfort trim of a regular 911S. The Carrera 2.7 did retain the 1973 car's Bosch mechanical fuel-injection, and performance was only slightly slower. Official 0-100kph times rose from 5.8 to 6.3 seconds, with top speed 2mph slower at 150mph.

Compared to the lightweight '73 icon, weight had risen from 975 to 1120 kilos. Versus a normal, narrow rear fender G series 911, width was up from 1610mm to 1652mm. In any case, it was a better deal than the North American Carrera 2.7. The Carrera had finally arrived Stateside for '74

MY. It had smog friendly Bosch K-Jetronic, and a mere 175bhp. Tighter 1975 emissions dropped that figure to 165 horses, with just 160bhp for California. Thank you federal government! The plusher Carrera enjoyed the 1974 911's galvanized outer panels, and came with fashionable black trim. In 1975 the Carrera's ducktail was replaced by the 911 Turbo's inspired whaletail spoiler. That year, a 911 Silver Anniversary commemorative model sold 1063 copies.

Peter Gregg & Al Holbert – Porsche racers

On the racetrack, pollution laws are of no importance, and Americans Peter Gregg and Al Holbert were two drivers who made good use of Porsche's trackside. Gregg had driven Bud Moore Ford Mustangs in the 1971 SCCA Trans-Am series, with teammate George Follmer. He achieved greater fame with Porsche. In 1971 Peter Gregg achieved three wins in an IMSA Porsche 914/6 GT. He took the IMSA GTU championship for the under 2.5-liter class that year.

Nicknamed Peter Perfect after the *Wacky Racers* cartoon character, because of his clean-cut image, Gregg got racing success with his dealership Brumos Porsche-Audi. Brumos was effectively Porsche's North American motorsport arm in the early 1970s. In 1973,

dealership owner Gregg was racing a 911 Carrera RSR, bearing his familiar #59 racing decal. The RSR was a 911 devotee's dream machine. Carrera RSR 2.8 racers had high butterfly mechanical fuel-injection, and five-stud racing rims.

The Carrera RSR 3.0 moved to throttle slide injection, with the expected Bosch twin plug ignition, and pit stop time-saving Porsche center lock rims. Brumos used a front compartment mounted ATL fuel cell with its RSRs, and Peter Gregg won the IMSA GTO championship, with the Carrera RSR 3.0 in 1973. That year, Gregg won the 24 Hours of Daytona in the Carrera, with co-driver Hurley Haywood. After the 1973 racing season, Peter Gregg hung up his racing helmet. He then occupied his time as a director of the Jacksonville National Bank, a club tennis player and a speedboat racer based at

Where there's a will, there's a way. Count Rossi of Martini & Rossi, got his Porsche 917 road registered, thanks to the Alabama DMV! (Courtesy Martini & Rossi)

The Martini Racing 1971 Le Mans Elford/ Larrousse 917LH is shown. Vic Elford had got pole position the previous year at Circuit de la Sarthe in a Salzburg 917L. (Courtesy Porsche)

John Wyer Automotive's (JWA) British engineer, John Horsman, worked up an aerodynamically stable, upswept shorttail, for the 1970 917K. (Courtesy Porsche)

Ponte Vedra Yacht Club. However, he did successfully return to racing and Porsches before his untimely death in 1980.[64]

A further Porsche legacy that Gregg left was the six special '73 Carrera RS coupés he built. The mechanically injected '73 911 Carrera RS wasn't emissions certified for North America. Brumos dealership customers wanted a car just like Peter Gregg raced. Even with his contacts, Gregg couldn't gray import such forbidden fruit, so he told the customers he would build cars for them! The Brumos built Carrera RS 2.7 used factory RS parts and the Brumos Race Shop facility.

The cars had a 2.7 race motor, gear ratio changes for second through fifth, special suspension and Fuchs. However, each car was unique in detail concerning spec. It is said the Brumos Carrera RSR 3.0's 24 Hours of Daytona win was the 911's first major international racetrack trophy. It all adds to the Gregg/Brumos legendary mystique, and makes surviving customer Carrera RS cars very historically significant.

Peter Gregg's victories weren't in a vacuum; he had competition from Roger Penske and Al Holbert. Racer Al Holbert's father Bob had raced a Porsche RSK between 1957 and 1963. Al's first SCCA C Production racing entry was in a 914/6. He had worked in the Penske organization as a summer intern, and became friends with Mark Donohue. In 1973, Al Holbert raced Team Penske's Carrera RSR, and challenged Peter Gregg. Holbert switched to the super effective Chevy Monza V8 for IMSA in 1976, because the turbocharged Porsches got banned. However, he did return with a Porsche 924 in SCCA production car racing. His racing number was 14, and he, too, had a dealership – Holbert's Porsche Audi VW.[65]

Mid-engined acers – 914 & 917

The 914/6 was a handy machine at the track. The 914/6 GT came sixth outright at 1970's 24 Hours of Le Mans. At the Nürburgring the little car achieved a 1-2-3 outright in the 1970 84-hour endurance race

Pedro Rodriguez and Leo Kinnunen's Gulf Oil JWA 917K, beat Vic Elford and Denny Hulme's Salzburg 917K, at a rain soaked 1970 Brands Hatch 1000. Both cars had the 4.5-liter flat twelve. (Courtesy Porsche www.YouTube.com/watch?v=K0YCGF3ncEY)

Left to right, Porsche racers 935, Manfred Schurti, Rolf Stommelen, Jochen Mass, Jacky Ickx and 936! Race boss Manfred Jantke (in black) is in the middle at this 1976 Dijon 6-hour event. (Courtesy Porsche)

Marathon de la Route. It also garnered a 1972 Targa Florio class win. Under Ferdinand Piëch's race car program two 914/8s were constructed. These 914s possessed the 908's flat-eight. One was given to Ferry Porsche in 1969 for his 60th birthday. This was all fine and dandy, but Porsche's main racing concern was the 908's successor and winning Le Mans.

Homologating the Porsche 917 for Group 5 Sports Cars wasn't easy. The act of building 25 917s, while racing the 908, was costly for a small company.[66] Ferry Porsche gave the green light to the 917 in 1968. The thinking behind the 917 was a 908 with 50 per cent more power. Indeed, the 908 contributed various parts, including engine items, to the 917. The new flat-twelve sports car made its debut at the 1969 Geneva Auto Show. A white car with green nose and '917' in black wowed the crowds, and the cost? That was 140,000 Deutschmarks, or ten Porsche 911s!

Pick a car, any car
At first, FIA officials didn't pass the 917. Porsche had completed three cars, the rest were at various stages of build. Zuffenhausen didn't want to build them and then have to take 'em apart prior to racing. However, on April 21, 1969 the FIA got a surprise. It was presented with a line of 25 917s. The inspectors met Helmuth Bott, Herbert Staudenmaier and Ferdinand Piëch. Piëch said, "Would you like to drive one? You can choose any one you like. Here are the keys!" The offer was declined and the inspectors sulked off, as bureaucrats usually do in such situations.

It's just as well they didn't try the 917s, since they had nasty handling surprises. Porsche thinking since the '30s Auto Union days was small frontal area, streamline, and let the driver's skill control the outcome. Brian Redman experienced the 917's problems in more ways than one. First, its high speed uncontrollability in 1969, and secondly, its bigness being no friend on tight tracks. The latter occasion was the 1970 Targa Florio with a 917K.

Jo Siffert gave the 917 a debut pole position at Spa in 1969, but discretion being the better part of valor, he raced the 908 longtail with Redman. The tight track problems were easily solved − let the smaller 908 deal with them. The 917 was designed by Hans Mezger, under Ferdinand Piëch and Helmuth Bott. To come up with the initial 4.5-liter flat-twelve, Mezger joined two flat-sixes. He produced a motor with dual spark, twin distributors and four cams. A magnesium block and aluminum heads were Beetle-like, but the class-leading 580bhp at 8400rpm was something else. So, too, was the Bosch mechanical injection system: it was derived from a commercial truck application!

The 917 was light, thanks to a 93-pound gas pressure-tested spaceframe, the use of titanium and magnesium in construction, a balsa wood shifter, and even the use of the aforementioned frame to pipe oil to the oil cooler. Due to the large engine, the driver had to sit far forward. It generated fear for Brian Redman when racing the 908/3. When the only thing in front of you is aluminum tubing and an oil filter, even the brave worry!

At least Spyders had headroom. On the 917 the doors were cut into the roof to aid driver access, but the racer sat in a poorly-finished interior. His head was kinked to one side, and by the driver's side the gas tank was under the rocker panel! Derek Bell subsequently said that drivers must have been mad to race them.[67] Porsche said the fender-mounted mirrors vibrated so much at speed they were useless, but don't worry, you shouldn't be overtaken in a 917!

Seeing how well John Wyer's JW Automotive (JWA) had handled Ford GT40 Le Mans wins in 1968 and 1969, beating Porsche two times,

Zuffenhausen figured if you can't beat 'em, join 'em. Porsche let JWA look after its factory cars in 1970. There would be a two-car campaign at championship races, and three at Le Mans, adorned in the blue and orange livery of the Gulf Oil Corp sponsor; JWA was backed by the oil company from 1967 to 1977. JWA secured the 1970 and 1971 World Sports Car Championships for Porsche, and it was on its watch that the 917 was finally made stable.

English engineer John Horsman worked for JWA – although not a pro, he was a good racer – and was greatly behind the safer 917K. He chopped the tail and built it up in shorter wedge form. There was more downforce, and it saved weight. The car was taken a stage further in 1971, with the 917LH. This was a longtail aerodynamic 917, with downforce, thanks to a concave rear fascia done by Robert Choulet. Porsche's big target was Le Mans; a race it had to win. So as not to place all its oeufs in one pannier, it shared factory involvement with Porsche Salzburg and Martini Racing.

Le Mans – mon amour

The 917 had a solitary win in 1969. It was the season finale, the Zeltweg 1000, where privateer team drivers Jo Siffert and Kurt Ahrens won. However, in 1970 the new bobtail 917K won all entered races, including Le Mans. By Monza, the flat-twelve was bored out to 4.9 liters with 600bhp, before finishing the year at an even five liters. However, next to the 24 Hours of Le Mans, these were mere details. Vic Elford

A 1976 Porsche 936 is shown. Privateer Reinhold Joest rebuilt his 936 chassis with 908 bodywork, and almost won Le Mans in 1980. The Porsche was just beaten by a Rondeau. (Courtesy Porsche)

got pole position in a Salzburg 917L, but Elford didn't win. Plus, the JWA cars all expired. The 1970 24 Hours of Le Mans was won by the #23 917K driven by Hans Herrmann and Richard Attwood. It was a 4.5-liter car owned by the Porsche Salzburg team. It was Porsche's first Le Mans victory and Herrmann's last race: he retired thereafter.

The Martini Racing 917LH came second, a 908 was third, followed by two Ferraris, then a Porsche 914/6 and 911S in sixth and seventh respectively. With the 917K's 1970 race season dominance, the 917 was in high demand. Porsche ended up building 59 917s, counting all permutations. In 1970, Ricardo Rodriguez and Leo Kinnunen won the 24 Hours of Daytona in a JWA 917. Younger brother Pedro Rodriguez dominated a very rainy Brands Hatch race to win in 1970 too.[68] There was still some competition from the Penske Sunoco Ferrari 512M Custom and Alfa Romeo T33/3. This prompted Porsche to keep improving the 917 and 908/3. Apart from the '71 season aero upgrades, the 917 received a flammable magnesium chassis. No matter, Jackie Oliver secured pole position for the 1971 24 Hours of Le Mans in a JWA 917LH. However, victory fell to the #22 Martini Racing magnesium-framed 917K, driven by Helmut Marko and Gijs van Lennep. This car still holds the Le Mans circuit lap record. 1971 also saw the 917 Spyder win the German Interseries Championship.

Porsche also conducted aero studies and Can-Am series parts durability tests at 1971's Le Mans race. The test car was a 917/20 called Big Bertha, or The Pink Pig. This one-off aero exercise was a product of Charles Deutsch and the French SERA consultancy. The racer's aim was low drag, without the long unwieldy length of the SERA 917LH. Except for military vehicles, Big Bertha was the widest Porsche to date and was stumpy looking. The Porsche styling department decorated the big piggy in a pink paint job, with dotted lines in the style of cuts of pork.

Campaigned by Martini Racing, this Pink Pig did just one race. Reinhold Horst and Willi Kauhsen qualified the 917/20 seventh, and it ran fifth in 1971's Le Mans. Unfortunately, the better aero meant the Pink Pig was harder on brakes. Adhering to the normal 917 brakes service plan caused Joest to crash after brake failure. The Pink Pig was repaired after the crash, and now oinks in Porsche's museum.

With FIA rule changes, 1971 was the end for the 917 in the Group 5 Sports Car class, and Porsche looked to the Can-Am series. American race legend and engineer Mark Donohue helped co-develop the Penske Sunoco 917/10K Turbo for Can-Am. Donohue suffered an accident in testing, and had to hand the car to George Follmer for the '72 Can-Am series. Follmer won the series, and in doing so ended McLaren's long-standing dominance. Going one better, Mark Donohue took out the 1973 Can-Am title, with the evil 917/30.[69]

Follmer's car had 850bhp, but the Sunoco/Porsche-Audi sponsored Penske 917/30 was the all time most powerful sports car to race. In qualifying guise, the 5.4-liter twin turbo flat-twelve Spyder ran 39psi of boost to make 1580 horsepower!! The 917/30 had better aerodynamics and a longer wheelbase. The car's dominance kind of killed Can-Am. The coming of the fuel crisis and new safety regs cooled things off also. The Penske 917/30 monster did only one race in 1974, and most racers moved back to atmo 917/10Ks.

On August 9, 1975, Team Penske took its 917/30 to Talladega. Here, Donohue set a new FIA record for a closed circuit, reaching 221.160mph. A week later Mark Donohue suffered injuries qualifying for the Austrian Grand Prix that would subsequently take his life. Today, six 917/30s survive, with one car having been built up from NOS parts. Indeed, many left over parts from the 917 program went towards the Porsche 936.

Germany's Joachim Grossman bought a spare frame and parts in 1975. He then satisfied German authorities to create a road legal 917 with registration plate CW-K917. The head of Martini & Rossi, Count Gregorio Rossi di Montelera, raced his Porsche-bought 030 chassis 917 in the Zeltweg 1000 in 1971. Count Rossi then had the factory road-compliance the car and paint it silver. To placate European authorities that it was a road car, he fitted Alabama license plates 61-27737.

Porsche 917 – at the movies

Steve McQueen had a vision to make a legitimate movie focused on motor racing. The result was 1971's *Le Mans*, made by Solar Productions. McQueen was a natural for realizing the dream of making the ultimate racing car flick. He'd had a passion for racing since driving his first race car in 1959. Plus, he had owned a Porsche 356 1600. There was another reason Steve McQueen preferred to be in Europe making *Le Mans* at this time. The actor had wound up on a death list drawn up by cult leader Charles Manson and his group The Family. So too had Doris Day's record producer son.

As *Thoroughbred & Classic Cars*' Ian Norris said,

the aim was to make a movie based on the 1970 race. The project had been delayed by the French student riots of 1968. There were some budgetary restrictions, such as a couple of Lolas made to resemble the Ferrari 512S. The financial backers prevented McQueen doing the 1970 Le Mans race in a 908. Solar Productions had bought the 908 and entered it at Sebring. Steve McQueen partnered Peter Revson, and the pair came second to Mario Andretti's Ferrari 512S. It was the only victory Ferrari had in 1970, and the 917K didn't visit Sebring![70]

At Sebring, McQueen had driven with his foot in a special cast: he had suffered a motorcycle race accident earlier. For the movie, McQueen had to pretend with a 917. Race-winner Richard Attwood was Steve McQueen's co-driver in the movie, where McQueen played Mike Delaney. His car was a Gulf Oil Porsche 917; the car crashes; he goes back to the pits to take over the other car and wins!

The film had big realism. A Ferrari (Lola) was crashed via remote control, and 25 cars from the 1970 race were used. These included five 917s, three 908s, four 911s and the real McCoy sixth place 914/6. The cars' real drivers turned up, such as David Piper with his 917. Suffering for art, Piper lost part of his leg when his 917 crashed during filming.

The Solar Productions 908 came eighth in the 1970 24 Hours of Le Mans. Driven by Herbert Linge and Jonathan Williams, it could have done better. However, its long pitstops were to change film magazines. 70,000 feet of film were recorded using the 908's three on-board cameras. In addition, the movie Porsche team wore Gulf Oil livery racing suits. Actor Ronald Leigh-Hunt even looked just like JWA team manager David Yorke!

Sadly, in spite of all the above, and Swedish beauty Louise Edlind, the film didn't do well at the box office. Real racing movies seldom strike a chord with the general public. This relegates most important racing figures and tales to documentary format. However, the 1971 Le Mans movie has its fans, and where would TAG Heuer be without the image of the immortal McQueen? According to Jack Heuer, customers didn't like the square-shaped automatic wrist watch – it cut shirt sleeve cuffs.

Car and racing fans appreciate when a genuine gearhead, McQueen, tries and succeeds in doing justice to motor racing, both on the track and the silver screen. Le Mans bankrupted McQueen's film company, Solar Productions. However, in 1971 the actor got paid one million dollars by Honda for a TV bike ad. In 1972 he did *The Getaway* with Ali MacGraw, and that's a great escape!

The 917 chassis number 013 driven by Steve McQueen in the movie was crashed and seriously damaged during filming. It was rebuilt in 1971, with the latest 630bhp five-liter flat-twelve, and won at Daytona, Monza and Zeltweg with driver Pedro Rodriguez. By the late '90s, owner Mark Finburgh had the car insured for two million pounds. He also had a dash plaque that read: "Pedro Rodriguez, Steve McQueen and David Piper. Hard driving men, all."[71]

On a less extravagant scale, a 917 replica featured in the 1977 movie *Herbie Goes To Monte Carlo*. The Lazer 917 GT coupe was driven by Herbie's arch rival, German driver Bruno Von Stickle. Herbie defeated Von Stickle on the Monaco Formula One Grand Prix circuit. Some irony there because the movie was a Walt Disney production, and the Monaco circuit has been considered a bit 'Mickey Mouse' since the Grand Prix racers of the '50s outgrew it. And the Lazer 917 GT? It was a replica based on the VW Beetle![72]

The 917's final curtain call

In 1981, the Porsche 917 made a comeback, when Le Mans rule changes allowed its return to the famous 24-hour race as the Kremer Racing 917K-81. Given the close links between Kremer Racing and Porsche, this may have been a Zuffenhausen strategy to help secure a Le Mans win that year. With the factory racing its 936/81, it was safety in Porsche numbers.

Bob Wollek, Xavier Lapeyre and Guy Chasseuil would drive the new old racer, which was based on an old Gulf Oil 917 that had resided in a British museum through the 1970s. This museum machine provided the pattern for the 917K-81's spaceframe, which had thicker gauge tubes. Outside, the racer had revised aero and a roof slit.

The 917K-81 was fast, but a broken crankshaft before the seventh hour, and then a collision unfortunately resulted in a DNF. The car's final outing was at the Brands Hatch 6-Hour. Once again, the 917K-81 was competitive, and even led the race. Sadly, suspension failure caused the car to expire.

CHAPTER Five

Blown out of all pro-Porsche-un.
Turbo times

Vittorio Strosek's 1984 'Auto-Vittorio 928SK' had two Roots blowers for the K-jet injected 4.7-liter V8.
The result was 462bhp, 0-124mph in 20.5 seconds, and more smoke than a forest fire!
(Courtesy www.strosek.de)

"A triumph of development over design." That was W O Bentley's take on the Porsche 911. *Thoroughbred & Classic Car*'s Brian Palmer felt the 911's unusual design may have lost it as many sales as it had won. There were two things beyond question: the 911 polarized opinion, and in H series 1975 guise, the 911 was still going strong. The 911 Carrera 2.7 returned that year. However, in Porsche's continued evolutionary road, it was the little things to keep track of.[73]

Welcome back, 912

Tightened North American emissions law saw the adoption of thermal reactors on 1975-77 911s. The consensus was that the 1974 911s ran cooler. Having a second external combustion chamber to deal with pollutants was no friend of engine durability or reliability. It was enough to make one wish for simpler times. A time when inflation wasn't running rampant, and insurance premiums weren't strangling. In the days prior to OPEC becoming a household name, the four-pot 912 was an affordable, entry-level coupe to Porschedom. In 1976, it would be so again.

As a stopgap model for North America, the 912E tided over Porsche fans between the demise of the 914 2.0 and the arrival of the much anticipated 924. The 912E was a very plain spec 911, with the familiar flat-six replaced by the even more familiar VW flat-four: to be precise, the Type 4 motor. It was Wolfsburg's first boxer motor with an oil filter! As a two-liter, it had been seen in the 914 2.0, but thanks to fed regs it was now rated at 86 net horses. Living up to its 'E' suffix, Bosch L-Jetronic injection was a pacifying refinement.

The new '76 912E was about 1.5 seconds tardier to 60, and 5mph slower in top speed compared to the 356-engined 912 of yore. However, the new motor was more tractable, and the 912E was well received with 2099 copies sold. In other respects, the 912E was like any other I series '76 911. One could order a targa top, and the bodies were now zinc-coated galvanized steel. The 912E had a five-speed as standard equipment. True to VW tradition, its 110mph top speed could also be a cruising speed. Capable of double the American speed limit, the 912E was a great way to save in Bicentennial year.

1976 saw all 911s utilize Bosch K-Jetronic fuel-injection, and the optional semi-auto Sportomatic now sported three speeds, not four. However, there were more pressing concerns for Porsche, namely the 2.7-liter flat-six magnesium block. The magnesium alloy crankcase expanded at a different rate to the Nikasil cylinders. In hot climates, like parts of North

Inside a 1977 930, the final year for the blown 3-liter. However, the Turbo's 4-speed would linger on into 1989. A short 4.22 final drive, and the Turbo's torque, helped that 4-speed. (Courtesy Porsche)

In 1975, the turbo in 911 Turbo stood for high-performance. In the 21st century, all 911s gained a turbo, as a smog law/gas mileage helper. (Courtesy Porsche)

The interior of a US spec 1976 911 2.7. One was in command of 157 thermal reactored horses. In spite of the EPA, Nader et al, this 911 could still do mid 15s. (Courtesy Porsche)

America, the cylinder head studs would pull out of the case. Given that southern California was 911 central, something had to be done about this. Enter the hurriedly done Carrera 3, or 1976 911 Carrera 3.0.

The third coming of the Carrera was a three-liter 911 with an aluminum alloy crankcase and 200 ponies, in European guise. The three-liter (2994cc) had 188lb/ft, and could have front and rear rims seven and nine inches wide respectively. 0-60 was 6.1 seconds, with top speed an even 150mph. The engine was really beefed up for durability, and the car was generally heavier and more luxurious, so it was no quicker than the outgoing 2.7L coupe, and you could specify Sportomatic. The semi-auto worked well with the three-liter, but Sportomatic ended in 1977 model year. It was replaced by a conventional torque converter, fully automatic three-speed box.

For improved reliability, Carrera chain tensioners, which tapped the engine oil's main supply, became a popular retrofit item. The tensioner went from the cam tower oil lines to the chain housing cover. Removing the chain housing cover reveals the possible retrofit. Porsche's design evolution made retrofits easier compared to other marques, a swaybar upgrade for example: even early Porsches delivered without a bar had provision for a unit stamped in the inner front fender panel. On a 911 or 914, a car suddenly sitting lower on one side could be due to a broken torsion bar.[74]

911 – Stayin' alive

The regular 911 2.7 was up to 165bhp and 176lb/ft by 1976; this was important because the normal 911 mattered. Other cars rise or fall by their halo or hero models. However, the general interest in the 911 itself kept the model going through thick and thin. In March 1975 *CAR* magazine chose the base 911 as the 'Best Buy' in its £4001 to £10,000 coupés and sports cars category. This group encompassed the BMW 2002 Turbo, Citroën SM, DeTomaso Pantera, Ferrari 308 GT4, Lotus Elite 502 and Maserati Merak.

Prices ranged from a little over four grand (BMW) to a smidgen over nine grand (Ferrari). The 911 cost £7497. It was the third slowest car, but its combination of 135mph top speed and frugal 22mpg economy, made it a standout according to *CAR*. It praised performance, engineering, finish, practicality, economy and roadholding. On the minus side, there was slightly old styling and wind noise above 110mph. The conclusion was that the 911 just gets better. It was noted that the 911S and Carrera 2.7 offered more go, but no matter.

Car and Driver's March 1977 *Porsche Brougham – Soft Porsche* story by Don Sherman, concerning the 1977 911S, was somewhat critical. In targa trim this car retailed for the princely sum of $15,495. However, when optioned to the level of the C/D 911S, the price was more akin to a king's ransom. The idea of a

A pair of 1975 911 Porsche Carrera 2.7s outside a dealership. By now no one could say "911," without "Carrera!" (Courtesy Porsche)

luxury Porsche simply gave buyers what they wanted, and they wanted plush. Plush in an AMC Concord, plush in a Vette and the 911S. With optioning, the 911 reached 20 grand, five years before the 1982 Corvette Collectors' Edition!

The 1977 911S Comfort Group cost $495. This included power windows and, rather oddly, Fuchs sports alloy rims. Cruise control was $195, leather interior with plaid/tartan seat inserts a 'mere' $965, and a leather wrapped tiller was 95 bucks. Without a heater core, heating in air-cooled VWs and Porsches was always an adventure. However, for $320 the automatic temperature control replaced fumbling with automation. No longer did drivers have to play with the heat lever between the front buckets.

To participate in the growing trend of Autosound, the $500 Blaupunkt Bamberg radio/tape system was a good start. Excellent Japanese sets with better tuners could be bought for less, but the 'S' in 911S stood for status as well as sport, so the Consumer Reports choice would never do. Rear parcel shelf speakers were optional and advisable. They brought

welcome shelf-located sound insulation to hush up that noisy flat-six. Factory a/c would push the sticker even higher.

With all this comfort, the 911 was still no Caddy, but was it still a Porsche? According to the C/D test the 157 horse, thermal-reactored 2.7-liter steed did the 1320ft fandango in 15.5 seconds at 87.8mph, recorded 0.77g on the skidpad, and top speed was an estimated 130mph. Of course, a Corvette could do all this at half the price; even less if the dealer owner was your father-in-law. However, weighing just 2530lb the 1977 911S was EPA rated at 16.5mpg for city driving

Porsche's two-car 1978 911 range. A base 911SC on ATS 'Cookie Cutter' rims, and the 911 Turbo 3.3 on Fuchs. Both finished in Porsche's iconic Guards Red. (Courtesy Porsche)

and 20mpg on the highway. The 3500lb Corvette couldn't do that. With CAFE starting in 1978, the plastic fantastic was headed for gas guzzler and downsizing pergatory. However, at least one didn't have to do valve clearance adjustments! Life is all about choices.

For the Porsche uber faithful, there was no choice or rival, not even the pending 928 V8. By 1977 it was 911 or walking. However, things could be improved. On the J series 1977 911, Sportomatic cars got standard power brakes and targas now came with black trim. There was also an historic moment. At noon on January 19, 1978, the final VW Beetle sedan made in West Germany rolled off the VW Emden plant assembly line.[75] Dr Porsche's Beetle sedan had been in continuous German production since 1938. Herbie was a long-time Porsche companion in Germany's auto industry. Porsche was going to do some range rationalization also.

The Carrera 3 was a high line model that sold 3700 units. It came well specified with powered and heated driver side reversing mirror, and powered headlamp washer jets. Technically, a four-speed was standard, but there was no charge for the five-speed or Sportomatic. To the end of '77 MY this Carrera had the 1652mm body width of earlier 911 Carreras. Porsche didn't really need the Carrera anymore. The ultimate 911 for road and race was now the 911 Turbo or 930.

In 1975, Zuffenhausen had three special models: the 911S, Carrera 2.7 and 911 Turbo. Now, with the 924 and 928 unveiled, and hotter versions of both pending, the 911 was scaled back. The base and Carrera 3 were combined into the 1978 911SC. With this new '78 K series 911, the SC stood for Super Carrera. The 911SC was basically the Carrera 3 with a detoxed three-liter, in a revised range where power assisted brakes were standard. With an 8.5:1 compression ratio, the 911SC and 928 could both drink low octane gasoline. This made them a natural choice for practical supercar buyers and North America, where federal regs had diluted many European dream machines, or turned them into nightmares!

The 1978 911SC weighed 1210kg and boasted 180bhp at 5500rpm and 189lb/ft at 4200rpm. *Autocar* tried one for its December 17, 1977 issue. The five-speeder did 0-60mph in 6.5 seconds and hit 141mph. In its August 26, 1978 issue, *Motor* magazine got that sprint time down to 6.1 seconds. Respective overall UK gas mileage readings were 17.9 and 17.2mpg. The 1979 and 1980 UK 911SC prices were a respective £14,549 and £16,109. In 1978, the 911SC was exactly the same price as the slower Lotus Eclat 523. The Porsche was considered an exciting, good value, economical and sensible choice.

According to *Autocar*'s stats it was quicker and cheaper than the five-speed Porsche 928. It was also equally roomy! For 911SC and 928, front/rear legroom was stated as a respective 40/28in and 41/27in, for the two coupés. However, Jonathan Empson had this to say concerning the 911SC in

In the 1978 movie *Good Guys Wear Black*, Chuck Norris' character John T Booker drove a modified F series 911... and raced a 934!
Insets: A 1/24 scale Bburago Porsche 911 kit with Krylon Gloss Paint, plus Testors Ultra Gloss, helped create this custom model. For his cameo in the 2012 movie *The Expendables 2*, Chuck Norris reprised the 'Booker' character name. Like the 911, the *Good Guys Wear Black* movie has a cult following. (Courtesy www.spencer1984.com)

The new 1975 3-liter 911 Turbo (930), provided a supercar alternative to the mid-engined, twelve-cylinder Lamborghini Countach and Ferrari 512BB.
(Original picture courtesy Edito-Service SA)

Thoroughbred & Classic Cars''70s coupe test: "If I had no head or legs, I'd have been perfectly comfortable in the back, but in compensation there was a wonderful turbine-like whirring going on somewhere in the small of my back!"[76]

Motor magazine also offered enthusiast directed comments in its November 15, 1980 issue: "Now with 204bhp to propel under 23cwt, the new 911SC is a very quick car indeed with enough acceleration to 100mph to embarrass all but the most powerful supercars. We doubt whether there is another production car which is so satisfying for a skilled driver to drive hard." However, it wasn't all warm beer and skittles for the UK magazine testers. The gearchange was of the usual VW/Porsche air-cooled seek-and-you-might-find variety. The clutch was heavy, and the revs had to be north of 3500rpm to make the 911 fly. Lazy drivers need not apply.

In spite of long-standing criticisms, W O Bentley was right concerning the 911's triumph of development over layout. In *Motor*'s view, the 911SC was one of the world's best handlers, and never mind the rear engine placement. The comment concerning lack of rear accommodation wasn't unique to the 911. The 928 was tight back there too, since the gearbox was within the wheelbase. The 924's gearbox was aft of the axle line, but that coupe was just plain small. Want a big Porsche? Wait for the Cayenne. However, concerning historical significance, the 911SC's time was now.

The 911SC was the 911 that turned the tables on the Corvette. Before this, the 911 was an expensive Euro handler, a modestly powered coupe that would lose its pink slip to a Vette in half a heartbeat, until now. At three-liters, not even the 911's awkward OMG shift, could hold Zuffenhausen back. The stats don't lie. *Road & Track* laid out the status quo in 1980 with records for its most recently tested 911 and Vette. The $25,900 (gulp!) 911SC weighed 2805lb and with five-speed did 0-60mph in 6.7 seconds and the quarter mile in 15.3 seconds at 91mph, with 0.798g skidpad, 59.7mph slalom speed and 18.5mpg overall for good measure.

The $13,140 four-speed U A W V8 love letter weighed 3345lb with equivalent readings of 7.7 seconds, 16 seconds at 86.5mph, 0.79g, 61.2mph slalom and 14.5mpg; so the Plastic Mastodon, as *Car and Driver* not-so-lovingly called it, was half the price, could stop 10ft shorter from 60mph (130ft vs 140ft), but was slower and implied a bigger OPEC donation. However, at least your auto loan officer didn't think you were ready for the funny farm. Still, in the needs

versus wants equation of life, the enthusiast deemed the 911 essential at any cost.

Even with the second gas crunch and Porsche model planning problems afoot, you can't keep a good 911 down. Revised ignition and cam timing post '79 L series models saw the Euro 1980 911SC A series move up to 188bhp, but it could still sup low octane gas. The 911SC's general 911 upgrades, including a sound external oil cooler, have endeared it to 911 aficionados. Of all the air-cooled 911s, it is seen as the best value for money, daily driver choice and, if ever a 911 could be seen as such, affordable. Earlier cars can be rather 'classic' in terms of fragility, while later cars are improved and faster but more complex and expensive to buy and run.[77]

Good Guys Drive Porsche – Chuck Norris

In the 1978 Chuck Norris movie, *Good Guys Wear Black*, the Porsche 911 was well featured on both road and track. Norris' character was Major John T Booker, a former CIA commando double crossed by a crooked senator played by James Franciscus. The movie starts with Booker's Black Tigers group getting ambushed while trying to free American POWs in the Vietnam War. The next scene shows Booker five years later, racing a white Porsche 934 at Riverside Raceway. The Major raced for fun, and now taught political science at UCLA.

While teaching class, Major Booker was informed by journalist Margaret, played by Anne Archer, someone was killing his old commando group, one by one. The two set out for justice, and to bring the crooked senator to account. As personal transport, John T Booker drove a custom black 1973 F series 911. This coupe had blackout trim, a 930 whaletail rear spoiler and special 'Booker' license plates. Even in heavily Porsche-populated southern California, such a car with custom plates would provide a handy target for an assassin.

It certainly seemed that way, with an oddly coincidental auto incident: the Major's 911 was pushed into an intersection from behind by a large truck. Booker was able to take evasive action, using his racing skills and the 911's lightning acceleration. Was it really just an auto accident, where the truck had a stuck throttle, or something more sinister? One is entitled to be a little jumpy, when you're a Black Tiger on the run!

930 – 911 Mit Puff!

Major Booker's whaletail spoiler, and the 911SC's three-liter motor both originated from the same source:

Porsche's 1975 930 or 911 Turbo. Whether by its job number title, or turbo suffix identifier, Porsche's forced induction 911 had its genesis in racing. Whether battling the BMW 2002 Turbo in the 1969 ETCC, or Can-Am 917s in North America, racing improves the breed, and thus the 911. So it was that the 911 Turbo made its world debut at the 1974 Paris Auto Salon, and wisely so.

The Porsche 911 Turbo was Europe's second turbo production car. A year earlier the BMW 2002 Turbo was the first, and with its boy racer bodykit and mirror '2002 Turbo' front spoiler script, intended to warn slower cars to get out of the way, it was chased out of town by a hostile press and environmental extremists (tree huggers on acid). Porsche waited for things to cool off, and Mercedes gave a further year to show its '76 450SEL 6.9. Unlike the Carrera RS 2.7 shown at the same French venue two years earlier, the 911 Turbo was a different kind of ultimate. It blended the most powerful powertrain seen in a roadgoing Porsche with a very complete luxury specification. A lightweight RS this was not, but it was the fastest 911 to date.

0-60mph in 5.5 seconds, 0-100mph in 12.8 seconds and a top speed of 155mph. It was performance heretofore the sole preserve of the twelve-cylinder Italian exotic contingent. Indeed, the January 1975 cover of *CAR* magazine showed the 911 Turbo, Ferrari Berlinetta Boxer and Lamborghini Countach with the title "The supercars face to face." The blown three-liter mill, boosted the 911 to the top Euro speed demon ranks. All the goodness came from a 2994cc single overhead cam flat-six making 260 DIN horses at 5500rpm and 253lb/ft at four to five grand, such were the torque properties of turbo motors.

The 911 Turbo, or 930, introduced what would takeover from the 2.7-liter as the 911's eventual base motor. It combined the 2.7's 70.4mm stroke with a bigger 95mm bore. The turbo's

prowess wouldn't have been possible without 11.8 psi of maximum boost delivered by a single KKK turbo. There was no intercooler early on. However, a new Bosch electronic distributor for the engine teamed up with Bosch K-Jetronic. It was the first time a Porsche turbo motor teamed up with Bosch continuous injection. The lack of computer-controlled engine management, an air-to-air intercooler and the use of 12lb of boost made detonation on pump gas a concern.

For engine longevity, Porsche, like others, had to adopt a low compression ratio: 6.5:1 for early 930s. With an electronic ignition cut out at 6500rpm, first through fourth gave theoretical speeds of 49mph, 85mph, 124mph and 160mph. Porsche felt that the 930's prodigious torque delivery made four on the floor and a 4.22 final drive ratio enough. On paper, the three-liter made more torque at 2300rpm than the 2.7-liter flat-six did at its peak. Even at the 6500rpm redline where torque usually goes well south, the 930 was still making 200lb/ft.

In December 1974, *CAR* reported on the 911 Turbo shown at the Earl's Court Motor Show. This right-hand drive prototype was in the hands of Nick Faure, who

The original, non intercooled 930 motor. The smallest KKK turbo Porsche could find, and 0.8 bar of wastegate regulated boost, minimized turbo lag and made 260bhp (DIN) at 5500rpm. (Courtesy Porsche)

was racing a Carrera RSR 3.0 for UK Porsche agent AFN at the time. Boost was judged useful from three grand, and way smoother than the all-or-nothing 2002 Turbo. There was a 0.1 second lag, so corners needed anticipation. However, the 930 would pick up from low revs in fourth from only 500rpm. Faure also mentioned the natural acceleration from boost build up. The 930 picked up speed without using more throttle.

In spite of the good word, many owners experienced pronounced turbo lag with blown cars of all makes, including the 930. The Saab 99 Turbo was noted for being more civil than most. So the 911 Turbo was still a case of change down, hold on and watch out! Speed fans liked it that way, and they also dug the 930's extravagant look. The Turbo was longer than a regular 911 – 4318mm instead of 4291mm – and wider than a Carrera – 1829mm against 1652mm.

It was quite a show, that wide-arched stance and whaletail spoiler, but it was all functional.

Early on, the 930 rode on 15x7in front rims wearing 185/70 VR rated gumballs, and 15x8in rear hoops with 215/60 VR rubber. A normal 911 had 6in wide rims times four. The blown 911 had spacers that widened the track two inches at the front, and nearly six inches rearwards, so it certainly used those flared fenders! Impact bumpers that recoiled were standard. The front spoiler and rear whaletail were edged in rubber, the rear between the taillights reflector panel had 'Porsche' writ large, and above it a black Turbo script badge. Apart from reversing mirror and rocker panel trim, there was a dearth of chrome.

The whole effect was different to previous 911s: all menacing wide body, crouched purposefully low on rear haunches. Matte black trim was in, and the color

Jean Pierre Nicolas' snowy oversteer on the 1978 Monte Carlo Rally recalled the 911 triumphs of Elford et al a decade earlier. (Courtesy Porsche)

keyed impact bumpers added to (rather than detracted from) the sporty flavor. It was 1975, but this was the 911 of the '80s. The 911 Turbo hinted at two qualities of tomorrow's car: it would be turbocharged and plush.

Although a high-performance racetrack refugee, many companies followed the 911 Turbo's lead. They could see turbos were the way to achieve high-performance, economy and low emissions. The approach was followed until the mid-80s, when cheaper gas and 16-valve engines saw turbos cool off for 20 years. The turbo warranty claims didn't help either. Then there was the 911 Turbo's high spec: on European cars, Hella's new high-power headlamp washers, heated windshield, two-stage heating for the rear window plus window wiper for the same, fast and tinted glass, fog lamps and power sunroof. Inside was the 911's normally optional automatic heating with sensors, leather seating with plaid inlays, deluxe carpet, electronic speedo and stereo radio/cassette deck with four speakers, a lot of which normally lived on the 911 option list. Right-hand drive 911 production was slated for February 1975. With a projected UK price of £14,000, almost twice a base 911, Porsche GB had already taken 12 deposits by Christmas 1974, and 8 maybes, for a coupe the price of a house in some parts of Britain.[78]

CAR magazine remarked that the 911 Turbo was the only supercar legal for American sale. There were some delays and federal smog control accommodations for the '76 MY 930. Power fell to 228 SAE net horsepower. The 0-60mph sprint was generally a half second slower than Euro cars at 6.5 seconds. Car and Driver's test 930 bettered that figure and reached 156mph. The Beetle was the people's car, so in the April 1978 issue of Car and Driver, Don Sherman was right in calling the 930 the people's racer. It was indeed the first federally legal car, capable of tripling the American speed limit, and it was popular. The 911 Turbo three-liter total came to 2873 pure coupés (no targa due to lack of structural rigidity) during 1975-77.[79]

During development of the 911 Turbo, Porsche built a Sportomatic prototype. This semi-auto 911 Turbo worked quite well, but wasn't put into production. It seemed Zuffenhausen had no trouble selling 911 Turbos, even in zombie shift loving America. It seemed the 34 grand price was no deterrent also, given the 350 930s allocated to 1978 model year Stateside buyers. Even at almost double the 911SC's sticker, buyers all over the globe were anxious to get the revised, more powerful 911 Turbo.

Cross-drilled 12in vented disks all around, finned aluminum four-piston brake calipers with Porsche script were a given. However, displacement was bumped up to 3299cc and European output an even 300 DIN steeds. The 3.3-liter motor featured a new crankcase, crankshaft, pistons, conrods and higher 7:1 CR pistons. There was a larger KKK turbo, happy to spin at 90,000rpm and deliver 11.8psi of boost. For the first time on a 930, an air-to-air intercooler dropped hot exhaust gas turbo driven intake charge from 265F to something akin to a hyperactive hairdryer. However, it was all connected to a four-speed.

The luxo 911 Turbo was never a lightweight in the Carrera RS mold. The 3-liter original was 2514lb, 144lb over a base 911 2.7. The whole enchilada 1978 US 930, with a/c standard, was a hefty 2844lb. Smogwise, its federalized 3.3L made 261bhp (SAE net) at 5500rpm and more importantly 291lb/ft at four grand. In Car and Driver's hands it equaled the 4.9-second 0-60mph sprint of its previously sampled 930 3-liter, but surged onto a higher 165mph. To make this last longer than one hot minute, the 930 had a new HD clutch. Its pressure plate had a heavier iron casting that reduced vibration. The clutch disk's big rubber hub also improved refinement.

Under that plush veneer lay a real race car. Curved radial 917 rotors, and a sensitive vacuum brake booster, demanded respect. So, too, did the crazy 36.2/63.8 percent front/rear weight distribution. The driver didn't need power steering, but did require life insurance, handy as that rear weight bias was for take off traction. The 930 was a four-wheeled racer between myth and reality. It could achieve 0.81g on the skidpad, but only with the driver fighting the steering on a razor's edge between understeer and oversteer. The 3.3L motor made big torque, but it also had big turbo lag.

For 1978, the 911 Turbo had a new type rear spoiler. The old 1975-77 whaletail was replaced by a high collar tray type spoiler, which would take the bigger engined Turbo onto a further 8209 sales to the end of 1985 model year.[80] The new style spoiler was 20% more effective at reducing lift than the old whaletail. It was 70 per cent more effective than no spoiler at all! This was one reason the spoiler became a popular factory option on the new 911SC, another was image.

The 911 had traveled to 16in rims for '78 MY. On the Turbo, footwear was 205/55VR rubber on 16x7in Fuchs at the front, and 225/50VR tires on 16x8in Fuchs rearwards. This, and the fact the latest US

The familiar Max Moritz Racing team's Jagermeister liveried 934, this time at the Norisring in 1976. (Courtesy Porsche)

Left: Derek Bell and Gunter Steckkonig, racing a 934 in the 1976 ADAC 1000, held at the Nürburgring. (Courtesy Porsche)

spec 930 could do 0-90mph in 9.9 seconds, meant nothing. So too the coupe's 17mpg highway gas mileage. Pulling up slowly to a fancy restaurant in a 930, with envious glances from valets and passersby, was priceless. Image is everything. I drive a wall poster car, how's your '78 Chevette?!

1979 would prove to be the final year for the 930 Stateside. Stricter pollution laws for 1980, the second fuel crisis, CAFÉ and Porsche's internal business problems all saw the 928 take over for a while as the fastest US Porsche. The 911 Turbo successfully continued in Europe. For 1981, Porsches went to the 17-digit international chassis number system. Plus, the

911SC got upgraded to 204bhp and 189lb/ft. This spelt a sub 6-second 0-60mph sprint and an over 145mph terminal velocity. However, it also implied that now the 911SC dined exclusively on premium gas. There was also increasing distance between Euro and US spec cars. More worryingly, there were concerns over the 911's future.

Racing the 934, 935 & 936

Magnesium block and all, John Buffam won a US PRO Rally event in 1977, with a 911 2.7L. The next time Porsche would win a PRO Rally event was March 1994. Shutterbug Jeff Zwart and world rally co-driver Tony Sircombe took out the Doo Wop event in Olympia, Washington using a 964 chassis 911 Carrera 4.[81] The 911 was still a good rally car, but Porsche had turned its attention to track racing by the early

Opposite, bottom right:
The Max Moritz Racing 934 re-liveried, and at the 1978 Nürburgring 1000. Sadly, the driver pairing of Gerhard Halup and Edgar Doren registered a DNF. (Courtesy Porsche)

Below left:
The 'flachbau' or flat front 935, was a 2857cc, 590bhp Group 5 911 Turbo with better aero. Jochen Mass and Jacky Ickx won the 935's debut race, the 1976 Mugello 6 Hour. Pictured is their 935 passing a BMW 320i. The 935 won the 1976 World Championship for Makes. (Courtesy Porsche)

Below right:
The Bob Wollek/John Fitzpatrick Porsche 935 at the 1977 ADAC 1000km race held at the Nürburgring. (Courtesy Porsche)

Main picture, bottom:
If Melville's Captain Ahab raced cars, he would fear this great white Porsche. It's the 935/78 'Moby Dick' at the Norisring in 1978! (Courtesy Porsche)

'70s. With the demise of big-engined Group 5 sports cars, Zuffenhausen utilized its 911 Turbo, making said coupe a Group 4 and Group 5 fiend. With the new FIA rules, soon everyone was turning to the turbo.

The relatively humble 934 was closest to the 930 in looks and engineering. This racer was directed at Group 4, and had GRP material for wheelarch extensions, engine compartment lid and trunk panel. The car was delivered to customers in a civilized state of attire. This included interior door cards and power windows, but that 32-gallon tank was for racing. In this 'regular trim' the 934 weighed 2403lb, with its 3-liter blown flat-six making 480 horse. This total would rise to 550bhp in 1977.

In Group 4 racing trim, the 934 weighed 66lb more to reach the rulebook required minimum weight. The 934, capable of 0-60mph in under four seconds and 190mph, was produced in 1976 and 1977. Driving for Kremer Racing's rival Georg Loos, Toine Hezemans won the 1976 European Touring Car Championship. The 934 was a familiar, and colorful, sight, as the Max Moritz Racing orange, Jagermeister-sponsored racer in the Deutsche Rennsport Meisterschaft (DRM) series.

A privateer favorite, the 934 was a common sight on both silver and small screens. In the TV show *Knight Rider*, a 934 replica took on the loquacious Trans-Am KITT, before spontaneously self-combusting under strain. Dr Porsche couldn't have envisaged a race rival like KITT. *Die Nacht Rider? Nein!* The episode, *Knights of the Fast Lane* of season 3, aired in 1984. It involved high-class, illegal street racers. This included the Dagger DX, a gold Ferrari 308 GTS modified by George Barris. By the late '70s, the Ferrari 308 and Porsche 911 were the highest profile sports cars in the world, hence their many TV appearances.

Racer Rolf Stommelen with his Porsche 936, 'Black Widow' at the ADAC 300 round of the World Sports Car Championship. The location was the Nürburgring, in April 1976. (Courtesy Porsche)

With aerodynamically-enhancing, factory-supplied bodykits, privateers were able to create 934/5s. This allowed them to take part in Group 5 racing. Group 5 was the realm of the Porsche 935. This was a more extreme version, further away from the production 930. With freer rules, it was faster and lighter than the 934. Its likeness was previewed at 1974's Le Mans endurance race. Here, the Porsche 911 Carrera RSR 2.1-liter turbo prototype, came fourth overall. The 935 was designed by Norbert Singer. Like the 930 it employed a four-speed, but distinguished itself by lacking a differential. The coupe raced under Silhouette Rules, where the basic production shape had to be maintained. That included retention of the stock rear window.

The 1976 Porsche 934 was 930 Turbo based, and aimed at Group 4 GT racing. This well known example was campaigned by the famous Max Moritz Racing team. (Courtesy Tamiya Plastic Model Co)

The 1976-79 Le Mans winners. The #20 Martini Racing 936 (Matchbox Powertrack), 1977 twin turbo #4 Martini Racing 936 (Tombow coloring pencils), 1978 Renault Alpine A443 (Matchbox Powertrack) and 1979 935 (Corgi). (Author collection)

With a minimum weight target of 970 kilos, and a 2.85-liter flat-six engine size, the 935 raced in the 4-liter class. The 1.4 multiplication factor made allowance for forced induction. The 935's debut win came at the 1976 Mugello 6-Hour. The factory Martini Racing 935 was driven to victory by Jochen Mass and Jacky Ickx. Journalist Ray Hutton predicted the racing and sponsorship position perfectly back in 1974. He wrote in *Autocar* magazine that Porsche was unlikely to compete in sports car racing in 1975, that is, the World Championship for Makes.[82]

Porsche was unhappy with the FIA CSI decision to have two endurance championships for 1976. In addition, Porsche's sponsorship deal with Martini & Rossi was expiring in 1974. Count Rossi had masterminded the coming together of brewery and sports car maker in the first instance. Martini & Rossi provided more sponsorship loot than the best Formula One sponsor of the day. Ray Hutton said the Martini Racing Team's Carrera Turbos would probably return in 1976, with the new Group 5 regulations. This indeed turned out to be the case.

The Martini Racing livery was iconic, so too was the 935's wind-cheating flat nose. The latter would eventually become a coveted 911 Turbo option. However, that flat nose came later in the 1976 racing season. To start with, the 935 looked like a 934, and the FIA were putting pressure on Porsche, not aero downforce! The powers that be made Porsche fit the 930's whaletail spoiler design to the 935. This caused a change in turbo intercooler type. It was Norbert Singer who spotted a rulebook loophole permitting said flat nose, with headlamps incorporated within the front spoiler.

As per Porsche tradition it was all about a small frontal area. Singer also added longtail Carrera RS-style rear fenders, which permitted more space for engineering and cooling components. The nice new 935 duds surfaced at the 1976 Nürburgring 1000. However, reliability gremlins sidelined the aero machine. It was a Loos 934 that came second to the winning Schnitzer BMW CSL coupe at this venue. Stommelen and Schurti brought honor to the 935 by finishing fourth at the 1976 Le Mans 24-Hour race.

At the Zeltweg 1000, BMW recorded a 1-2 finish, with a privateer 934 third. In the Group 5 battle Porsche's pure sports car, the 935, took on BMW's grand tourer CSL coupe. To level things against the smaller 935, BMW gave its coupe lots of power. Going into the Dijon 6-Hour finale, it was Porsche on 90 points to BMW's 85 points. Gearbox failure ended the pole position BMW CSL Turbo. Porsche completed a 1-5 finish: the Group 5 World Championship for Makes title was in the bag.

With the Bavarians largely out of it for 1977, Porsche focused on Le Mans, but did do a revised 1977 935. Front fenders were now above the trunklid line and carried side mirrors. There was a slight rear fender reshape, and second rear window above the stock 930 item, for improved aero. The sting in the tail was a twin turbo flat-six. Two turbos were tried to reduce turbo lag, but the motor suffered cracked heads. However, a customer 935 came third outright at Le Mans in 1977. The 935 still secured the World Championship for Makes throughout 1976 to 1979.

For the junior Division II two-liter class of the DRM, the factory cooked up a 1.4-liter turbo flat-six 935. It had a lightweight aluminum tubular spaceframe. For the 1977 German F1 support race at Hockenheim, Jacky Ickx set pole and won the event. With point proved, the 935 Mini was placed in the Porsche museum. Privateers handled Porsche honor so well that Zuffenhausen concentrated on Le Mans again for 1978. The Porsche 935/78 was designed to do just one race: Le Mans.

The 935/78 was nicknamed Moby Dick, with reference to Melville's literary nemesis of Captain Ahab. With white paint, added length, and bluff aero form, the 935/78 did indeed share a visual kinship with Melville's great white whale. The coupe carried aero fairings for the doors. Utilizing an allowance granted to BMW to make the CSL mid-'70s competitive, the floor was cut away to lower the body. The gearbox was even turned upside down to reduce driveshaft angle. A reworked twin turbo flat-six registered 750 ponies. To overcome head cracking, Porsche went with four-valve water-cooled heads.

As a custom Le Mans exercise, Moby Dick had a right-side driver seat position. The coupe was fast; in fact the fastest car down Mulsanne Straight that year. In addition, Moby Dick qualified third, just behind the Renault Alpine that would win the race and the pole-setting Porsche 936. However, reliability woes meant Porsche's great white whale was more of a white elephant. Moby Dick eventually came eighth outright.

Moby Dick didn't like twisty, tight tracks but its legacy would be a successful engine with water-cooled heads. This motor would power the 936/81, 956 and 962C. The 935s did the winning, like the special version created by Kremer Racing. Porsche didn't do customer 935s until 1977, and wasn't into selling evolutionary versions of the 935. Eventually, Zuffenhausen moved to the humble 924 Carrera GT-based prototypes for Group 4 and 5, feeling that the 936 had passed its peak as a competition car, and seeing the 924 Carrera GTR as a 934 successor. No problem – for a winning 935 go to Kremer Racing.

The Kremer Brothers' team was based in Cologne, and had a close association with Porsche. In the opinion of racer and journalist Tony Dron, who came 12th at Le Mans in the factory 1980 924 Carrera GTR, the work of Kremer was as much from Zuffenhausen as it was from Cologne.[83] Kremer Racing's 1976 935K1 came second to the factory's effort in that year's Mugello 6-Hour. Kremer's 1977 935K2 had much in common with Moby Dick. Then there was the very successful 935K3 of 1979.

With the ground effect tricks of a contemporary Formula One car, the K3 also featured an upside down gearbox and double rear window aero improver. These tech aids were reminiscent of Porsche's own 935 work. The 935K3 proved its worth at 1979's Le Mans. The Kremer coupe driven by Klaus Ludwig/ Don Whittington/Bill Whittington came first overall. The fancy Group 6 protos faltered. It was a Porsche 935 1-2-3 finish, and the last time a normal car won Le Mans, given the 935 was 930 based. Rolf Stommelen came second in a customer Porsche 935/77A. This coupe was part of the Dick Barbour Racing team. Stommelen, Barbour and Paul Newman shared the driving.

As Tony Dron observed, the 935 was a Porsche 911 at heart, and as for its many achievements in the face of specialized prototypes, "Memories of 935 glories in that era bring tears of pride to the eyes of strong men in Stuttgart to this day."[84] In the 1980 Le Mans 24-Hour race, John Fitzpatrick put the Dick Barbour 935 on pole. The 930 890 0022 chassis no 935K3 bought by privateer Dudley Wood for the 1980 season – at a cost of £40,000 – came fourth outright and first in Group 5 in 1980's Le Mans. Wood was sharing the driving with John Cooper and Claude Bourgoignie. It came second outright and first in class at the 1981 Mugello 1000.

The 935's competition pedigree is hard to ignore, winning the Daytona 24 Hours and Sebring 12 Hours outright six times each! With pedigree comes appreciating value. In December 1989, at the peak of the market, and moments before the early '90s world recession, a near unused, unmodified 1977 935 sold for £484,000 at a Christies' auction. This was back when that was a *lot* of money. However, when you win that much, you get a reputation. Racer Tony Dron dismissed the 935's reputation for severe oversteer. On a damp day at the Silverstone track, he found it almost impossible to slide the tail out. In his view, the overster story was "complete cock unless you don't know how to drive."[85]

The real skinny on the 935 was that understeer was its enemy. In slippery conditions the coupe didn't want to turn. This made it difficult getting back on the power early. The 935 also took out Category 2 of the 1979 Trans-Am series. Plus, Kremer Racing did a 935K4 in 1981 to challenge the Zakspeed Ford Capri. The 935's last big triumph was winning the 1984 Sebring 12-Hour in IMSA GTP. Thereafter, an inability to achieve ground effect, or accept a rear diffuser, sidelined the 935. However, its legacy as the last road-car-based outright sports car victor is secure.

For the Group 6 3-liter prototype sports car class, Porsche had its 917 successor: the Porsche 936. In Zuffenhausen evolutionary fashion, the 936 had a 908/3 frame, 2140cc single turbo two-valve per cylinder, SOHC flat-six, plus 917-sourced brakes, gearbox and titanium driveshafts. The 936 moniker was an amalgam of 930 and Group 6. Whatever you want to call it – evolved 917, sports car proto – the 936 was a winner. Reinhold Joest got the 1976 World Sports Car Championship for Porsche with 20 points. Jacky Ickx and Gijs van Lennep won that year's Le Mans in dominant fashion.

The winning car was chassis no 002. The racing number was 20, but the 001 chassis car (#18) driven by Reinhold Joest and Jurgen Barth suffered engine failure and recorded a DNF at 1976's Le Mans. The famous Spyders sported Martini Racing livery, but the iconic supersize humped airbox was only fitted later in the 1976 season. This fairing accommodated the turbo's intercooler. In 1976, the Renault Alpine team had done poor pitwork, and its car proved unreliable.

In 1977, La Regie concentrated on Le Mans, as did Porsche. Zuffenhausen's factory effort was again sponsored by Martini & Rossi, but the 936-77 had some modifications. Now with a reduced frontal area and twin turbos, it was chassis no 001 that did the Le Mans honors, with Jacky Ickx again at the wheel. However, Renault had its revenge in 1978, with the new Renault Alpine A443 prototype of Pironi and Jaussaud winning Le Mans. Bob Wollek, Barth, and Ickx were second in a 936, with Haywood, Gregg and Jose Dolhem third in the other 936. They were the upgraded versions of the previously successful 001 and 002 chassis 936s. Porsche's new, pole-position-setting 003 chassis 936 crashed out.

The 001 and 002 chassis 936s were back for 1979's Le Mans, with Essex Petroleum sponsorship. Ickx and Redman were in one car, Wollek and

Haywood in the other, but electrical gremlins lay the half baked campaign low. It was up to the Porsche 935K3 to save the day for Zuffenhausen and win Le Mans that year. A Porsche nearly won Le Mans in 1980 too. Victory fell to the French Rondeau, but privateer Joest's 908/80, with driven help from Jacky Ickx and Michel Leclère, narrowly lost.[86]

The 908/80 of Joest was a strange beastie – a 908 in name but a 936 underneath. This was odd because Porsche didn't sell 936s to customers. At this time, Porsche was concentrating on Group 4 924s, but was the 908/80 an arm's length way of testing the prototype waters? History shows that Porsche's new CEO Peter Schutz was behind getting a Le Mans factory effort back on track for 1981 and beyond. When asking the racing department what they were up to, they said not much. So Schutz commanded the elves to get a 936 out of the museum.

This, the Zuffenhausen elves did, and while they were at it, they added a 2.65-liter turbo flat-six, originally intended for Indy racing. This 936/81 had a Can-Am 917 gearbox, plus Jacky Ickx! Ickx had come out of retirement on one condition: that Derek Bell join him. This was granted and Ickx won his fifth Le Mans.

In the hot conditions, only 20 of the 55 starters finished! Derek Bell declared, "This car is absolutely incredible." De-tuned to 640bhp perhaps, but using its Type 920 gearbox it could hit 235mph on the Mulsanne Straight.

Bell judged the Porsche 935 as having a fantastic, brutal feeling of power, but not much handling. However, he felt the 936/81 had both qualities. Even so, like Didier Pironi in 1978, Bell fainted on the podium; such was the strain of driving a turbo car at Le Mans. So much turbo lag, and going from understeer to neutral on boost, was mentally and physically wearing.

Derek Bell had mixed emotions concerning the 1981 Le Mans victory. The third French Rondeau had crashed, killing French endurance race specialist Jean-Louis Lafosse. Marshall Thierry Mabilat also died during the course of the race. It was the first Le Mans with a safety car. A Mercedes 500SEL was used four times, for a total of 50 minutes under the safety car.

With the 936/81's triumph, Porsche also got a positive test of its upcoming 956 motor. There would be no customer 956s until 1983, so privateers created roofed 936 replicas. Examples were Joest's 936C JR005 and Kremer Racing's CK5 01. They chose Porsche because in sports car racing there was no substitute! 🐎

CHAPTER Six

911 meets the 'yuppie' & Le Mans dominance

With a low comp, soft tune, hydraulic lifter V8, the 928 was a friend of Fido and the environment. However, was it the enthusiast's choice? (Courtesy Porsche)

911SC – Everyone loves the old kid in town

It was easy to make a case for the 911 on pure stats, like comparing it with the Maserati Merak SS. *Motor* magazine tested both the 180 horse 911SC and 220bhp Merak SS. In 1980 model year it was £18,096 versus £16,109, and the cheaper Porsche was winning all the way. Comparing 0-60mph, fourth gear 30-50mph acceleration, and overall fuel economy, it was 6.1 seconds, 6.3 seconds, and 17.2mpg for the 911SC (*Motor*, August 26, 1978), against 7.8 seconds, 7.2 seconds and 13.3mpg for the Italian. In addition, the 911SC could do all the above on low octane two-star UK leaded gas. The Maserati needed 98 octane four star.

Motor magazine estimated the Porsche's top speed as 145mph, and Maserati claimed 154mph. Somehow, you kind of believed the Porsche estimate more. The 911 really satisfied heart and mind. It had 9.8cu/ft of luggage space, against the Maserati's 6.6cu/ft. As for the relative reliability of the two cars, it can be summed up in four words for the Merak: got a warranty claim? In an era when stuff fell off, even before getting home from the dealer, the 911SC was judged by *Motor* to be beautifully made. The journal noted improved ventilation for '79 MY, as well as an electric fan for the heater.

Concerning that 911 heater, in 1978 *Road & Track* noted that it could practically fry eggs and burn toast! Compared to the tepid heater in the Testarossa, Zuffenhausen had a better chance of impressing *Consumer Reports* than Maranello. As an indication of the sports car ownership experience in those times, *Motor* took on a 1982 911SC Targa long-term test car. They picked it up with 9500 miles on the odometer in August 1982, from a Porsche AFN authorized Guildford dealer.

There was wind noise around the targa top, the rear electric wiper arm was poorly located, the windshield washer was faulty, and the heater was out to lunch. In his 5500-mile 1985 update, *Motor's* Howard Walker reported on a broken power window switch, and that was it. No engine fires; the coupe always started first time and left no one high and dry. This was good for the time, but then again, the 911 has always been timeless!

Back to 1963

For '82 MY the new C series 911SC had a 'Ferry Porsche' special edition. Plus, in 1983 the 911SC's D series arrived, though what we really had here was a time machine. There was no need to wait until 1985 to get a DeLorean with aluminum siding attached

and dub in V8 sounds; the 911 was taking people back in time now. One person was ex-F1 champ Phil Hill. In April 1983, *Road & Track* pitted the 928S, 911SC and Audi Quattro against each other at Sears Point International Raceway. Hill remarked that the 911 had predated his racing retirement!

Here was the 911, still around after 20 years, with most of the old foibles intact. Every magazine article was becoming a 911 retrospective piece. They revisited the car's … charms. That great driving position was intact, but so too were the floor-hinged pedals, scattered dash switches and floor controls, awkward Beetle shift and tail end wag. Yes, the 911 was now easier to drive, but many commented that the steering had been numbed to save potential victims. It was still slow in, fast out and tread carefully. Expert Phil Hill posted 928 and 911 lap times of 1:10.20 and 1:10.35 respectively. However, the 928 was more precise, and fun, in his view.

R&T staff members Peter Egan, Bill Motta and Kim Reynolds drove the cars between Newport Beach and Sears Point. They track tried them too, with expected views aired. The 911SC was described as the Peter Ustinov of coupés: eccentric, characterful and entertaining. One still had to saw away at the 911's tiller. Many also remarked on the slow, rhythmic basketball bounce of the front footwear. But hey, when the 911 started out, the Vette had just kicked the straight axle habit. The plastic fantastic was still riding on bias belted rubber, and clinging to four wheel drums!

In the words of *R&T's* John Lamm, "If this were an engineering test, the 911 would get a F; in a talent contest, A-plus." As for the 928? It seems competence earns respect, but not friendship. Also in *R&T* in 1983, Paul Frère expressed his thoughts concerning the 928. The Belgian engineer, Le Mans winner and journalist, first raced the French enduro in 1953 with a Porsche 550. In a choice between the 928 and 911, he wouldn't have dreamt of buying the former. Poor Dr Fuhrmann. You can lead a horse to water, but you can't make it race!

Motor's Howard Walker had similar praise for the 911SC, a difficult but rewarding coupe. The magazine's long-term test silver 911SC Targa five-speed brought the comment: "The most exciting machine on the streets? Without a doubt."[87] Watch out for tail-happy handling on wet roads, but most of the time the tester was happy. Walker said it was a difficult car to put away in the garage. You just wanted to drive more! As ever with Porsche, it seemed like good sense, tempered with practicality.

Motor's 911SC Targa had been traded in after just one year (the warranty length) by its first owner. He said he bought 911s due to low depreciation and service costs. He was now on his fourth 911, and got back 100 per cent of what he paid for the silver targa when trading in his latest red 911. It was fast becoming an '80s phenomenon. All aided by Porsche's good reputation and the 911's model constancy. Detroit used to say there was nothing older than last year's model. Porsche would say, there's nothing better!

With the Maserati Merak ending in 1983, it seemed like only a Porsche, Ferrari or Lotus were in the mix. For 1983, there were even more 911s. First seen as a design study at the 1981 Frankfurt Auto Show, the full convertible 911SC Cabriolet was a show stealer. It was the first ragtop since 356 days, and the public went nuts! Porsche rushed this good thing into production, and John Davis and the folks at TV's *MotorWeek* tried one out.

911SC – praise unlimited!

In 1983, a base 911SC Coupe was listed for $29,950, at a time when a Mustang GT 5.0 cost around ten grand. One had as much chance of impressing Christie Brinkley with the latter, as a Timex digital watch. 911SC Targas and Cabrios retailed at $31,450 and $34,450 respectively. The North American 3-liter flat-six made 172bhp at 5500rpm and 189lb/ft at 4200rpm. *MotorWeek* found its five-speed cabrio could do 0-60mph in seven seconds, the quarter mile in 14.5 seconds at 92mph, and reach over 135mph, nerves and light front end permitting. It could also stop from 55mph in 133 feet.

For comparison, *MotorWeek* tried the new C4 Corvette that year. The Chevy brought forth 0-60mph and quarter mile times of 7.8 seconds and 15.8 seconds respectively. *MotorWeek* got 25mpg on test with the 911SC Cabrio, so it was faster than the Vette, and federally CAFE compliant too. *MotorWeek* speculated how much faster the 911SC would have accelerated, were it not for its awkward shift. Statistics were for the birds and Robert McNamara, not 911 devotees. A Porsche-Audi dealer salesman could have informed you the 911SC was EPA rated at 16mpg while city driving and 26mpg on the highway. But all that stuff was for Chevy Cavalier buyers.

The Porsche faithful wouldn't have bought a Crossfire Vette, even if it could do a 14.5 second quarter, which it couldn't. In spite of the Rube Goldberg, EPA-mandated, tacked-on pollution controls, the 911SC was still plenty strong and loved. In *European Car*, Jay Jones wrote that the '83 911SC was revered in Porsche circles as one of the best. *MotorWeek* offered some wonderful comments concerning its 911SC Cabrio, saying it was capable of "stopping on a dime, and giving nine deutschmarks change." It was also a "sophisticated, macho car of nearly unmatched exclusivity."

Yes, every interior gadget was like an add on, but this was one throwback that had been successfully updated. It proved that in the end "there's no Porsche, like an old but new Porsche."

Room for improvement? A little. Borla Performance Industries of Oxnard, CA acknowledged the 911SC's popularity by doing three stainless steel (non-magnetic T304) sports systems. Each carried the firm's one million mile warranty.

The single tip version was coded # 11163, dual tip was # 11122 and quad tip # 11159. The last edition was the most popular, and necessitated cutting the rear valence on the passenger side. The dual tip and quad tip versions were dual parallel exhaust tip systems with 2.5in diameter outlets, and involved a rear muffler change aft of the cat converter. This 'cat-back' system worked. *European Car* magazine oversaw dyno tests. In stock trim with Bosch CIS injection, the 911SC test subject made 101 rear wheel horsepower at six grand. The Borla quad tip system lifted rear wheel horsepower to 105 units, and 110rwhp after some tuning. That was a 9 per cent improvement in high end power, with better mid-range response, but no compromising of low end torque. It also sounded nice and deep on four wheels![88]

It was 1983, and Porsche was still making the 911: to be precise, 54 cars per day, including four Turbos. This was up from 44 cars per day in 1981. Wasn't the 911 supposed to have ended by now? Yes, unofficially the 911 was going to be discontinued by the end of 1981. However, Ferry Porsche and a new Porsche chairman had other ideas.

The 928 was going to replace the

Ferry with the new Porsche 928! Even after his active Managing Director position ended in 1993, Ferry Porsche remained an honorary chairman. (Courtesy Porsche)

Porsche

Dr. Ing. h.c. F. Porsche Aktiengesellschaft,
Porschestraße 42, Postfach 40 06 40, D-7000 Stuttgart-Zuffenhausen, Deutschland

Porsche 924

92 kW, 200 km/h

Porsche 924 Turbo

125 kW, 225 km/h

Porsche 911 SC

138 kW, 225 km/h

Der erste Porsche entstand 1948/49 auf der Basis des Volkswagen. Sein vor der Hinterachse eingebauter Motor leistete 40 PS. Mit dem Typ 356 begann 1951/52 die Serienproduktion. Erfolge auf allen Rennstrecken untermauerten den Ruf, Sportwagen der Spitzenklasse zu bauen.

Porsche 924

Mit dem 924 begann bei Porsche ein neuer Abschnitt. Das 1975 vorgestellte Auto zeigte kaum noch Familienähnlichkeit mit traditionellen Porsche-Modellen. Die Karosserie mit weichen, fließenden Linien und versenkbaren Scheinwerfern war bis auf das Emblem frei von gewohnten Porsche-Attributen. Mittlerweile überzeugte der 924 auch Porsche-Fans. Im November 1978 folgte die Vorstellung des 924 Turbo. Die Technik: Frontmotor, Heckantrieb, Getriebe an der Hinterachse (Transaxle). Motoren: 2,0 Liter-Vierzylinder-Einspritzer 125 PS, 2,0 Liter-Turbo 170 PS. Beide Fahrzeuge mit Fünfgang oder Automatik (kein Viergang mehr). Modelljahrgang 1980 mit nur leichten Detailänderungen (Innenausstattung und Lackierung).

Porsche 911 SC

Der traditionelle Porsche mit luftgekühltem Sechszylinder-Boxermotor im Heck bekam acht PS mehr Leistung. Jetzt also 3.0 Liter 188 statt 180 PS. Der 911 SC begnügt sich als einziger Porsche noch mit Normalkraftstoff. Weiter im Programm bleibt die Targa-Version für das Fahrvergnügen oben ohne.

Porsche 928

Sportwagen der oberen Luxusklasse, vorgestellt 1977. Jetzt, zwei Jahre später, erweitert der 928 S die Modellreihe. Motoren: 4,5 Liter-V8 mit 240 PS (928), nun mit höherer Verdichtung und größerem Drehmoment, dazu der 4.7 Liter-V8 mit 300 PS (928 S). Frontmotor, Heckantrieb (Transaxlesystem). Fünfgang und wahlweise Automatik. Besonderheiten der Modellreihe 928 sind eine spursteuernde Hinterachse, stoßabsorbierendes und regenerationsfähiges Front- und Heckteil, höhenverstellbares Lenkrad zusammen mit Armaturenträger. Der 928 S erhielt vorne und hinten Spoiler und seitlich schützt eine in der Wagenfarbe lackierte Leiste die Außenhaut.

Porsche 930 Turbo

Das Spitzenmodell entwickelte Porsche aufgrund der gemachten Rennerfahrungen aus dem 911. Der 3,3 Liter-Sechszylinder-Boxermotor leistet 300 PS. Für das Modelljahr 1980 wurden nur kleine technische Änderungen vorgenommen: neuer Ölkühler und Zweirohr-Auspuffanlage. Einziges Modell mit Viergang.

Porsche 930 Turbo

221 kW, 260 km/h

Porsche 928

177 kW, 230 km/h

221 kW, 250 km/h

Porsche 928 S

Porsche was conservative. The 924 Turbo and 928 did 0-62mph in 7 seconds flat, with the 911SC on 6.5 seconds. (Courtesy *Vereinigte MotorVerlage*)

PORSCHE MODEL	ENGINE SIZE	BHP (DIN)	0-62MPH	TOP SPEED
924	1984CC	125HP	9.9 SECONDS	125MPH
924 TURBO	1984CC	170HP	7.8 SECONDS	140MPH
911SC	2994CC	180HP	7.0 SECONDS	140MPH
930	3299CC	300HP	5.3 SECONDS	162MPH
928	4474CC	240HP	7.8 SECONDS	143MPH
928S	4664CC	300HP	6.8 SECONDS	155MPH

The new 928, at the 1977 London Earl's Court Motor Show. Porsche now had two supercars!
(Courtesy Porsche)

911, and the 924/944 would take care of volume sales business in the '80s. With the NHTSA unclear concerning safety tests, the EPA still tightening emissions and noise levels, plus CAFE gas mileage restrictions, it seemed the sensible course of action. Porsche's chairman of 1972-1980, Dr Ernst Fuhrmann, thought so. Porsche didn't want to have a range of cars that it couldn't legally sell in North America. It's always the federal government's prerogative to change its mind – on anything.

Through the '70s, there were many warnings from esteemed fellows in the automotive media. They said air-cooled VWs and Porsches would soon be banned. Fortunately, Ferry didn't fear 'Nader and the Nay Sayers,' and 1980 provided an opportunity for Zuffenhausen climate change. Porsche had posted its first ever annual corporate loss. Much of this was due to the world recession, triggered by the second fuel crisis, something all automakers suffered. However, part of it was due to the major investment Porsche had made in the new front-engined ranges.

For the first two model years, the 928's chassis

number had a coupe digit '1.' It seemed Porsche planned a convertible, and early on there were stripper and upscale 928s in West Germany. It seemed that, in Porsche tradition, a full range of 928s were in the offing. However, the 928 just didn't sell anywhere near as well as hoped. Porsche had a lot of models in play, and the 911 was the one supposed to go?! Ferry Porsche always considered the 911 to embody the true spirit of the company.

It was time for Dr Fuhrmann to move on, and Ferry appointed a new CEO in January 1981. The new chairman was German-born, but American-raised, Peter W Schutz. In his great wisdom, Ferry realized he needed someone with a handle on the American market, because Fuhrmann & Co had been clueless. By the third week of Schutz's tenure, he had saved the 911 from extinction. Walking into the product planning office, he saw the timeline board for the various model ranges. The front-engined cars stretched far into the distance, but the 911 was due to die soon. Well, Schutz picked up a board marker, and extended that 911 timeline clean off the board, onto the wall and into Zuffenhausen's parking lot! Apparently, Helmuth Bott was pleased.

Such folklore has been verified. After leaving Porsche, Peter Schutz became a motivational speaker based in Florida. Car commentator Doug DeMuro had a friend that knew Schutz. This friend had put the question to Peter Schutz, concerning the veracity of the above mentioned tale. Schutz confirmed that the story was 100 per cent true, and that he had a Cheshire Cat grin while wielding said marker! And so it was that Porsche altered course. The 928 was scaled back to mainly a single model GT status cruiser, and the 924/944 were pizazzed up. Most importantly, development of the dormant 911 was restarted.

Schutz was behind the new 911 Cabriolet and returning Porsche to full Le Mans campaign mode. These two moves gave a real boost to Porsche's 1980s street cred. To think the firm was going to give up on both areas pre-Schutz! During his 1981-87 stay at Zuffenhausen, Peter Schutz oversaw the 1985 Frankfurt Auto Show arrival of the 959. He also pushed for the 944 Turbo, and the S2/3/4 928 and 944 evolution programs. The 968 was originally going to be the 944S3. Trebling the company's sales and five record sales years vindicated Ferry's choice. In 1985, the normally talkative Peter Schutz was asked why Americans perceived West German cars as possessing the highest quality. His reply was brief: "There are three reasons for that: Mercedes. BMW. Porsche."[89]

Managing Porsche

Through the decades, Ferry Porsche had kept an overall guiding hand on Porsche. This would continue until 1993 and was certainly apparent in the 1971 'family purge,' which saw Ferdinand Piëch move to Audi, and Butzi Porsche set up a design consultancy in Australia. Various members of the Porsche and Piëch families could agree on little. Journalists likened them to the characters in the TV show *Dallas* − "He ain't a Porsche mama!" or words to that effect in German. Ferdinand Piëch's son, and then daughter, both received offers of 100 million Deutschmarks from the Middle East, when they were seeking their tenth of Porsche AG.[90]

Ferry Porsche had the solution: move all family members out of the company, and go public. Outside buyers were limited to preferred, non-voting stock, in 10,000 DM parcels. Of the 327 million Deutschmarks raised by this method, two thirds went to existing family shareholders, so there was no longer a need to consider tempting outside offers. Strong Porsche sales during the Schutz years, plus

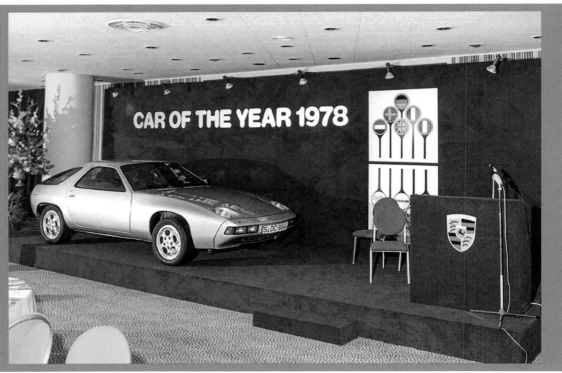

Coinciding with the new 3.3-liter 930, was the European 1978 Car Of The Year, the Porsche 928. This was the press unveiling in Monaco. (Courtesy Porsche)

CAR OF THE YEAR 1978

that Porsche stock mystique, saw the price rise from 780DM to 1100DM before the sale. As mentioned above, Ferry was right to get Dr Ernst Fuhrmann to take nephew Ferdinand

Piëch's place. He was also right in 1981 to get a CEO with an ear for the North American market. Well, North American buyers, but what of Porsche-Audi dealers?

In its April 1978 issue, *Car and Driver* described an individual it called 'Porsche Freak.' Porsche Freak was a prototype yuppie, complete with designer sunglasses, Gucci belt

"YAH ... ACTUALLY, IT'S: 'POR-SHERRRR' ..."

JOHN VAN TOL
Caledonia, MI

Paraphrasing the title from a 1981 movie with the Bigfoot monster truck, V8s have been shoehorned into Porsches for the longest time. More commonly Chevy SBs than Ford 429 BBs though! (Courtesy www.cartoonsmag.com & Rod Simpson Hybrids)

They drive Porsches

Margot Werner, prima ballerina and show star.

Uli Hoeness, forward for Bayern and the German national soccer teams, soon to be Bayern manager.

Barry Sheene, motorcycle world champion with girlfriend Stephanie.

Daybreak in a 356. Erich Green of Vermont recalls that his very first childhood memories concerned his father's silver-blue 356, the first Porsche run in Canada. The 356 model became a part of the young painter's life style: at 18 he bought a blue 356 A from 1956. Green explains that this car, "is part of a legend" for him and carried him through many highs and lows of his life. In his picture entitled Daybreak he presents it as a monument. A small series of this painting was reproduced.

Three months of painting went into this picture by R. F. Britten from Crayford in Kent, England. Along with the basic idea of showing the harmony between man, landscape and the auto, there are countless further connections within this presentation. For instance the contrail embodies the song "Amelia" by Joni Mitchell and the word "boom" is connected to a film script by Tennessee Williams. The 924 alongside a college friend of the painter was put into this picture because Mr.

and loafers, plus tailored jeans. He was probably the type that corrected people concerning the two-syllable nature of the Porsche name, and lived on Chardonnay – imported, naturally. Mr Freak followed the *C&D* staff by invitation to Briggs Cunningham's museum. Racer Briggs Cunningham was one of the first people in North America to get involved with the Porsche marque. He was going to try out *C&D*'s new Porsche 928 five-speed. Porsche Freak knew all about the 928, had one on order, and had even bored three people to death concerning the V8 supercar within the last week. Freak was in awe of the 928, up to the point Briggs Cunningham started the coupe and drove off. At that point, after a pause, he said, "Gee, it sounds just like a Pontiac."

Peter Schutz understood Porsche Freak. He knew the individual loved the 911 to the point of designer label overload. Jack Cook probably did too. Cook was the new boss of Porsche Cars North America (PCNA), after holding the same position at BMW North America. Both Schutz

Left: Motorcycle champion Barry Sheene, was one of the first UK owners of the new Porsche 928, seen here in 1977 with future wife, Stephanie. (Courtesy Porsche Christophorus)

Porsche never admitted it, but the 911SC was going to be the final 911. Zuffenhausen was betting on the 928 to take over. The 1980 911SC Targa and Coupe are displayed. (Courtesy Porsche)

and Cook also knew that Porsche's North American fans had been stung by sticker shock at the hands of Porsche-Audi dealers for years. Said dealers really focused on the second word of MSRP: manufacturer suggested retail price. Load it up with options, charge what the market will bear, and take advantage of that popular new model.

Porsche-Audi dealers went a step further, trying and succeeding in renegotiating price and spec, even after a car was ordered! On the very popular 1982 Porsche 944 that meant even more than you thought, or pass and let someone else get the car you had waited ten months for. There was a long waiting list. To redress the customer/dealer balance of power, Schutz and Cook had a plan they felt was sound and legally okay. It was also rather ambitious: they wanted to get rid of the dealers! Instead, there would be a Sales Agency Plan. Here, factory-authorized agents, on a modest 8 per cent mark up, would replace existing franchised dealers.

By the by, Porsche's agreement with VW was coming to an end in 1984, so no more Porsche-Audi dealers!

In addition, there would be limited partnerships in the new distribution centers for wealthy Porsche owners. There were going to be 40 factory stores, aka Porsche Centers, in Schutz's new deal. Then came the ultimate tidal wave. Existing dealers, regional distributors, dealer organizations, and even kids that sold Porsche pins on Sunday, brought three billion dollars worth of lawsuits against Porsche! Naturally, Ferry wasn't pleased about this furore. The plan had been announced in January 1984, and withdrawn by April of the same year. Ferry stepped in, yanked the checkbook out of Schutz's hands, and smoothed things over.

By mid-1984, nearly all the lawsuits were settled. Jack Cook said: "We tried to be a crusader …" Unfortunately, the dealers thought Peter Schutz and Jack Cook were communists. Gentlemen, back to price gouging! Porsche Cars North America admitted the plan was a failure and a tactical error. In a subsequent interview, Ferry Porsche said such a failure would normally result in the chairman being fired. However, Porsche believed in second chances, so Peter Schutz stayed.[91]

That Porsche Mystique
The 911 was given a second chance. On January 10, 1980, the last Karmann-built VW

Beetle Cabrio rolled off the production line. But don't worry; bug production may have stopped in West Germany, but it would continue in Mexico until 2003. The Porsche 911 didn't have this option, so it's just as well Peter Schutz picked up that board marker. There were second chances for people and cars at Porsche. By August 1984, all Porsches were in *CAR* magazine's 'Interesting' section of its infamous Good, Bad & The Ugly segment. The summation had the 924, still chugging with VW/Audi two-liter, as a robust car, offering a lot of name for the price. The 944 was judged a terrific development of the 924. The 911 was denoted the traditionalist's car, and the 928S2? A great pan-European GT machine.

The front-engined Porsches were noted for their failsafe handling. What brought 924 acceptance, 944 perseverence, 911 evolution and the 928's acknowledgement? It had to be that Porsche mystique. The charm that was perfect for the brash, 'I've got something you don't,' 1980s. Little wonder

It was 1981, and time to celebrate. Break out the champagne, 100,000 924s were sold, and Peter Schutz was Porsche CEO! (Courtesy Porsche)

Porsche was featured so greatly in contemporary TV and movies. In the 1981 *Simon & Simon* episode *Love, Christy*, the investigative agency brothers AJ and Rick, were helping a college co-ed find her stolen Porsche 924 Turbo. This led them to a car theft ring, specializing in upscale sporty machines. In this episode, AJ and assistant district attorney friend Janet Fowler visited a Porsche-Audi dealer, looking for the stolen 924 Turbo. Posing as a yuppie couple fallen on hard times, AJ was the well-dressed lawyer, seeking to impress the neighbors with a new Porsche. However, "retail was out of the question."

The beloved 911SC had a big part in TV's *TJ Hooker*. Sergeant Hooker's partner, Vince Romano, had replaced his Datsun 280ZX with a Porsche. He had been fixing up the 911SC for quite some time. Mention was made of a blueprinted motor and milled heads. Ebullient about the classy coupe, Romano was taking Hooker to a nightclub to show him "how the other half lived." That was Porsche by the 1980s. Not just a sports car, but an entry ticket to a jet set luxury lifestyle, envied by others.

In spite of a fancy car alarm, the 911SC was boosted from the nightclub parking lot! Once again, this 1984 episode *Grand Theft Auto* involved a prestige car theft ring. The 911SC was going south of the border, where it would fetch 25 grand.

Under Peter Schutz's 911 revival and range expansion plan, there was a 911SC Cabrio for '83 MY. It was part of the long-lived 911SC's final D series. (Courtesy Porsche)

The 3.2-liter 911 Carrera of 1984-87 was the 911 that was never meant to be. However, the 928 didn't replace the 911, and the new Carrera became an '80s icon. (Courtesy Porsche Cars GB Ltd)

Sadly for officer Romano, the 911SC got wrecked when in hot pursuit. The thief couldn't handle the 911's shift, nor its oversteer! At the end of the episode, Junior looked wistfully at a red 911SC being driven out of the police academy parking lot, while Hooker consoled his partner.

There was also a red 1983 911SC Cabrio in the 1984 movie *Against All Odds*. Here, Jeff Bridges' Porsche raced James Woods' black Ferrari 308 Quattrovalvole GTSi on LA's Sunset Boulevard.

So great was Porsche's image during the Schutz years that the 944 even made it into song! In the 1985 episode of TV's *Moonlighting, Brother, Can You Spare A Blonde?*, David Addison's conman older brother sings a song in an underground parking lot that had 'Porsche 944' in the lyrics. They really were aspirational times.

Even the UK's *Motor* magazine couldn't resist the 911SC's star power for its 1981 car testing documentary *Road Test*.[92] This 18-minute film, featuring staff journalists David Vivian and Jeremy Sinek, covered the process of car magazine evaluation. The 911SC was joined by a Rover 3500S and Ford Fiesta 1.1S at the MIRA proving ground. A cameraman mounted his equipment on the 911SC's Targa bar/rear window for steering skidpad tests. The documentary was shot on 16mm color film. It was part of the Argus Film Library (London), and was available for loan to car clubs.

The 911 featured in *Motor*'s documentary had the license plate 'A PR911.' It was a publicity trend started by UK Porsche importer AFN. It used this license plate on its press cars. By the mid-'80s, UK tested 911s were often seen with the 1963 license plate 'A 911.' UK Porsche dealers, numbering just 28 in 1985, were value adding by including a new Porsche with custom plates as part of the purchase price.[93] Porsche mania was universal, and touched all models bearing the sacred shield. With the license plate THE 928S, an automatic 928S4 equaled a DeTomaso Pantera in being the joint fastest car *Autocar* magazine tested during 1986. The terminal velocity in question was 160mph.

During the year's testing of a 911 Carrera Cabrio, *Autocar* noted the cabrio's full power top was reminiscent of American luxury cars of the '50s and '60s, and so it should have been. For this ragtop conversion, and subsequent 944 convertible, Porsche sought ASC (American Sunroof Corporation). Even the humble 924 wasn't that humble. At the 1986 Essen Motor Show, there was a Testarossa converted 924! The real Testarossa was a no-show at this event.

However, this custom 924 provides an insight into the modified Porsche scene of the time.

Porsche had a different relationship with West German tuners than BMW. The Bavarians got on well with the tuners. They worked with them in racing, extended the factory warranty to their cars, and sometimes even adopted their ideas. To big BMW, tuners were minnows and no commercial threat. Given Porsche's small sales volume, tuners were kind of a rival. Prior to Peter Schutz's arrival, Porsche didn't acknowledge that they even existed! Very quickly, such tuners became professional operations, and TUV recognized small automakers. They did things the source company either wouldn't or couldn't do.

By the early '80s, Rainer Buchman's Frankfurt coachbuilding firm B&B was doing 930 Targas and 928 convertibles. You couldn't get this kind of car from Porsche in 1981. The B&B 928 convertible had a blend of luxury and high-tech gadgets, perfect for the conspicuous high consumption of the '80s. Wealthy West Germans may have had a Porsche, but did they have a b&b or a Gemballa? Exclusivity has its own value and price. Gemballa was founded in 1981 by engineer Uwe Gemballa. In the automotive realm, Uwe Gemballa had done some trick interiors. Now, he turned to customized 930s.

From 1985, Gemballa became well known through three special 930 flat-nosed cars. The convertible Cyrrus, and companion Avalanche and Mirage models, were visually distinctive, expensive and very exclusive. Only ten Cyrrus ragtops were built. Gemballas were noted for their wide bodykits, featuring Testarossa style side strakes.

Three-piece BBS rims and triple splitter exhausts were distinctions. If the Red Baron drove a sports car, it would be a rouged Gemballa! In keeping with Gemballa tradition, the interior was plushly trimmed and gadget laden. State of the art touches ran to eight-disk CD autochangers, and sometimes even cameras were utilized in place of conventional side reversing mirrors.

By the 1990s, Gemballa's bodykits had become milder. The company diversified into BMWs, and a dedicated SoCal installation facility was built. As an automaker offering complete Porsche-based customized cars, Gemballa continues to the present. Even the Dutch police recognized the visual impact of Porsche. The *Rijkspolitie* have been using Porsches as visual deterrants for decades. To celebrate the 25th anniversary of using Porsche cop cars, the Dutch police assembled its fleet of

The 1984 Carrera 3.2 was Porsche's star of the 80s. Yuppies were price limited to the 944, and the expensive 928 was overshadowed by the evergreen 911.
(Courtesy Benny Proot)

The wider the tyre, the greater the g

DUNLOP SP LOW PROFILES.

25 911s, mostly targas, for a group picture. Showing in diamond formation, the *Rijkspolitie*'s first Porsche, a 1961 convertible, joined the picture!

With image comes reputation, good and bad. Porsches were famous for wild oversteer, with that pendulum rear-weight bias coming into play. The *MotorWeek* TV show demonstrated this using its 1983 911SC Cabrio. During the show's emergency, high-speed swerve test, which was conducted on a dry test track, the 911SC Cabrio did well enough. However, repeating the test with the driver taking his foot off the throttle mid-turn, resulted in the whole tail slewing sideways. The convertible missed its intended path, completely. Twenty years on, the 911's handling was safer, but not failsafe. This was part of the motivation, for the front-engined Porsches.

In 1983, *Autocar* magazine tested the 911 Turbo. They stated the coupe's rear engine layout and tremendous, and sudden, power output, with

Above: The 944 was a big part of Porsche's image and soaring sales in the 1980s. (Courtesy Dunlop Tyres Ltd)
Its big wheel, flared arch look was even copied by Mazda, for its second generation RX7! (Right, courtesy Wikimedia Commons)

USA, CANADA, $2.00 GERMANY 5.50DM SINGAPORE $5
DECEMBER 1980 75p

car

Supercar survivor:

Why Porsche's 911 refuses to die

Porsche's new 1981 CEO, Peter W Schutz, affirmed Ferry Porsche's sentiment, that the 911 embodied the spirit of Porsche. No 911, no Porsche! (Courtesy CAR)

controlling the car in the realm of the expert. In 1984, Porsche Cars North America (PCNA) paid legal damages when a lady driver accelerated a 930 over 60mph in a 25mph zone, lost control and killed her passenger. On the face of it, driver error seems at hand. However, the 911's tail happy reputation being well known, in the land of the lobby group, Porsche saw incident closure as the best option.

On the plus side, there is ample evidence confirming Porsche's reputation of making high quality, long-lived cars. The central West German motoring organization Technischer Überwachungs Verein (TÜV), had roadworthiness data from its actual 1984 inspections. Rust wasn't a problem for the larger BMWs, Mercedes W123 or the Porsche 911. The 911 was also in the top class for inspected six to eight year old cars, concerning brakes. Rotten exhaust systems were also unknown on the 911. The affordable 924 also displayed excellence in TÜV durability testing.

In maintaining quality at all price levels, and achieving racing success with all models, Porsche secured great resale value. Buyers were willing to pay top dollar for Zuffenhausen's wares. This included the upcoming Porsche 959, which *Autocar*'s Michael Scarlett called the emperor of supercars. By mid 1985, Porsche AG had received 450 orders for the 200 959s to be homologated for spring 1986, at an equivalent of £100,000. Porsche were carefully vetting the orders to avoid speculators. This had occurred with the recent Ferrari GTO.

From Lohner to 959 – Porsche high tech

"One giant leap for mankind, one small step for Porsche," the 1984 ad told people. NASA's lunar

In the late '80s, pre 1974 911Es were still numerous and affordable enough to race in the Pirelli sponsored UK Porsche Club Championship. Today, they are too valuable to flip on their roof! (Courtesy Pirelli)

buggy was predated by Porsche's own front-drive electric buggy, the Lohner. This horseless carriage was commissioned for Emperor Franz Joseph, and displayed at the 1900 World Exhibition in Paris. Then there were the mid-engined Auto Union GP racers, the people's car aka Herbie, and what about that AWD Cisitalia GP racer? Add in torsion bar suspension, and concepts covering aircraft, seacraft and tanks, and that's quite a design resume. That's Porsche.

Ferry Porsche always insisted that Porsche started in 1931, with the Stuttgart Design Consultancy. In modern times, Porsche thinking has been embodied by the Weissach Center. This facility had clients from the aero industry, NATO, governments, car makers and component manufacturers. For example, when SEAT needed an efficient inline 1.5-liter four-pot for its '80s Ibiza and Malaga, they got Porsche to design it. By 1983, 40 per cent of Weissach's work was for outside clients. This included secret car projects. As technical boss Helmuth Bott said at the time: "It's quite a problem hiding 80 plus cars from visitors."

Porsche needed space. Race testing was done at nearby Flacht village. A large new building was in the works for emissions testing. Porsche was at the forefront of the World Spec Motor. One capable of satisfying all pollution laws. Even those of the Golden State. So, by 1984, the Weissach Center covered 123 acres, with 16 acres for experimental workshops, and 500 projects on the go. Even so, Porsche needed more. It had been using VW's Wolfsburg aero tunnel for streamline testing, but it wasn't handy for secret client projects; Porsche needed its own wind tunnel.

An immediate result one could see was the new '86 MY 944 Turbo. After over 60,000 Porsche 944 sales, Zuffenhausen launched what it called, third-gen turbo tech, with greater refinement, less lag and more reliability. It was 911 Carrera 3.2 performance, with a sliderule or two. Porsche were on board with the West German government's unleaded cat route. Its 32-valve 928 5-liter V8 would soon be for all. Then there was the Porsche 911 Turbo. In 1983 it was still the fastest accelerating volume produced car in the world – 0-100mph in 12 seconds, and the standing start kilometer in 24 seconds – but it had stayed frozen since 1978!

The 924 had moved to Siemens-Hartig digital ignition for 1981. This had allowed a commensurate increase in CR from 7.5 to 8.5:1. However, the 911 Turbo was still on 7:1, as a detonation failsafe. No knock sensor here, like on the upcoming 944 Turbo. With the arrival of CEO Peter Schutz, 911 development was reanimated, so no more waiting. In addition, Weissach had been working on the new ultimate 911, the 959. This coupe had more high tech than anyone could ask for, and only a few journalists were permitted to try this car in April 1986.

Eschewing the simpler viscous coupling, British-invented FF AWD system (seen on cars before and later, like the Jensen Interceptor and VW Golf Synchro), Zuffenhausen went for something more complex. The 959 had: computer-controlled hydraulic multiplate clutch; automatically adjusting ride height & tire pressure/wheel crack monitoring system; 0.31 drag coefficient; sequential dissimilar size turbos; 24-valve, 2.85-liter water and air-cooled flat-six; slightly larger rolling diameter front tires; and Wabco-Westinghouse ABS greatly sensitive to individual wheelspeed changes. It cost a lot, but with the 959 one got a lot, and probably more high tech image than all the Italian marques combined![94]

Dr Porsche's thinking involved continuous improvement of an existing design. Others went clean sheet every few years. (Courtesy Porsche)

911 Carrera 3.2 – a new beginning

Hans Mezger's 1963 two-liter flat-six had room to grow. By 1978 it was up to 3.3-liters with the 930. Ferry Porsche said that had he known the block had that much capacity, he would have started with a smaller, lighter unit. It would have reduced rear end weight bias, and made handling more 912 neutral. On the other hand, the 901 flat-six allowed the 911 to become the powerhouse of people's imaginings. It also allowed Porsche to compete with exotic Italian 3-liter rivals when they came in the '70s. Reflecting on the value of hindsight, and the move to a smaller six, Ferry eventually said, "Now I'm glad I didn't!"[95]

The big block six was perfect for Peter Schutz's restarted 911 program. The 911 had somewhere to go, and that place was the new '84 MY E series 911 Carrera 3.2. The 911's new 3164cc capacity came from a 95mm bore and the 930's 74.4mm stroke. In Euro trim, power was 231bhp at 5900rpm, with 209lb/ft at 4800rpm. The flat-six now sported Bosch DME (digital motor electronics) LE fuel-injection. Improved engine oil fed chain tensioners for better durability, and a front passenger, fender well located oil cooler did that too. The latter replaced serpentine lines.

The 911 had a chain tensioner problem. When Peter Schutz arrived at Porsche, he found out this mechanical malady was at the root of the 911's two current customer complaints: unreliability and high price. He asked the Porsche engineers why nothing had been done concerning the chain tensioner arrangement. They said that with the 911 due to die in 1981, there was no point. Think again boys!

Other engine upgrades included higher compression dome pistons, as well as new intake and exhaust manifolds. Porsche claimed the latest E series was 80 per cent new, but, as ever, similarities with older 911s were apparent. The wheelbase was 2271mm, with length and width at 4291mm and 1610mm respectively, the same as 1977! Overall, the integration of front foglamps in the front valence was the most notable visual change compared to the outgoing '83 911SC. Of course, when people think of a 911 Carrera 3.2 its usually with the M491 option fitted.

911 Carrera 3.2 – handling & power

The M491 pack provided 930 upgrades for the atmo 911 Carrera 3.2. Most obviously, there was the wide-body 930 look, enveloping suspension, brakes, and rim/tire combo. The 930's tie-rod ends weren't included, but larger cross-drilled brake rotors were aboard. Compared to the stock 11.1in vented front and 11.4in vented rear stoppers of the Carrera 3.2, you were now on 12in front disks and 12.2in rear disks, all vented. That was a lot of brakes for a sub 2800lb Euro spec car. Standard Carrera hoops involved 15in cast alloy rims, 6in wide at the front and 7in wide at the rear. Tires were Pirelli P6s sized 185/70-15 front and 215/60-15 rear.

The normal 16in upgrade option took one to 16x6 in front and 16x7 in rear, with 205/55-16 tires front and 225/50-16 tires rearwards. Both the 15 and 16in tire sets were VR rated. However, M491 took one on to 16x7 in front and 16x9 in back rims. Monster 205/55-16s and 245/45-16s were the VR-rated rubber fitted front and rear respectively. On the inside, M491 brought 930 buckets, on the outside that famous tray type rear spoiler. Everyone kept calling 'em 'whaletails,' but that style was gone at the end of '77 MY. The M491 package was very popular in North America in 1984-85. This was partly because the 930 had left the building at the end of '79 MY.

Some magazine testers and fans remarked that they preferred the plain, non tray spoiler base Carrera 3.2. It looked more '60s, more classic 911. However, the M491 Turbo look pack brought objective, measurable gains in handling and braking. The Turbo chassis plus 3.2L atmo motor, equaled a safer 911, with higher limits and less susceptibility to wild oversteer. In 1984, *Car and Driver* was searching for the best handling car in America. Out of the imported cars tested, a 911 Carrera with M491 pack came first on the objective portion. It scored 61 points in *C&D's* July 1984 issue.

In achieving first place, the 911 Carrera had beaten out the Porsche 944, 928S, Ferrari 308 GTBi, Lotus Esprit Turbo and the Audi Quattro. The test considered skidpad, slalom, LA's SCCA Pro Solo Gymkhana course, emergency lane changing and Willow Springs race course. The 911 got a 0.84g reading on the smooth skidpad, 0.82g on the bumpy one. However, it didn't bottom out on the latter, but the 944 on stock suspension did! Overall, the 911 did well and was controllable as long as its limits were respected.

The 928S was the big, ponderous machine that displayed plow understeer and tail wagging. It lapped Willow Springs two seconds slower than the 911. The 911 matched the lap times of the Lotus and Ferrari. The 911's assessment was: "Porsche 911 Carrera hanging in there." In more ways than one, it could be said. Trouble was, the 911, M491 or no, required a lot of driver concentration. The 944 was a piece of cake. The 911 with 930 pack beat the Lotus and Ferrari on the subjective test portion, and tied with the 928S. However, in the end, it was that easy feeling 944 that went on to represent the imports, and vanquish the Camaro Z/28 to become *C&D*'s best handler in America.

Porsche's 0-100kph time of 6.1 seconds was a conservative factory figure. Objective magazine testing showed that the latest 911 was faster and more economical. *Motor* magazine tried the 911SC Cabrio in its June 4, 1983 issue. 0-60mph, top speed and overall fuel economy were a respective 5.8 seconds, 147.3mph and 20.1mpg. On February 4, 1984, *Motor*'s 911 Carrera 3.2 managed, respectively, 5.3 seconds, 151.1mph and 21.1mpg. The new 911 was also more flexible concerning in gear 30-50mph and 50-70mph acceleration. It was 6 and 9.3 seconds, for the two respective increments, using the 3-liter SC. The 3.2L coupe brought respective stats of 5.6 and 8.2 seconds.

There seemed little penalty concerning a 3.2L coupe or ragtop. On January 8, 1986, *Autocar* tried the 911 Carrera SE, a 911 with the M491 kit. On June 11, 1986, the same journal sampled a 911 Carrera 3.2 Cabrio. Respective 0-60mph, 50-70mph, quarter mile, top speed and fuel economy were 5.6 seconds, 4.1 seconds, 14.4 seconds at 95mph, 148mph and 19.2mpg for the coupe. The ragtop scored respective stats of 5.7 seconds, 4 seconds, 14.2 seconds at 98mph, 147mph and 21.2mpg. It was even all the way. The coupe and convertible weighed a respective 2780lb and 2674lb. Both were five-speed stick shift cars.

Coupe or convertible, the 911 Carrera 3.2 was the car that shouldn't have existed, in more ways than one. *Motor*'s John Simister brought up the concept when testing a 1986 911 Carrera Cabrio in Dunwich. This was an historic English coastal town in Suffolk that was eroded by the North Sea. The idea was to take a car that logically shouldn't exist, to a town that doesn't! Rear-engined cars, with that much weight behind the transaxle, were illogical by 1985. The 911 as a model, should have gone too, sensibly replaced by the front-engined coupés.

However, the 911 did still exist, and its electrifying performance was very real and entertaining. As Simister said: "It's a spine-tingling soundtrack that starts as an uneven, Ford V6-like beat, blares a bit as the revs build up, and culminates in the hard yowl that sounds so unlike anything else." Simister tried power oversteer on a wet deserted

roundabout, and it proved controllable. It seemed the 3.2-liter Carrera was safer than earlier 3-liter editions. In the end, "Dunwich beckoned, and so did the Porsche. Catch them both while you can."[96]

911 pricing & value
The Porsche 911 seemed like the odd man out by the 1980s. In the age of the slippery 0.30Cd Audi 100, the 911 Carrera 3.2 registered a barn-door-like 0.40Cd! Even so, the general public viewed the 20-plus-year-old 911, as a high tech bastion of speed and efficiency. It was certainly fast and efficient: compare it with the more expensive £29,100 Ferrari 308 GTB Qv. With 0-60mph and top speed of 6.7 seconds and 150mph, Maranello couldn't match the £25,227 911 Carrera 3.2's 6.1 seconds and 152mph. Both factory figures going into '86 MY. In addition, the tardy Ferrari could only offer gas mileage equal to a 160mph 911 Turbo. That is, the Ferrari was 8mpg thirstier than an atmo 911!

The 911's out-of-step drag factor was of no concern. Dream cars have no interest in wind tunnels, or the humdrum. In August 1986, *Modern Motor*'s Paul Gover said, "With more curves than almost anything produced in the angular '80s," the 911's body design was one of the most beautiful things about the 911. With Porsche's venerable coupe still held in such high regard, the strategy of pricing the new 1986 944 Turbo slightly higher, seemed questionable. The almost identical pricing underlined the one-time intention of replacing the 911. It also turned the 944 Turbo versus 911 decision into a Pepsi versus Coke taster's choice, and guess which car was Pepsi? Poor Dr Fuhrmann obviously didn't know much about Corvettes or soda pop.

In Britain, it was £27,546; equal with the 911. In Australia, $92,723 against $92,415 for the base 911. Porsche always stressed that the 944 Turbo would sell to a different buyer profile. Even so, it's a tough showroom contest when the 911, with better resale value, costs the same. Porsche Cars North America neatly side-stepped the issue by pricing the very well equipped 944 Turbo at a competitive $29,500. *Road & Track* considered that a bargain.

Paul Gover's 1986 *Modern Motor* 944 Turbo versus 911 Carrera 3.2 comparison test showed the two cars performing very similarly. Porsche Australia claimed 0-100kph in 6.32 seconds for 944 Turbo, and 6.23 seconds for ye olde 911. In the real world and trackside driving, the two were hard to separate. However, it was the 944 Turbo, not the 911, that bottomed out more and was trickier on the limit.

The blown 944's pokey power supply was partly to blame.

The 911's linear, atmo power delivery and clear suspension warnings made the older coupe an easier visitor to the razor's edge. Gover asked and answered the question, concerning which was the better car: "The Porsche, of course." Objectively, this was true, but preference is a subjective thing. On the 944 Turbo, you had the 924-sourced, small tilt-and-slide sunroof. The 911 offered a larger power roof. As George Orwell said in *Animal Farm*, some are more equal than others. Unfortunately for the 944 Turbo, in the capitalist world, folks got to choose.

Pricing in the various markets was uneven. In Britain, the mid 1985 price for a 911 Carrera 3.2, was £25,227. The targa was a no cost option (a NCO). The Sport (M491 – 930 kit) was £27,078, the cabrio was £26,462, and the cabrio sport was £28,192. The 911 Turbo and 928S2 were £39,300 and £35,524 respectively. Automatic was an NCO on the 928S2. In Australia, importer Alan Hamilton's Porsche Cars Australia operation charged an extra 30 grand for the M491 option! It was standard operating procedure for importers to bring in small numbers of prestige cars and rip off buyers.

Behind the scenes, the 911 had been kind to mankind. 1985's F series 911s had a cat converter option. It was the West German government's smog device of choice. The formerly optional four-spoke wheel became standard too. '86 MY G series 911s gained sports seats as a no cost option. In America, Carrera was the name, and unleaded was the game. The base 911 in this market was called Carrera, so was its 3.2L motor. The figures for this smogger 3.2L were 9.5:1 comp, 200 SAE net horses at 5900rpm and 185lb/ft at 4800rpm.

Road & Track's '86 911 Cabrio did 0-60mph in 5.7 seconds, which was almost equal to the Euro version. 1986 was also the year the 911 Turbo returned to America. It still had that four-speed box, 4.22 final drive ratio and Bosch K-Jetronic mechanical injection. It was more powerful than in 930 days, now with 282bhp at 5500rpm and 278lb/ft at four grand. These days it was running less boost, but was emissions compliant on unleaded gas.

It all called into question Porsche Cars Australia's failure to provide a 1986 911 Turbo for this also unleaded market. PCA's excuse was that the blown 911 couldn't handle unleaded gas and a catalytic converter. The 911 Turbo had been available in Australia up to 1986, in Euro leaded gas form. America could have a 1986 911 Turbo with unleaded gas and cat, but Australia could not. A mystery for the ages.

By 1986, the blown 911 was called 911 Turbo in America, not 930 anymore. It was in keeping with world markets. 0-60mph arrived in five seconds flat, and a 13.4-second quarter mile and 155mph were on offer. Even faster if you were, well, let's say brave. In truth, the 911 Turbo was no faster than the 930, and it didn't need to be. At 48 grand, the 911 Turbo announced its big kahuna status without

Porsche returned to Formula One in 1983 as an engine supplier. The TAG Turbo V6 powered the McLarens of Nikki Lauda and Alain Prost to driver's titles in 1984 and 1985 respectively. Prost was '86 champ too! (Courtesy Shell)

turning a wheel. The base 911 Cabrio cost $36,450 with five-speed and a/c standard. Then there were the options: 16in rims ($1580), full leather ($1202), stereo ($625), power passenger seat ($380), cruise control ($320), power door locks ($250), sports shocks ($200), alarm system ($200). With the 911 Turbo … driving was optional!

On effectively the fastest car in North America, the 3060lb 911 Turbo could have LSD ($595), and the feds slugged you with a 500 buck gas guzzler tax donation to Uncle Sam, but why worry? Racer Danny Ongais didn't. What was Ongais' technique for fast cornering in his 930? "I don't go around corners fast in my Turbo." And, according to racer Al Holbert, the 911 Turbo was best driven with three feet!

Worried about your 911 getting stolen? In 1987's September issue of *What Car?* a security expert was able to gain access to a new 911 Carrera in 11 seconds. However, the trunk and engine covers were pretty secure from the outside. *What Car?* said

this was a concern, given the 911 Carrera was one of the most desirable cars on the road. It's one time when the Porsche crowd envied Hyundai owners; Kia anyone?![97]

Rallying, F1 & Le Mans
The reborn Tour de France Auto featured classics from the '50s to the '70s in stage type rallying. Cars like the Ferrari 250 GTO, Ford GT40 and Lancia Stratos. They visited classic venues like Magny-Cours, Paul Ricard and the ascent Mont Ventoux. The Porsche 911 was a star of the original Tour de France, and was prominent in the 1992 edition as well. The French crew of Sevin and Baratta won the modern event in a pre '74 911. A Ferrari 250 GT came second.

The 911, with its rear engine traction advantage and compact length, was always a fine rally car. In the '80s Group B era, it had a chance to shine once again. The impetus came from Porsche and sponsor Rothmans. Porsche, chiefly Helmuth Bott, wanted to show the link between production cars and racing.

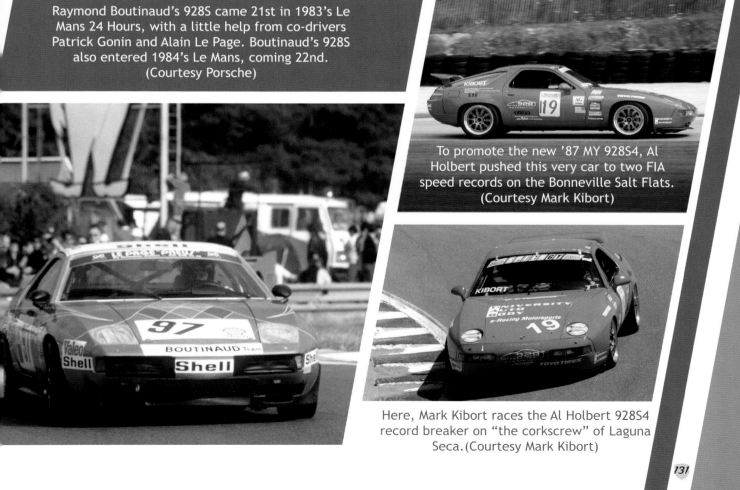

Raymond Boutinaud's 928S came 21st in 1983's Le Mans 24 Hours, with a little help from co-drivers Patrick Gonin and Alain Le Page. Boutinaud's 928S also entered 1984's Le Mans, coming 22nd. (Courtesy Porsche)

To promote the new '87 MY 928S4, Al Holbert pushed this very car to two FIA speed records on the Bonneville Salt Flats. (Courtesy Mark Kibort)

Here, Mark Kibort races the Al Holbert 928S4 record breaker on "the corkscrew" of Laguna Seca. (Courtesy Mark Kibort)

The all-wheel drive 953 911 Carrera at the Paris Dakar Rally on the 26th of April 1984. A relatively conventional rally car, in an age of space framed, turbocharged Gruppe B monsters! (Courtesy Porsche)

Below: At the 1984 Paris Dakar Rally, René Metge and Dominique Lemoyne's 953 achieved an outright victory. (Courtesy Porsche)

Rallying was a great showcase for the versatile and durable 911. Rothmans was buoyed by its successful sponsoring of the Porsche 956 sports cars in 1982 and 1983. It wanted more sales in the Middle East, and the FIA's new '84 Rally Raid Championship, covering Europe and the Middle East, seemed just the ticket.

Everything fortuitously dovetailed into the 1984 911SC RS. The new 911 Carrera 3.2 couldn't meet homologation requirements, so the outgoing 3-liter coupe sufficed. Porsche built 20 911SC RSs, and new rally team David Richards Autosports (DRA) got six. This outfit eventually became Prodrive. The homologation machine had a 911 Turbo chassis,

lightweight body panels, lexan glass (bar the windshield), special torsion bar springs, and two 18mm swaybars. The 3-liter motor featured a sportier cam, simplified mechanical fuel-injection and 935 heads, which boosted power to 255bhp. Torque was 184lb/ft with factory figures of 0-100kph in 5 seconds and 159mph.

Custom touches saw DRA strengthen the A pillars, front bulkhead area, and rear semi trailing arms. The coupe was a winner for Saeed Al Hajri. As Middle East rally champion in 1984, Al Hajri got his third successive Middle East series victory in 1985's Qatar International Rally. A Toyota Celica Turbo was second. The Group B era was a difficult one. Outright victories were achieved by increasingly

The dominant Porsche 956 at Kyalami in 1983, with the superstars of sports car racing. From left to right the driver pairings of Jacky Ickx/Jochen Mass, Derek Bell/Stefan Bellof, and Al Holbert/Vern Schuppan. (Courtesy Porsche)

Stefan Bellof and Derek Bell's Porsche 956KH, in the 1983 Nürburgring 1000. Bellof set a new lap record on the Nordschleife. (Courtesy Porsche)

specialized designs. At the 1985 Acropolis Rally, Timo Salonen's Peugeot 205 T16 mid-engined AWD racer won, and indeed dominated the whole 1985 World Rally Championship. Stig Blomqvist's Audi Quattro Sport was a distant second on the Acropolis. Even with AWD and a 420bhp 20-valve turbo I5, the Audi was too close to a production car.

Saeed Al Hajri came fifth on the 1985 Acropolis Rally. It was only his second time on the event. During the rally's first leg, he was in third place. Al Hajri's Rothmans factory 911SC RS's window winder broke off in the heat of battle, and jammed under the clutch pedal, and then the rear suspension collapsed! Not an easy business, rallying. However, Al Hajri's 911SC RS did finish the event, and the 911SC RS did win races.[98] The DRA Rothmans # 110-008 chassis

911SC RS did 13 rallies, with five wins. Successes included the 1984 Belgian and Portuguese rallies, and the 1985 Jordan rally. In 1987, this car helped Saeed Al Hajri secure the Middle East Rally Championship with wins in Kuwait and Qatar, and it came second in Jordan. The car had been previously driven by Henri Toivonen and Juha Kankkunen.

A little more specialized and also successful was the Porsche 953. This 959 stepping stone resembled a jacked up 911SC RS, and was designed for the 1984 Paris-Dakar Rally. The 953 had a manually controlled AWD system, much modified suspension and 300 horses from flat-six punch! Three 953s were entered in the 1984 Paris-Dakar Rally. René Metge and Dominique Lemoyne achieved first overall in this event, with their Rothmans liveried 953.

Porsche knew something about rallying. It also knew

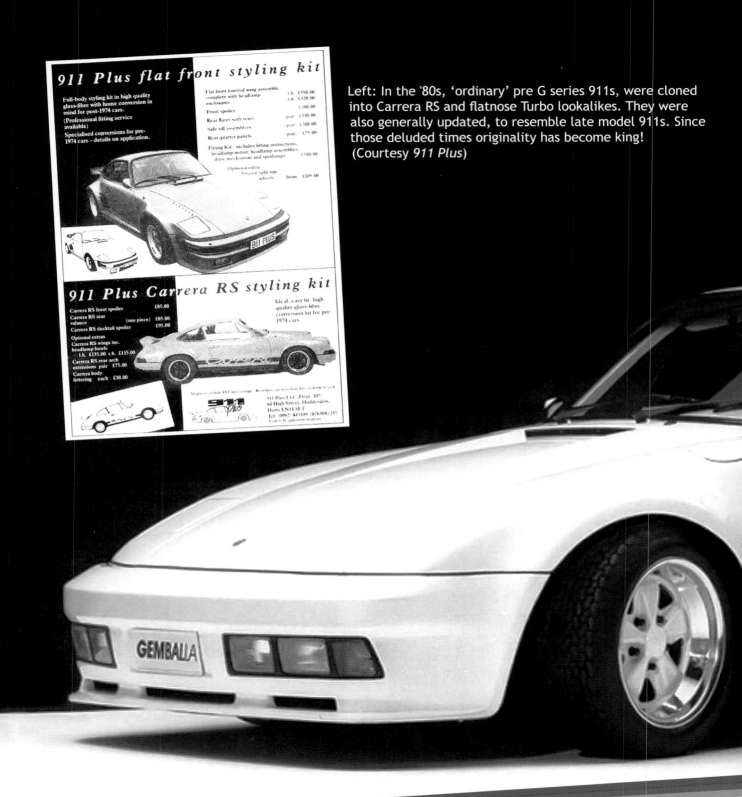

Left: In the '80s, 'ordinary' pre G series 911s, were cloned into Carrera RS and flatnose Turbo lookalikes. They were also generally updated, to resemble late model 911s. Since those deluded times originality has become king! (Courtesy *911 Plus*)

Penthouse model Maria Whittaker added even more glamour to the 911-based Gemballa Cyrrus in 1986. (Courtesy Gemballa GmbH)

something about turbocharging, so Zuffenhausen was the perfect engine supplier to a Formula One series increasingly dominated by 1.5-liter turbo motors. Porsche got into an exclusive relationship with McLaren, under Ron Dennis control, in this era. Its reliable TAG Turbo V6 delivered the power. Porsche hadn't raced in F1 since 1962 with its own car. This time, lots of success came. In 1984, Nikki Lauda narrowly beat his team-mate, Alain Prost, to become World Champion in the McLaren. The next year it was all Prost; he became the first French F1 World Champ.

Between the 1984 Dallas GP and the 1985 Detroit GP, at least one Porsche-powered McLaren finished a race. After bungling Renault Sport in 1983, Prost was glad to be in a McLaren at this time. McLaren secured the Constructor's Championship in 1984 and 1985. In 1986, Alain Prost, aka The Professor, snicked through the chaos of the Williams F1 team in the aftermath of Frank Williams' car accident. Prost out-pointed Nelson Piquet and Nigel Mansell, to be '86 World Champion. He was the first driver to achieve back-to-back F1 driver titles since Jack 'Black Jack' Brabham in 1959-60. More than a little of the thanks for this went to Porsche power, displayed in 25 GP wins in the 1984-87 era.

By the early '80s, Porsche was synonymous with sports car racing. Just two words: Le Mans. Indeed, the F1 TAG Turbo V6 had been trialled in the Porsche 936's successor. So it was that, in 1983, chassis no 107 Porsche 956 provided the F1 motor's debut. The 956 was designed by Norbert Singer as a racer for the new sports prototype racer Group C. As such, the first prototype chassis was completed on March 27, 1982. It was Porsche's first aluminum monocoque, and complied with a 1764lb minimum weight requirement.

The 956 made its debut at the 1982 Silverstone 6-Hour. However, all eyes were on Le Mans. Le Mans 1982: a new Porsche, the same drivers (Ickx & Bell), and a new sponsor. In 1981's Le Mans, the factory Porsche 936/81s were sponsored by Christian Dior's new 1980 fragrance for men, 'Jules,' already a top French seller (the fragrance, not the 936). In 1982, sponsorship for the Jacky Ickx and Derek Bell factory 956 switched to Rothmans. A different fragrance to be sure, but the sweet smell of success was evident nevertheless.

Since Ickx and Bell were basically recycling the 936/81's motor in 1982, their 956 carried the No 1 marking from their 1981 Le Mans victory. The pair won again in 1982, and with Porsche 956s coming second and third, it was a Porsche 1-2-3! Jacky Ickx and Derek Bell went on to achieve their fourth joint Le Mans win in 1983. Once again, they were driving a Rothmans Porsche 956. The 956 helped Porsche win the World Endurance Championship (WEC) in 1982 and 1983. Even so, as with the 936, the factory kept a tight rein over supplied 956s.

The 956 only became available to customers in 1983, but with conditions. The factory had control over the sale of every chassis or replacement. The factory Rothmans 956s had a one-piece undertray. This produced a ground effect that sucked the car to the road. There is a 956 mounted upside down in the Porsche museum, a testimony to the 956's legendary downforce. In its career, the 956 had two rear wings. A large wing with high downforce was used for most races. There was also a lower, smaller, low-drag wing for Le Mans, and high speeds on the Mulsanne Straight.

Customer 956s had a two-piece undertray. Some teams tried small front wings on tight tracks. The addendum wasn't compatible with the two-piece undertray on fast circuits. Less, not more, downforce was the result. And, well, Porsche was to be cagey with the 956, lest privateers gain the upper hand. This was the case with Le Mans during 1984 and 1985. In these years, the very professional Joest Racing Team

The 1989 model year 911 Speedster 3.2 was a nostalgic revival of that 356 ragtop from the 1950s. Porsche boss Peter Schutz told racer and Speedster fan Al Holbert that modern Porsche buyers liked things plush. (Courtesy Porsche)

won. The 1984 event even saw the works Rothmans cars withdraw, and the driver pairing of Henri Pescarolo and Klaus Ludwig triumph in the privateer 956B.

1984 had seen the revised 956B introduced with an improved chassis and Bosch Motronic fuel-injection. It was also with a 956B that Joest Racing won 1985's Le Mans 24 Hours. They did so with a very frugal car. So frugal that it could run faster than the Rothmans 956Bs, sans frequent refuelling. The winning 1985 driver trio was Klaus Ludwig, Barilla and Winter. The first dual clutch gearbox was used on the 956, being joined to a normal five-speed box on the test car. During 1986's Le Mans, one works Rothmans 962C debuted the high tech as PDK. A 962C, the 956's successor, had set the fastest lap at 1985's Le Mans: 3 minutes and 25.1 seconds.

The popularity of Le Mans was in decline by the early '80s. For 1986, there was an admission charge reduction, made possible by axing a local tax. Porsche's success at La Sarthe was undiminished either way. So was the 956's significance. With Stefan Bellof as driver, the 956 set a Nürburgring Nordschleife lap record that would stand for 35 years! It was 6 minutes and 11.13 seconds. Bellof set the record while qualifying for the 1983 Nürburgring 1000. The record was eventually beaten by another Porsche: a 919!

The 956 was a winner with problems. Stefan Bellof died at the 1985 Spa 1000 when he collided with Jacky Ickx's 962. Privateers were switching to the safer 962. The 962 was a stretched 956; in Europe the FIA mandated a safety transition from the short tub 956 to the 962 monocoque. The front axle was extended for more safety. However, the 956 ended on a high. Joest Racing gave the design its last win in the final race of 1986's WEC. In addition, that year had seen Derek Bell raise the second highest charity contribution to the BBC's *Children In Need* telethon. The World Sports Car Champion raised £16,000. Six grand came from an enthusiast treated to a three-lap drive in a works 956, with Bell doing the driving honors, naturally![99]

The 911 Turbo 3.3L was up to 320bhp by the 964 era. However, the special order '92 MY Turbo S version had 381bhp. Eighty cars were so built. (Courtesy Porsche)

911 – business as usual

CAR magazine kicked off 1988 with a January issue piece titled *Porsche 911 Carrera,* and said, "Those who love the 911, revel in the car's unforgiving behaviour." This traditional enthusiast sentiment was echoed by Ian Kuah in the May 1995 edition of *911 & Porsche World*: "The 944 was better, but I preferred the engine of its Italian contemporary, the Alfa Romeo GTV6, and the handling of the Lotus Excel. I bought none of the above, as I was working my way towards a 911."

A different decade, different rivals, but the result was always the same. The Porsche 911 was the enthusiast sports car lover's number one choice. Corvettes were nice, but not pure enough sports cars. The Italian rivals from De Tomaso, Ferrari, Lamborghini and Maserati were either going, gone, or prohibitively expensive, so fans kept liking the 911, ignoring the 928, and Porsche played the evolution game. The most significant, practical change for 1987's H series 911 was replacement of the 915 five-speed with the easier-to-use Getrag G50 five-speed. The new box had Borg Warner synchronizers and hydraulic clutch. It was heavier in action than the 915, but, using contemporary jargon, was 'user-friendly.' The new shift linkage and pattern helped.

1987 also brought a new thermo fan and reworking of the Katalyser unleaded motor. October 1986 saw a fuel remap and rechip for the Bosch DME. It increased SAE net power from 200 to 214 horses at the same 5900rpm. It was more power for US drivers, and tax credits for environmentally aware West German buyers. So much better than a Trabant. *Autocar* reviewed Porsche's '87 MY wares and noted: "To many, the 911 is still the only 'real' Porsche, and this year it celebrates its 23rd birthday." Normal 911s marked the milestone with a rear body panel that now accommodated fog lamps. However, most attention shone on the 911 Turbo SE, a car that made a real statement.

This year, for the first time, one could factory order a 911 Turbo in Targa or Cabrio forms. Porsche updated the Turbo with the ordinary Carrera's annual refinements. However, the base Turbo was still on 1978's 300bhp, and still had a four-speed! That said, the SE (Sport Equipment) version offered more for a pretty penny: as usual with the SE pack, front and rear spoilers, sportier shocks and forged alloys, plus the 911's best footwear. For the British market, the ultimate 911 had the flachbau in all the publicity shots. The flat front became a factory option in 1987. Your 911 now had fashionable pop-up headlamps, and behind them lay louvered air intakes.

The rear fender's air intake aperture had three horizontal black strakes. There was also the expected rear tray spoiler. The 911 Turbo SE had an uprated 330bhp (DIN net) version of the familiar 930 motor, but it had something even bigger than that. With a UK price tag of £86,443, the 1987 911 Turbo SE was the most expensive Porsche going, and more than double a base 911.

At first glance this seemed very expensive, but then one only had to look at the Cabrio version. With the flachbau and rear side strakes, it resembled a Gemballa Cyrrus. A Targa and Cabrio 911 was something only a Porsche tuner used to do. Compared to tuners, the factory car was much cheaper. Closing the door on tuners may have been part of the Porsche plan. In addition, 1987 saw all Cabrios come with a power top as standard. That wasn't always the case for all markets.

Going into '87 MY, Porsche had two major non-911 things going on: the 944S and 928S4.[100] Here, Porsche treated its front-engined models to multi-valve single world emissions market engines. It was a 2.5-liter I4 16-valver for the 944, and a 5-liter 32-valve V8 for the 928S4. The former was basically half the latter. They were big news at the time but have faded into obscurity since. As ever, the 911 was where the action lay. 1988 saw the J series 911 debut with the now blueprinted 3.2L flat-six, uprated 10 horses to 241bhp. It was the final dalliance with 98 octane leaded gas before Brussels bureaucrats weighed in with their Care Bears pollution policy to save My Little Pony!

Happy birthday 911!

For '87 MY, Ferrari had increased its junior supercars, the 308/Mondial, from three to 3.2-liters. Zuffenhausen kept the 911 on-guard. Even with all the changes, the 911 still looked much the same as ever. *MotorWeek* said as much when it met up with the evergreen racer in 1988. The 911 was now 25 years old, so the TV show carried the title, *Happy Birthday and Many More.* One big change was the price. In 1965 America, a new 911 cost five grand; now, it was $43,585 base list: adjusted for inflation, pretty much its always-expensive self. Standard equipment was described as 15in wheels, a/c, power windows and part power seats. Options mentioned by John H Davis were ABS, sport shocks, 16in rims, full power seats and automatic heater.

The auto heater saw a dial replace the standard 911's between-the-seats, VW Beetle-like levers. One lever, as per tradition, handled how much engine

No, it's not a
Porsche pincushion.
It's our new warranty on
pre-owned Porsches.

Key to illustrations

1 A 1993 964 911 Carrera 2 Targa is shown. The Targa name was familiar, but the 964's standard 3.6L flat-six and AWD option were newbies. Porsche claimed the 964 911 was 87% new, not 86% nor 88%, they were precise like that!

2 This US spec 964 911 Carrera 4's 3.6-liter flat-six made 250bhp at 6100rpm. The 964 was the first 911 with the controllability advantage of all wheel drive.

3 The 964's styling was attributed to the work of Benjamin Dimson, in 1985-86.

4 A 1991 964 Carrera 4 3.6 Coupe. Racing did improve the breed, an AWD system for Gruppe B racing, was shown at the Frankfurt Auto Show a decade earlier.

5 Porsche CEO Heinrich ('Heinz') Branitzki announced the new 964 as, "The 911 for the next 25 years." Thank you Peter Schutz!

(Original 964 images all courtesy Porsche)

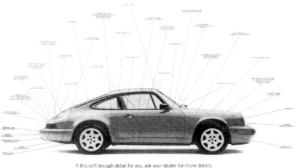

No, it's not a Porsche pincushion.

It's our new warranty on pre-owned Porsches.

If this isn't enough detail for you, ask your dealer for more details.

Porsche Pre-owned Limited Warranty Program.

Porsche already had the best new car warranty for a sports car company. By the early '90s it was getting into the approved used car schemes offered by prestige car brands.
(Courtesy Porsche Cars North America)

MotorWeek's 911 stopped in 109ft from 55mph, and needed hot brakes for best results.

Such hot brakes showed the character difference between Porsche and Lexus. The 911 worked well with hot brakes, the Lexus did not. *Auto Motor und Sport* magazine conducted its usual mountain road driving test of cars, from small and cheap to large and expensive. After 12 miles of downhill driving, the brakes of the Lexus LS400 were dangerously hot. Hot enough to crack a rotor. It showed Porsche's engineering distinction. The 911 was designed to be driven. The Lexus was designed to be sat in. The latter was perfect for the average luxury car buyer, happy to waft along half tranquilized on the turnpike. However, the 911 wasn't average, it demanded more.

Problems with the 911 still centered on the great driver concentration needed to keep the tail at bay during high-speed driving. The coupe was classed by the feds as a mini compact. It's true, the 911 can't seat four adults in comfort. The space saver spare was also on the negative side of the ledger. That said, as a no compromise road racer that one could use as a daily driver, with very small kids in tow, the 911 was unique. Celebration came in the form of the 1988 911 Silver Limited Anniversary Edition, now a serious collectible.

Interior accoutrements included silk gray leather with black accent striping, complemented by silk gray velour carpets. There was a stitched leather console, outside temperature gauge, CD or cassette holder and small bronze '25th Anniversary Special Edition' badges. A short shift kit and LSD were mechanical improvements. 500 Silver Limited Anniversary Edition 911s journeyed to America. The 300 coupés saw 240 in Silver Metallic and 60 in Satin Black Metallic. Of the 200 Cabrios, 160 were silver and 40 were black. In the end, 76,473 911 Carrera 3.2s were constructed. This broke down to 35,670 coupés, 19,987 Cabrios and 18,468 Targas.

Always look on the light side of life – 911 Club Sport

There was another way to celebrate the 911's birthday, and *CAR* magazine thought it was the best one of all, the 1988 Carrera CS (Club Sport): "This, perhaps even more than the out-of-court 959, is the proper Porsche." Using the 'less is more,' Mies van der Rohe approach, the 911 Carrera CS was also the cheapest 911 one could buy. As of January 1988, it was introduced to the UK at £34,390. A veritable bargain, given a contemporary 959 had a telephone number price tag. The surprises continued with

compartment hot air was admitted to the interior. The second lever concerned heat distribution between front and rear compartments. As ever, driving position was very sound, interior controls were scattered to the four winds, but not as chaotic as an Italian exotic! The rear seats had seatbelts, but could only accommodate children under 8 years old. However, the rear seat backs could be folded flat to create a luggage or oddment platform. The Super Beetle could do this too.

Interior materials were top notch, and the whole car was well built, in a way that the Corvette was not. The gear changes were still tricky, but at least the new hydraulic clutch was very smooth and easy. Performance on test turned out a 14.6-second quarter mile at 98mph. 0-60mph was 5.7 seconds, and 135mph was registered on the straights of Georgia's Roebling Road Raceway. The 1988 Carrera 3.2 was EPA rated 18mpg city driving/25mpg highway driving. The coupe got a real-world 21mpg on test.

This racer was converted from a 964 C4 to two-wheel drive C2, and has been racing in the Porsche Club GB Championship since 2006.

The car was originally white, then orange & white, before adopting German flag colors in 2013!

For better weight distribution, the 964 marked the return of the within wheelbase located 911 dry sump, for the first time since 1972.

David Botterill's 964 chassis 911 started as an AWD C4 model. (Images courtesy David Botterill)

the fact that this lithe variant was available in America. No doubt the latest way Dr Porsche foiled Ralph Nader!

The 911 Carrera CS option code was M637, and 340 cars were made between August 1987 and September 1989. Intended for intrepid club racers, the 911 CS was a stripper with a heart of gold. Specifically, a blueprinted 3.2L flat-six with hollow intake valves. The rev limiter was lifted from 6500rpm to 6840rpm. Weight dropped 120lb, and the 2670lb stat implied a 0.2-second fall in 0-60mph times. To achieve this, there were no power gadgets. The sunroof and a/c were gone (gulp!), the radio, rear seat and PVC undercoating were also absent. Reduced sound deadening was heard, and joined the also absent rear wiper, door pocket lids and 'who needs 'em?' fog lamps. Front hood locking mechanism, plus the engine and luggage compartment courtesy lights were deep-sixed. The Club Sport was so minimal that lockable wheel nuts and rear Carrera engine lid badging were left off too!

One 911 Carrera CS did have a sunroof, and two had a/c. The latest lightweight 911 did have 'SP' stamped on the crankcase and cylinder head. Outside, a left front fender 'CS' call-out decal weighed little, but had a heavy visual impact. Some exterior colors could be special ordered. However, the official UK color scheme was a Grand Prix White exterior, with red Carrera CS decal script on each side of the car,

and red rims. The UK market received 21 cars in 1988 and 7 in 1989. Canada got 1 CS in 1988, and 53 cars officially made it to the US.

In America, the light 911 carried the 911 Club Sport title. It cost $45,895, more than a normal 911 but less than the marginally swifter 944 Turbo S ($47,432). Both Porsches could out-accelerate a new (but sub 30 grand) L98 Vette. *Road & Track*'s 911CS experience brought 0-60mph in 5.7 seconds, and a 14.3-second quarter mile at 99mph, along with 18mpg. Equivalent 944 Turbo S readings were 5.5 seconds, 14.2 seconds at 100.5mph and 18.5mpg. The 911CS was tested in May 1988, and the 944 Turbo S in June's issue. Stats, competence and the 944 Turbo S' 250bhp aside, the 911CS was judged the more likeable coupe. *R&T* praised the responsive engine, quick and direct steering, and called 911CS "a no-nonsense sports car." However, the ergonomics were dated, the price high, engine noisy, creature features were absent, and there was that lift throttle 'take a set' oversteer.

Blown 944 conclusions saw that "this is an enormously competent car, but it isn't fun the way a 911 is," and "still expensive and still not a 911." Which goes to prove you may have a/c, but that doesn't make you cool! Porsche applied the same formula on a larger scale with the 928S4 Club Sport in 1988: a CS decal on the left front fender, redline raised to 6775rpm, stick shift only, lighter a/c system and 201lb less. A real gas to drive for the equivalent of $69,400, but not available in North America. PCNA feared too few takers.

In West Germany, it was white graphics

on red exterior. A gas station attendant gave his thoughts to journalist Georg Kacher in the November '88 issue of *Automobile* magazine. His boss wasn't too happy with the 911 Club Sport. It was too spartan, too stiff and too expensive. Kacher felt the 928CS was an ideal compromise between the 'race me' 911CS and the 'boudoir on wheels' powerhouse that was the 944 Turbo S. The 928CS provided a preview of the upcoming 928GT's motor. It also showed the engineering department still held sway over marketing. Porsche legend, and Weissach Chief, Helmuth Bott retired in 1988. Bott offered this view on the 928CS: "This car is strictly for the performance-oriented customer." A little less luxury for a lot more driving pleasure.

911 on the small screen – TV
In spite of the wisdom of Herr Bott, television chose the 911 Carrera 3.2 Cabrio. Two silver gray examples were driven by the leading characters in two new fall debut shows of the 1987-88 TV season. The shorter lived of the two was *Leg Work* starring Margaret Colin as Claire McCarron. McCarron was an ex-district attorney turned private investigator on the streets of New York.

Colin's character had a Porsche, and in keeping with the times, lived beyond her means. She was always dealing with debt collectors and trying to get clients to pay up. In one episode, she questioned her mechanic about the high maintenance cost of

her Porsche. This was also in keeping with the times.

A much more successful show, in terms of ratings, was *Jake and the Fatman*, starring Joe Penny as policeman Jake Styles and William Conrad as his LA district attorney boss J L McCabe. Styles was J L's special investigator. In the show's plot, there was speculation about how Styles lived at such a high level. Nice threads, an expensive pad and that Porsche 911 Carrera 3.2 Cabriolet, an '80s icon if ever there was one. He explained that the apartment belonged to a landlord friend who was awaiting a new tenant. How Jake afforded the Porsche was never explained.

The 911 Cabrio was Jake's transport through the show's first season. The only times the top was up was one occasion during surveillance work and another incident when tree sap on the top was worked into the episode's plot. The second season saw the characters move to Hawaii, where, unfortunately, Jake took over his late buddy's Fox Mustang 5.0 convertible. Jake kept the Mustang for seasons two through five. However, the 911 Carrera 3.2 was featured in some more episodes, twice as a Guards Red coupe driven by good and bad guys. It also featured prominently in the 1990 fourth season episode *Round Midnight.*

Round Midnight had Jake on a date, for which he borrowed a friend's 911 Carrera for the evening,

Left to right: The reborn 964 chassis 911 Carrera RS, was an exciting 260 horse coupe. However, *Autocar* magazine didn't like the ride comfort, or lack thereof. (Courtesy Porsche)

The Jubi had the Turbo's wide rear arches and full leather interior. That meant cowhide on the seats, dashboard and door cards. Jubi also had a 250bhp 3.6-liter atmo flat-six sting in the tail! (Courtesy Unity Media plc)

The 964 Carrera 4 Anniversary (Jubi) of 1993, celebrated the 911's 30th birthday. Most were painted Viola Metallic, with a Rubicon gray leather interior. (Courtesy Porsche)

The 1993 911 Carrera 2 3.6 Speedster. The reincarnated roadster, was a 964 based homage to simpler 356 times. Inset: 3000 964 Speedsters were planned, but only 936 were actually built and sold during 1993-94. (Courtesy Porsche)

Above: A 1991 964 chassis 911 Turbo, with the long-serving 3.3L blown flat-six, established 1978! Now making 320 horse and 332 lb/ft, a 3.6L turbo replacement started production in January 1993.

Below: The hard riding stripper, known as the '93 MY 911RS America, weighed just 1,250 kilos. No Chevy LS V8 conversion required! (Courtesy Porsche)

Above: Unlike Lamborghini, Porsche was always linked to racing. From left to right this 1993 group picture shows: (front row) 911 Turbo IMSA Super Car, 911 Turbo S Le Mans GT, (rear row) 968 Turbo RS, 911 Carrera 2 Cup Edn, 911 Carrera RSR 3.8. (Courtesy Porsche)

Below: A 1993 964 Supercup 911 is shown. This was the year the competition started as a Formula One support race, for identical 911s. (Courtesy Porsche)

Below: Kremer Racing continued its association with Porsche sports cars, in the form of this 962CK6 shown at Silverstone. (Courtesy Andy)

only for the coupe to be stolen by car thief Slick. Jake then went to the Porsche dealer to get a second 911 Carrera as bait. In keeping with the aspirational times, it seemed all the TV shows were going upscale. A decade earlier, New York's Kojak had a Buick Century, and LA's Jim Rockford drove a Pontiac Firebird. In the '80s, *Miami Vice* had a faux Daytona and real Testarossa. (Sonny Crockett was once seen driving a 1978 Porsche 911 SC Targa, in a flashback to 1980 in the season 3 episode "*Forgive Us Our Debts.*") The show *Moonlighting* used a BMW 6 series. So, it comes as no surprise that this image hungry era gave rise to the reborn Porsche Speedster.

The New 911 Speedster

The new 911 Carrera 3.2 era Speedster represented the meeting of '50s beatnik and '80s yuppie. An awkward and uneasy encounter. How do you combine the spirit of '50s sports car minimalism, with the '80s ethos that everything is still not enough? Well, you don't. Porsche applied the famous Speedster name from the past to an expensive, uber upscale '89 MY Carrera 3.2 built from January 1989 to July of the same year. Option code M503 saw 2104 Neu Speedsters made. Most were Turbo style wide body cars, with M491 upgrades. However, 171 narrow-bodied Speedsters were in the mix, and 823 went to North America.

The reborn Speedster project started under Helmuth Bott in 1983, before Bott retired in September 1988. Peter Schutz told Al Holbert about the new Speedster over dinner in 1986. Holbert, PCNA's boss of racing car operations, had just been part of the driver team that won Le Mans that year in a 962. He was having dinner with the Porsche factory race team, when Porsche CEO Schutz delivered the skinny on the new roadster.

Al Holbert told Schutz that the new Carrera Speedster lacked the spirit of the original. Schutz said Porsche management thought today's buyer wanted things plush. It was a commercial reality. However, Al Holbert and designer Tim Everett were motivated to cook up their own Speedster. Everett was also of the opinion that Porsche was merely capitalizing on the Speedster name. Holbert's Porsche credentials were faultless. Plus, Everett's dad, Bert, won the 1967 under two-liter class of the SCCA's Trans-Am Championship, driving a 911. Both Al Holbert and Tim Everett owned original '50s Speedsters in their younger days. The Holbert & Everett Speedster was based on an '80s 911 Carrera

Targa. Understandably, it looked like a cross between a 356 and 911.

The factory and Everett designed Speedsters had to be longer than the 356 original to accommodate the longer 911-sourced transaxle/engine complex. However, Everett's take on the concept spelt minimalism, which equalled a 400lb weight saving and 12.8-second quarter mile at 106mph. Unfortunately, it involved a spartan nature that the average '90s buyer would have been frightened by. No power windows, hold the a/c, forget power seats, and fold a truly low Speedster top to enjoy a chopped windshield. There were new front and rear fascias, and a car bra with 'Porsche' front bumper script. No bumper, just nerf bars and no heater blower motor!

Reproduction Speedster seats and 356-style door panels were neat retro touches. One could even mount side curtains in the new alternative roadster. Tim Everett completed the retro Speedster as a memorial to Al Holbert in 1993. Holbert was busy with the Porsche Indy car project and PCNA racing car operations when he died in a privately-chartered plane in September 1988. The Holbert & Everett Speedster was available from Memory Motorcars Inc PA, a non-profit company that supported Holbert's Lehigh University scholarship fund. In the mid '90s, its special roadster was a $14 grand turn key conversion for existing Targas and Cabrios. Alternatively, one could choose the $9500 kit. The basic car came with original-style 356 carpeting and German vinyl upholstery, or optional leather.[101]

The factory M503 Speedster was perfect for the power dressing '80s, and they are super collectible today. The 1989 wide body 911 Carrera Speedster saw 139 right-hand drive examples made, with six sold in Australia. A left-hand drive Speedster in good original condition (but no concours car) sold for over $300 grand in California in August 2014! With looks that some say only a mother could love, beauty is indeed in the checkbook of the beholder.[102]

Sales, price & image – an all-time high!
The 911 Carrera K series-based Speedster of '89 MY was seen as very 930 related; it was even available with a flat front (flachbau). It was also judged a slightly retrogressive machine, because it shared its 1988 Frankfurt Auto Show debut with the truly new 964 chassis 911 Carrera 4. The final K series iteration of the classic 911 saw 16in wheels become

Above: It's the Porsche 968RS Turbo, in the ADAC GT Cup. Magazines loved this blown big four-pot, but it didn't do that well in the race series. (Courtesy Porsche)

Above and below: A 1995 PCA 968 racer is shown. The 968's balanced handling and even atmo 3-liter torque delivery, made the coupe a racetrack natural. (Courtesy Gary Grigsby)

standard for the first time. A small point, since in an overall sense Porsche had never been bigger. Over 50,000 sales per year, and the four-cylinder volume sellers played their part.

"Porsche has always had a soft spot for children," so said the company's '87 MY ad for its 2.5-liter four-pot coupés. These now covered the 924S/944/944S/944 Turbo, referred to as "Porsche's 2.5-liter series." Concerning passive safety, the torque tube of the transaxle system was called an impact shock absorber. The ad concluded with: "Our 2.5 family is waiting eagerly for yours." Porsche script was written all over the rear seat upholstery, just about the only inviting thing about the rear +2 seat!

If you've got it, flaunt it. This was the '80s and Porsche was riding high, in more ways than one. Airship Industries' AD500 airship utilized two 911 engines with a 2.5-tonne payload capacity. The aircraft had a 24-hour range, and 48mph cruising speed. On a more private level, what about a Cessna light plane with 911SC motor? The 1984 plane had a duplicated electrical system, an aviation safety prerequisite. To promote safety on the road, Porsche Cars GB Ltd organized track days at the UK's leading circuits, with the support of distributor AFN Limited. Aside from circuit driving, Porsche engineers worked out cadence braking, obstacle avoidance tests and steering maneuver training, tailored to the various models.

There weren't many owners attending track days in the late '80s. Porsches were some of the few production cars that could survive racetrack usage sans overheating and terminal brake fade after a couple of laps. Then again, Porsche was in a special position. *What Car?* magazine's Tony Lewin made the observation that if Jaguar is the king of cabrios, the Porsche 911 must be the prince. Going into the late '80s, image wasn't a problem for Zuffenhausen, and Porsche was ready to deal. Porsche Cars GB had an impressive new HQ located in Reading. The UK importer predicted the pricey new 16-valve 944S would take over from the ordinary 944 Lux as the new volume seller. However, problems were brewing.

Porsches were starting to attract the wrong people. No longer purely sports car fanciers, but now arrogant image seekers too. Like a 911 Turbo clone parked illegally in late '80s London, England, with the personal plates 'JR Ewing.'[103] The storm clouds were gathering, and 1987 saw sales fall appreciably in most countries. This was very apparent in the important North American market. Here, stockpiles of unsold four-cylinder Porsches were reaching worrying levels. By Spring 1988, Porsche had 15,000 cars unsold worldwide. Most were 924/944s, and production of these cars was cut 50 per cent.

DIAL 911

The 30-something 911 is older, faster and more refined

BY DAN SANCHEZ
PHOTOGRAPHY BY CHARLIE RATHBUN

Many people dread turning thirty, but in reality, it's not all that bad. Usually, you're stronger than you were when you were twenty, much wiser, less rebellious and much more refined. Coincidentally, the new Porsche 911 has these same characteristics now that it too has reached the 30 year mark. Although the 911 has matured, it is definitely not ready to slow down or even think about retirement. In fact, its great combination of old style and new refinements puts the '95 911 at the peak of its performance.

The updated 993 911 in Jellybean Blue. Porsche did some funny 993 TV ads, including one showing their new color range's inspiration:

JELLYBEAN Blue

Testing times at Porsche

Peter Schutz was gone, replaced by new CEO Heinz Branitzki. As sales went south, people inside and outside Porsche started playing the blame game. When they were riding high with the Schutz plan, they loved it. Now, voices were saying they had sold too many cars! Early '90s thinking was that the Porsche brand had become diluted, and was no longer able to charge a premium price. Well, at the start of 1988 the top 911 Turbo cost over £100,000, came with a ton of turbo lag, and still had a four-speed. That sure looked like premium pricing. You can be expensive and exclusive, like Lamborghini. Then you make a few hundred cars no one has heard of and get gobbled up by an econobox hatchback maker looking for street cred.

Even during the high-sales years, and afterwards, Porsche's image was always golden. In fact, the biggest companies of the last 100 years, GM and Toyota, benchmarked using Porsche cars. Jack Turner was in charge of the 1977 Chevy Camaro Z/28 program. Chevrolet had bought a Porsche 924 to figure out how to design a coupe that rode and handled well. For the downsized 1986 Buick Riviera and Olds Toronado respectively, chief engineers Dave Sharpe and Ted Louckes stated the Porsche 928 was their handling benchmark.

With the modern Toyota 86, chief engineer Tetsuya Tada bought a new Porsche Cayman every

SPEED Yellow

RUBYSTONE Red

www.YouTube.com/watch?v=xZkErbU_1LE.
(Courtesy McMullen & Yee Publishing Inc)

year for four years, to help develop the also boxer-motored Toyota. In fact, the 86's middle dash vents look just like those on the 996 and Boxster. With the original Mazda RX7, the Porsche 924 was the benchmark. One was on hand at the press drive held at Mazda's proving grounds for comparison. The second gen RX7 and Mitsubishi Starion studiously used the Porsche 944, as the go-to sports coupe development template.[104]

By the end of the fiscal year in July 1992, Porsche sold 22,481 cars worldwide. It decided to set a 35,000 unit production ceiling, with no single market taking more than 25 per cent. How did the company reach this point? At the time, much blame for Porsche's sudden fall from grace was attributed to the 1987 Wall Street stock market crash. It shook financial markets, and the financial high flyers that worked in them. It seemed a disproportionately large percentage of Porsche's customer base worked in the financial sector. However, Mercedes, BMW, Audi and Jaguar were still doing reasonable business.

The financial market crash of 1987 did herald that the high riding days of the '80s were coming to an end. Plus, that the early '90s recession was on

the way. This recession affected all automakers at all price levels. People just didn't buy cars. However, Porsche's late '80s predicament was more due to an over-produced and over-priced supply of aging four-cylinder models. It seemed the public could only accept the concept of the 911 evolving. Porsche refined and improved the 924/944 over the years. However, by 1988 it was a twelve-year-old design facing newer and more sharply priced European and Japanese opposition.

By the fall of 1989, a plain 944 was £25,990, a Nissan 300ZX Turbo was £23,516, and the Renault Alpine GTA Turbo was £28,500. In America, the 924S and Toyota Supra were well matched overall. Acceleration, handling and economy were a wash, but the Supra cost two grand less and came with more toys. The 911 flew at a higher, safer price altitude. It was out of the turbulence of value for money Euro, Japanese and American competition. In the words of *Autocar & Motor* concerning the 1990 Nissan 200SX, "Ferrari looks Porsche pace Ford price." Ian Kuah, a 911 devotee, said in *World Sportscars* that the new flat fish 300ZX offered an unrivaled balance of speed, comfort and refinement.

Below: Porsche's local autobahn police would have been unwise to choose anything but a 993 Carrera! (Courtesy Stuttgart Baden-Wurttemberg Autobahn Police)

Ferry Porsche with the one millionth Porsche. For the police in Porsche's neck of the woods, a 285 horse 993 cop car! (Courtesy Stuttgart Baden-Wurttemberg Autobahn Police)

In late 1989, the old pre 964 911 Turbo started at £57,852, with the 911 Turbo Cabriolet Sport at £109,078. At least these '89 911 Turbos now came with a five-speed stick! *Autocar & Motor* tested one in its March 15, 1989 issue. It did 0-60mph in 4.9 seconds, 50-70mph in 2.4 seconds, the quarter mile in 13.1 seconds, 156mph and 16.6mpg overall. The 911 Turbo's performance was described as shattering. It was a rich man's plaything, in more ways than one. However, commercially that wasn't helping Porsche.

Covering the 1988 Geneva Auto Salon, *CAR*'s Georg Kacher said, "The only German maker desperately short of aces is Porsche." He added that American 924/944 sales had been especially poor, and that Porsche's Indy racer hadn't done well. There were buy-in and takeover rumors involving Daimler-Benz, BMW and Deutsche Bank as interested parties. Workforce layoffs and management shake ups were in the works. To get the product line right, Kacher mentioned that Porsche engineers were trying one crash program after another.[105]

In such troubled times, even the automotive press weren't completely in awe of the 959. *Motor*'s Daniel Ward felt the 959's tremendous high tech might be to keep its 450bhp and 911 handling in check. He found the 959's bi turbo powerplant glorious, but turbo lag was in evidence and so, too, the 911's oversteer prone handling. Looking back at the test year, Ward noted *Motor*'s '87 MY 911 was the best 911 *ever*. That said, the rear window defogger was DOA. In spite of the slings and arrows of outrageous fortune, Porsche's image was still golden. After all, what was on the cover car of *Motor*'s Road Test Annual 1986? Answer: Porsche 911 with custom plate 'A911.' In *Motor*'s year of evaluation, no Porsche had come first or runner-up in any category, but when it came to glamor only a 911 would do!

Right: With 300bhp at 6500rpm, from 3746cc of air-cooled flat-six wunder, the red 911 Carrera RS 3.8 Clubsport and yellow RS were a powerful 1995 pair. Below: The '95 MY 911 Carrera 3.6, red 911 Carrera 4 and 911 Carrera Cabrio. All 993s got the Porsche's Weissach Axle design, to fight oversteer. (Courtesy Porsche)

A 1996 993 911 Targa 3.6L. Today, the 993 911s sell for around 40 grand more than the first water cooled 911s (996). (Courtesy Porsche)

With the 1996 Carrera 4 3.6 Cabrio, Porsche figures said 272bhp at 6100rpm and 275kph. However, with a classic in its lifetime, stats mean nothing! (Courtesy Porsche)

A 1996 911 Cabrio Tiptronic is at hand. Porsche did the sequential shift Tiptronic before Audi. In the air-cooled era Tiptronic's mere four speeds, limited performance. (Courtesy Porsche)

911 – bargain hunting

The world being a much more complicated place in 1989 compared to 1959, Porsche had more things to consider than in the 901's days. On June 28, 1985 the European Economic Community (EEC) agreed on its first set of emissions regulations. They would run through 1990 to 1993 model years. West German greenies had wanted the tough American regs, but fortunately failed! However, European buyers of the K series 911 Carrera 3.2's successor would experience a taste of what US Porsche fans had been enduring for years.

1990 was the final year the 944 range tried for anything approaching volume sales. Who would want the £42,296 944 Turbo when that new 964 Carrera 2 was starting from £44,058? There was no 911 Turbo. Zenith of 911 affairs was the C4 Cabrio at £56,089. Cruiser or sportster, the 928S4 auto and 928GT five-speed both cost £60,792. Who would buy them when the Tiptronic C2 and AWD C4 911s cost less? The latter even served as a relatively poor man's 959, no less!

In March 1991, Zuffenhausen took over 944S2 production, so limited was the four-cylinder car's demand by this time. The arrangement would continue with the 944's successor: the 968. Once again, Porsche would build all 968 variants, a total of 2776 units in three years of production. The 912E managed 2099 sales in just one North American market year. The 912E was another four-cylinder coupe made by Porsche. However, the 912E looked like a Porsche and had its engine in the traditional location. And so it was that Porsche and others looked hopefully towards the 986 (Boxster).

The Boxster concept car was a star of the 1993 Detroit Auto Show. With an exterior by Grant Larson and interior by Stefan Stark, this concept stirred the imaginations of even jaded industry insiders; visions of 550 Spyders, and memories of James Dean no doubt. However, behind the glitz, things weren't cool at Porsche. Heinz Branitzki's successor as CEO, Arno Bohn, had moved on suddenly in late September 1992. He was replaced by Wendelin Wiedeking.

It's felt Bohn left because he thought Porsche needed a partner to bring the 986 to market. Porsche and Piëch family members wanted Porsche to stay independent. So out went Bohn, and 1849 other Porsche employees. In came a razor gang to cut costs 20 per cent and boost productivity 30 per cent. Well, if fewer people are doing the same amount of work, things are going to get productive. The early '90s weren't easy times. Even Mercedes had lots of unsold Helmut Kohl-sized S-class sedans. They also brought in the bean counters to make ends meet.

At Detroit '93, Porsche's spokesman for the board, Wiedeking, said: "This year will be another tough one for us, but the Boxster demonstrates that this company does have a future." Board member in charge of sales and marketing, Dieter Laxy, said the 986 would take 10 per cent of a 150,000-unit global market for this class of vehicle. Meanwhile, Porsche's American sales had hit rock bottom for recent times, just 4115 cars in 1992. In Peter Schutz's last winning year of 1986, it had been 28,000!

So, it was time to go bargain shopping. If you couldn't find a Porsche dealer offering 20% off list and the hand of his daughter in marriage, the used car market had some real peaches. Or, in the words of *CAR*'s James Ruppert, "There are more Porsche 911s out there than you can shake a Sportmatic stick at." How about a two-year-old Carrera 2, for less than half its new price?! Yes, the early '90s recession was the time to get a 911. According to Ruppert, the 1990 Carrera 2 with 81,000 miles cost £19,950. It drove like a mint condition car with 20,000 miles. He judged the new-shape 911 (964) to have good build quality.[106]

There seemed to be a permanent Ferrari 308 clearance sale going on, *caveat emptor*. Ferraris were still not the most durable, and a well cared for, 40,000-mile, 5-year-old Lotus Esprit Turbo creaked and squeaked constantly on the test drive. Dash and door trims were starting to fray, but the a/c and fast glass worked … for now. It seemed that new or used, recession or not, the 911 was the enthusiast's best bet. The Porsche marque was safest of the other exotics. Porsche parts and prices came in a wide, readily available selection, be they new, used or 'pattern parts.'

Things don't remain stagnant forever. There was an improvement in US European car sales through early 1994. Comparing April 1993 to April 1994, Porsche North American sales increased 131 per cent! The American and World economy had turned the corner. The prosperous '90s had started. Although much expectation surrounded the upcoming Boxster, aka the 911's cute little sister, it would be the Porsche Cayenne that truly boosted the bottom line. After all, what does a sports car maker do when the world stops buying sports cars? Sell lemonade. Stepping out of the recession, and taking over volume sales before the Boxster and Cayenne had even turned a wheel, was the Porsche 911! That immortal sports car now had a new internal code … 964.

The 1995 911 Carrera RS 3.8 Clubsport. Add Weissach Axle to Carrera, RS and Clubsport, to make this 993 a veritable 911 lexicon on wheels! (Courtesy Porsche)

964 – all the right moves

On its debut at the 1989 Frankfurt Auto Show, Porsche CEO Heinz Branitzki referred to the new 964 as "the 911 for the next 25 years." And he was right, but not in the way he thought. Up to this point the 911, like the VW Beetle, had evolved gradually. Small changes were made from year to year. However, the latest 964 was 87 per cent new according to Porsche. From this time on, new 911 coded chassis cars would come more frequently. They would also bring a raft of changes, introduced at one time. The 911 was blending into modern model cycle development.

The first 964 taxi off the rank was the 911 Carrera 4. This stick shift only variant was the first all-wheel drive (AWD) regular production 911 in history. It was only Porsche's second series production AWD road car, after the 959. AWD would help tame the 911's infamous oversteer, and the engineering was something to behold. The gearbox and rear final drive unit had two hydraulically-controlled wet clutches. These limited slip in both the center and rear differentials. Taking a leaf from the front-engined Porsche's book, the 964 C4 employed a torque tube. With 964, the torque tube connected the center and front differentials. With a 30/70 per cent front/rear torque split, the C4's AWD system was rear biased, to keep the classic 911 feel but with more safety. The C4's AWD was oversteer insurance, if you will.

The new 964 range saw the first use of power steering on the 911 as a standard item. ABS was also standard, and '90 MY US spec 964s came with dual airbags at no extra cost. There was a new climate control system, revised instrumentation and dashboard warning lights. The 964 body had flush, integrated bumpers with built-in fog lights. There was also a new powered rear spoiler that rose at 50mph, but stayed flush at lower speed. It was all good enough to reduce the 911's drag coefficient from 0.40 to 0.32; better than the 924's 0.36Cd, and nearly as good as the ground breaking 1982 Audi 100's 0.30Cd. Once again, this 911 represented a triumph of development over design.

With all these refinements, the 911 C4 weighed in at 3252lb. To deal with increasing 911 weight, Porsche turned to a larger 3.6-liter flat-six. It was still air-cooled, and a SOHC two valves per cylinder design, but had contemporary twin spark ignition technology. The 964 motor also had a knock sensor that permitted a compression ratio of 11.3:1. This one-style-suits-all, unleaded fuel motor was more powerful with 250bhp at 6100rpm and 228lb/ft at 4800rpm. It was also more economical at 24mpg overall. Bore and stroke for Porsche's latest flat-six, coded M64, was 100mm by 76.4mm, and yielded exactly 3600cc.

At this time, the first Euro market, cat-ready smog motors were unenthusiastic. The latest detoxed BMW M20 2.5-liter and VW Golf GTi two-liter weren't as nice as their leaded gas predecessors. However, with a 6700rpm redline, up from the 3.2L's 6500rpm, the latest Porsche motor was as free-revving as ever. A five-speed stick was still the enthusiast's first choice, but here the 964 had a problem. Zuffenhausen introduced a dual mass flywheel to the new 911. This

item was improved on the 968, but on the 964 it spelt maintenance problems for some.

By now, Maranello was on its all-new 348, with 3.4-liter V8: a somewhat unloved junior Ferrari that probably drove customers to the good-looking 964. The new Ferrari's styling and handling shortcomings may have contributed to the strong-selling 964's sales total of 63,762 units. Factory performance figures for the 964 were 0-62mph in 5.7 seconds, and a 162mph top speed. With the 911, Zuffenhausen was still conservative with its claims. When it came to handling and chassis, Porsche honored history by looking to the Beetle.

Well, a very big Beetle; the 964 had the same suspension layout as the VW Type 4! Like that first luxo VW, the 964 decided to ditch the long-lived VW & Porsche torsion bars. Front and rear, it was now all coils: MacPherson struts at the front, and semi trailing arms at the rear. To overcome the long feared 911 sudden oversteer, the 964 was the first 911 since 1972 to place the flat-six's dry sump within the wheelbase. That is, in front of the rear axle line.

By 1996, the standard 911 Turbo's 3.6L motor made 398 lb/ft. If 0-60mph in 4.5 seconds and air cooling sounds good, run this way! (Courtesy Porsche)

During the 911's long evolutionary path, this change plus other refinements helped.

The 911 was still a car of modest dimensions. More 2+2 in name than deed. Sitting on the same 89.4in wheelbase as before, the 964 was 168.3in long and 65in wide on debut. In its class, the 911 was still reasonably tall at 52in, providing good front seat headroom, as per earlier incarnations. The 964 was also historic in being the last 911 with raised front fender tunnel port styling. It was also the final air-cooled 911 with a Targa body choice.

Coupe, Targa and Cabriolet options were available on the AWD 911 C4, and two-wheel drive C2. The latter, apart from being seen as a purer 911 interpretation, also offered Tiptronic automatic transmission. Since 1977, Porsche had utilized a three-speed torque converter automatic. Tiptronic took things to four speeds, and brought a sequential racing car shift. Introduced with the 1990 C2, Tiptronic had a mini gate to the right. Once the shifter is knocked to this plane, just push the stick forward to go up a gear, and back to downshift. There were no mechanical linkages, it was all electronic.

Tiptronic's manual mode would see the system change up by itself if you forgot. Plus, it wouldn't downshift if the engine speed was too fast. Come to a halt and it automatically engaged second for take off. With the 964's successor, the 993, the system was refined to feature two rocker buttons on '95 MY cars. The buttons were on the airbagged steering wheel's spokes, placed just under the thumbs, '+' for up and '-' for down. Using the buttons produced quicker shifts than normal kickdown, or even a real manual gear change. The trouble was the limitation of just four speeds on the 964 and 993 Tiptronic 911s. There was no room in the air-cooled 911 body for a longer transmission. The 996 went to five-speeds, but given the 911's modest displacement and high revving nature, even five ratios weren't enough.[107]

The 964 earned a place in *CAR* magazine's 'Interesting' part of its infamous GBU (Good, Bad & Ugly) section. For: sharp tool; Against: can slip; Sum-up: rewarding, but use carefully. The 911 C4 was seen as safer, but not as enjoyably sensitive as the C2. The 964 was a successful 911, the best at that point in time, and it has built up a loyal following. However, in its interim years it was overlooked. That said, as a new car, it was an industry leader, as most Porsches tend to be. VW's Scirocco successor, the Corrado, adopted a powered rear spoiler that automatically rose at a predetermined speed. Audi took on Tiptronic in name and nature for its all-new '95 Audi A4. BMW followed with its own version called Steptronic. If you build it, they will copy!

Speedster & Turbo, wherefor art thou?

Well, you can't keep a good turbo down. The 911 Turbo, being the institution that it was, returned with the 964 chassis in three main versions. The first made a March '90 debut with 320bhp at 5750rpm. This new 911 Turbo represented the first major tweak of the 3.3L flat-six since 1978! The familiar motor was 20 horses stronger. Carrera Cup style reversing mirrors also distinguished the new machine. The truck-like torque of the M30/61 turbo motor, 332lb/ft, helped produce a 0-62mph time of five seconds flat, and a 168mph top end. The 1470kg coupe had respective front and rear tracks of 1442mm and 1448mm.

The trouble with the new 911 Turbo, apart from the perennial river-long lag and mountain-high price, was the reality that this force of nature wasn't much quicker than a C2. Total 964 Turbo 3.3L production saw 3660 cars fly off the line. So, for '92 MY in came the further tweaked 911 Turbo S, with 381 DIN bhp. It was a case of bigger injectors, more boost, sportier cam profile, and limited creature features to cut weight. A front strut brace helped tame chassis flex. With no power steering and just 86 Turbo S cars made, it was a real specialty number. For a truly revised blown 911, look to the 911 Turbo 3.6. This started production in January 1993, with the M64/50 turbo motor.

CAR's Georg Kacher noted that the 964 Turbo 3.3 was antiquated and lag-ridden. He also observed that the limited edition Turbo S 3.3 (964) nearly killed the base model, due to the resale value freefall its introduction induced. Who indeed would want a mere 320bhp? However, the 964 Turbo 3.6 was redeveloped with true Porsche thoroughness, and there was no price change! This made the Turbo 3.6 much better value. It had a lot of new stuff. The 18in Speedline three-piece alloys were much lighter than the old Carrera Cup style rims. Indeed, the latest 911 Turbo had an unchanged weight of 3234lb.

The rims wore 225/40ZR-18s at the front, and 265/35ZR-18s rearwards. Yokohama A008Ps were a popular and ride-compliant choice. The wheels covered bright red, Porsche white script brake calipers. While the rear brake hardware was a carry over, the front saw larger, light alloy, four-piston calipers and drilled/vented 11.5in rotors. The latest rims/tires wouldn't fit earlier Turbos due to suspension changes. The new Turbo 3.6 sat 0.8in lower, and the slightly amended rear valence had the expected two large tailpipes.

The rear suspension semi trailing arms were reinforced to cope with greater cornering G forces. Springs were 15 per cent stiffer, to be in sync with firmer shock absorbers. The latest 911 Turbo could corner 20 per cent faster, but the ride wasn't as taxing as the 964 RS. Improved active safety saw the Turbo 3.6 stoppable from 100kph in 2.63 seconds. It was a certified record for the *Guinness Book of World Records*. The latest brake pad design covered the brake rotor's full width.

Horst Marchart was chief engineer, and his team reworked the 964's 3.6L flat-six for turbo duty. The crankcase and cylinder block were pure C2, but the heads, intake and exhaust manifolds were new. Pistons, connecting rods and cam profiles were redone, as was the Bosch DME injection. For stat lovers, the new Turbo 3.6 made 360bhp at 5500rpm. Torque was up from 325lb/ft at 4500rpm to 376lb/ft at 4200rpm. From 2400 to 5500rpm, the new motor made more torque than the old Turbo 3.3 at its peak!

Keeping things balanced were stronger, redesigned driveshafts. The LSD, also stronger, had a power on locking ratio of 20 per cent. Trailing throttle locking was 100 per cent. The clutch was stronger and lighter and had a more progressive action. For all markets, the Turbo 3.6 came with standard equipment of at least dual airbags, a/c, ABS, top audio, power/heated front seats, trip computer, alarm system, metallic paint and full leather interior. The tab was £72,000 in the UK.[108]

With the revised motor and thermodynamically improved combustion process, Porsche claimed 5-10 per cent less gas usage between 90 and 135mph. At 75mph the Turbo 3.6 did 27.4mpg (UK gallon). There was an optional 20-gallon tank, but compared with the stock 17-gallon unit, it ate into luggage space. Now with a KKK K27 turbo and 1.5psi more boost, 12psi total, the latest engine was more responsive. The old 3.3L was an on/off light switch in comparison, but the Turbo 3.6 was still a big horsepower single turbo installation nonetheless. That meant no go under 3000rpm, and almost two seconds to build full boost.

CAR's Georg Kacher said that before, torque was picked up like an aggrieved Rottweiler. Now, it was more sensitive, but power still came in with a bang! The Turbo 3.6 tramlined badly, got light with its steering at 125mph, but was stable on uneven surfaces. It could do a progressive tailslide with concentration. With 0-62mph in 4.8 seconds and a 175mph top speed, Kacher declared the 964 Turbo 3.6 to be the last Jekyll and Hyde sports car. He urged fans to get one before the new, less controversial, 993 came out.

In spite of the heads up warning, and the fact the Turbo 3.6 was well made, reliable and robust, less than 1500 were made during its 1993-94 run. The final 90 964 Turbo chassis went to Porsche Exclusive, to create the 964 Turbo 3.6S. It was your choice of the normal Turbo body, or flachbau, a US $60,179 option on top of the usual 99K list price. Utilizing the no charge 36S option, it included X88 to get the X92 Exclusive front spoiler, X73 Exclusive rear spoiler and X99 Exclusive rear fender vents. For flachbau, 968 parts and Japan's 964 Turbo 3.3S front were used. The X88 uprated motor made 385 DIN bhp at 5750rpm, and 384lb/ft at five grand. A LSD and ZF clutch allowing 20% locking action on power and 100% lock off, like the normal Turbo 3.6, tried to keep the rear end back where it belonged.

964 Turbo 3.6S allocation saw 39 cars go to America, and ten to Japan, all in Polar Silver, even though the asking price required plenty of gold or folding green! For North Americans lacking that kind of disposable income, BEGI had the answer. Bell Engineering Group Inc (BEGI), founded by Corky Bell, had a special conversion for C2 and C4. Bell was a one-time agent for Haltech programable ECUs, in the guise of Car Tech. His turbo conversion used the stock fuel-injection computer for 50-state emissions compliance on 93 octane gas. It all worked with the stock North American 964 11:1CR, and a max boost of 5psi by 1400rpm.[109]

Boost enrichment was handled by a special variable rate of gain fuel pressure regulator. The second part of VATN was the aerocharger variable area turbine nozzle turbo. It needed no wastegate or external oiling, and could have a vertical shaft axis. The two turbos were on the driver's side, with hot gases going into one intercooler. The special fuel regulator lived downstream of the stock Bosch regulator. It had programed limits to the fuel return into the fuel return line. This raised fuel pressure to a limit of 85psi. Boosted air went through the stock Bosch AFM, and the intercooler lived behind the passenger side rear wheel. 0-60mph was cut 18 per cent, and the factory turbo lag was history. Turbo tech had come a long way since the 1975 930.

Never before had so many 911 variations been available, and the 964 Speedster added to the tally. The latest Speedster was a C2-based roadster,

At the 1986 Paris Dakar Rally, the 959 managed a 1-2 finish in the all-wheel drive category and outright car win, utilizing 450 horse turbo flat-six power. René Metge and Dominique Lemoyne were driving an AWD Porsche once again! (Courtesy Porsche)

Right: The Porsche 961 endurance racer was a 959 descendant. It was the first all-wheel drive vehicle to compete at Le Mans. Here, it came seventh overall, and first in GTX class. (Courtesy Tamiya Plastic Model Co)

All descendants of the Porsche 935, the roadgoing and Paris Dakar Rally 959s, and 1986 Type 961 circuit racer. Ultimately, all developments of the 1963 901! (Courtesy Porsche)

available in standard or lightweight Club Sport trim. It had the civilized C2 suspension, but the spartan nature of the 964RS. It came standard with power windows, but a/c and stereo were options. In this troubled sales era for Zuffenhausen, 3000 units were planned in 1992. However, just 936 were made in total, and sold during 1994 and 1995 model years. America took 427 units, with only 14 cars done in right-hand drive form. Truly rare were the 20 Turbo-look wide-body 964 Speedsters done at Porsche Exclusive's Werk 1.

If a 964 Speedster didn't catch an American buyer's fancy, then one of 250 America Roadsters might have. This was a Turbo-look wide-body Cabrio, with standard 964 electric rear spoiler, Turbo Cup 17in rims and Turbo suspension. The America Roadster was available during 1992 and 1993.

Someone with a hand in all of the above was Porsche's Helmuth Bott. Joining Porsche in 1952 as a production assistant, he became the engineer in charge of experimental and racing departments, driving test director, test director, deputy development director and eventually director of development. In 1978, he attained the board-level post of director of R&D, which he held until retirement. A spiritual father of the 911, Bott was a driving force behind the 911 Turbo, 959, 911 Speedster and 964 Carrera 4. Helmuth Bott retired from Porsche in September 1988. He passed away after a short illness on May 14, 1994, in Munsingen, Buttenhausen, Germany.

964RS – Rennsport returns!

With the 964, it seemed racing still improved the breed. It also allowed the fabled RS tag to return to 911 land for the first time since 1973. This time it was Porsche's own one-make regional and national racing series, the Porsche Cup, that provided the purpose. The series was thought up by Roland Kussmaul and engineer Helmut Flegl, and the road car that arose was the '92 MY Carrera C2 RS. At its heart was a mildly reworked 964 3.6L flat-six, the M64/03. The motor made 260 horses and 240lb/ft. It was hooked up to a lightweight flywheel, and G50/10 close ratio transmission. Performance was similar to the C2. Factory figures showed a 0.4 second improvement in 0-62mph time, and the same 162mph top speed. However, this 911RS majored in spirit, not speed.

A sporting highlight of the 964 range, the C2 RS avoided power windows/seats, rear seats, a/c, cruise control and sound deadening. The coupe came with new racing buckets, and a stereo was optional.

An aluminum trunklid, thinner door glass and rear window were complemented by a seam-welded chassis, steel synchromesh, asymmetrical LSD and chassis mods.

Ride height was 40mm lower, springs and shocks were firmer and swaybars were adjustable. Power steering was junked, except in the UK. The official weight reduction compared to a C2 was 100kg. This made the C2 RS 1250 kg. Unfortunately, under the less-is-more banner, while the RS lost a lot of equipment compared to the regular C2, it actually cost the equivalent of $20,000 more!

Then, there were the variations. The 964RS Touring put back all the luxury, including a/c and dual mass flywheel. So it only saved 30kg. More dedicated was the 964RS Sport, with basic carpet, no undercoating and just a three-year anti-rust warranty. The M002-coded Touring saw 76 cars made, the Sport 2039 units. For the very committed, the RS N/GT had more letters than features. This M003-coded racer possessed Kevlar shell Recaros, four-point Schroth harness, Matter rollcage, racing clutch and lightened flywheel. With M003, 290 were constructed. The 964 C4 RS Lightweight was a real oddity, with just 22 cars made. Weissach-built and costing 285,000 Deutschmarks, it had plastic side windows, aluminum doors/engine cover/luggage lid and an AWD system more akin to a 953, than a 964.

Naturally, none of the above could be had in North America. In '93 MY the 964RS America arrived. However, in 1992 some quasi C2 RS coupés were brought over. Their purpose was to participate in a one-make CART-supporting race series that never happened. Lack of sponsor support saw the 45 cars offloaded to the public. These coupés did without airbags, power windows, and an alarm system, but did have US lighting/bumpers and standard rims and seating. Even so, they were still a handy 200lb lighter than a US 911 C2. For '93 MY, the official US RS came, with a dash plaque stating: 'Carrera Cup US Edition.' Based on the US C2, the North American RS came in standard colors of red, black or white. Midnight Blue, Solar Silver and Speed Yellow were optional.

The RS America had the rear tray spoiler, a part stripped interior, Euro type flat door cards and basic carpeting, plus no rear seats. The sports seats were cloth trimmed, and went with the absence of power steering, cruise control, power side mirrors, a/c, sunroof and radio. The absence of equipment saved the North American buyer ten grand. Air-conditioning, sunroof, in-car audio and LSD were optional. Standard were 17in rims, M030 sports suspension, 'RS America' call-out on the decklid and RS logo in front of the rear wheel arches. The RS America was 77lb lighter than a US C2. Weight was officially 1340kg.

The top RS in Europe was the 964RS 3.8, with M64/04 stroker motor and 1210kg weight. A 964 Turbo 3.6 was 1470 kg! This special RS had a bore of 102mm and 76.4mm stroke. It made max power at 6500rpm and 360Nm at 5250rpm. The compression ratio was raised to 11.6:1 for the first-ever atmo 911 road car to reach 300 horses. Factory figures were 0-62mph in 4.9 seconds, with a 169mph top speed. Build numbers were 55 road-going RS 3.8s, with the remainder of the 104 total for racing. Only two cars were right-hand drive, and racers wore the time-honored RSR suffix.

A RS 3.8 cost 225,000 Deutschmarks from Weissach. The RSR was 270,000 Deutschmarks. The 1994 model year machine was 964 Turbo body related. However, the front spoiler was deeper, and the biplane rear wing was adjustable, so too the combined spoiler/engine lid. The trunklid and doors were made of aluminum, lightweight glass was present, and the bodyshell had extra welds. The coupe's fine touches marked it out as a racer of fine distinction. Individual throttle butterflies, revised ECU, gas-flowed head with polished ports and monster 51.5mm intake and 43.5mm exhaust valves. Steel synchro for the G50/10 five-speed was a given. The LSD had 40% locking action. Cross-drilled rotors came from the 964 Turbo 3.3S. There were split-rim Speedlines, 18x9in front and 18x11in rearwards. Naturally, power steering was deep-sixed.

It was racer Jurgen Barth who broached the reborn RSR idea, to Porsche competition director Peter Falk in 1988. Barth, Dominique Dupuy and Joel Gouhier achieved a GT class victory with the 964RSR 3.8's 1993 Le Mans debut. Class victories for the RSR followed at Spa and the Nürburgring. The 964RSR 3.8 certainly honored Porsche racing pedigree. It all justified the financial R&D outlay, during a financially difficult hour at Zuffenhausen. It went further than even the M004 road car's optional M545 92-liter gas tank would allow![110]

The Carrera Cup started in 1990, and the 964 Cup car had 265bhp, welded rollcage, 55mm lower ride height, stripped interior, no sound proofing, special gear ratios and no power steering. However, the cars did have a catalytic converter and ABS. In 1992, the Cup car was revised with 964RS bodywork, 275bhp, and drivers could

now turn the ABS off. The last item was handy for emergency braking and when going backwards after losing control. The 964 Cup machine now had 18in magnesium rims, not aluminum, and the coupe now rode 20mm lower than previous Cup cars. Vehicle weight was still 1120kg, but torque was uprated from 310Nm to 314Nm at the same 4800rpm.

On an international basis, the Porsche Michelin Supercup was a similar one-make series. Starting in 1993, it provided support races for the Formula One Championship. Like the Carrera Cup, the Supercup was run by Porsche AG. The European Supercup was broadcast on ESPN and ESPN2. The initial nine-race series had at least 30 new 964s. Jochen Mass, Jean-Pierre Jarier and Jacques Lafitte were former F1 stars taking part. They were joined by American racer Nick Ham.

All 911RS cars were atmo in nature, but in 934 and 935 days, turbos were the winning ticket. The 964 Turbo S LM-GT upheld the blown 911 track tradition. LM stood for Le Mans, and the Turbo S LM-GT was a prototype 964 Turbo S for racing. It had a deep chin spoiler and two air inlets above the rear arches. Putting an adjustable racing wing above the stock Turbo tray spoiler was truly form following function. Flared rear arches housed 12in-wide racing slicks, and a stripped interior, rollcage, and plastic windows came as no surprise. Firepower came from a twin turbo 3.2-liter flat-six making 475bhp.

On debut at the 1993 12 Hours of Sebring, a Brumos Porsche Racing Turbo S LM-GT came first in class and seventh overall. The factory entry expired with engine damage. The Turbo S LM-GT then moved to the Larbre Compétition outfit, where a 993 3.6L turbo motor was inserted. The coupe did four races in the BPR Global GT series and won them all! This included the 24 Hours of Daytona, which was its debut race under Larbre Compétition, and the Suzuka 1000. The racer finished with Obermaier Racing in 1995. In some ways, the Turbo S LM-GT inspired the 993 GT2: a mass-produced racer for privateers.

A Jubi-lant 911 celebration

In the rollcall of rarity there were 3660 3.3-liter 964 Turbos, and 1437 964 Turbo 3.6s. However, there was a 964 that was rarer still by design. It was all in connection with the 911's 30th birthday, so 911 examples were planned for 1993. The Jubi was based on the 964 Carrera 4, but had the wide-body Turbo look and an interior trimmed like said Turbo too; it was full leather for seats, dashboard and door cards, plus 30 Jahre badging. A rear window-facing metal plaque stated '30 Jahre 911 Limited Edition/Nr.xxx,' indicating the build number of the car at hand.

Most Jubis were Viola Metallic outside, with a small powered 964 rear spoiler, and Rubicon Gray leather inside. The UK market saw 41 RHD examples imported. Jubis are currently worth the most in their home country of Germany. In this neck of the woods, the €100,000 barrier was crossed in 2015, and their value is rising. However, they are still worth less than a 964 Turbo. Powering the Jubi is the same 250 horse 3.6L seen in the 20,395 worth of normal C4s produced; a birthday special that kind of inspired the 993 C4S!

959 – on all paws!

When it came to global exposure and raising Porsche credibility (if that was even possible) the Porsche 959 was hard to beat. In the *Daily Express'* 1987 *Guide to World Cars*, Gordon Wilkins described the 959 as a 200mph car of the 21st century. The public caught their first glimpse of the supercar at the 1983 Frankfurt Auto Show. Here, it carried the Gruppe B moniker. This design study car was shown at many events, including the 1984 NEC car show in Birmingham, England. It was a headliner that couldn't be ignored. In January 1985, *Four-Wheel Drive* magazine had the story title, *Porsche to build the ultimate 4x4 road car.*[111]

Four-Wheel Drive stated three different versions would be built: the luxo Komfort, road-going Sport, and 20 units of a pure competition version. Living up to the design study name, it would all be part of a minimum 200 car, Group B homologation racing requirement, with an engine descended from the mighty 935/936, and front to rear power split varying according to road surface. The latter could be manually overridden. How much would you pay for a car like this? Try 420,000 Deutschmarks, or $225,000 in 1987. It was a bargain, for some.

For starters, Porsche was asking less than half the break-even price. Speculator action saw a profit for anyone willing to sell, up to the 1990 recession. Porsche insider Walter Rohrl got a rebuilt prototype for a 310,000 Deutschmark trade price. Two weeks later he was offered 1.2 million Deutschmarks, but kept the car for 15 years anyway. Just before the 1990 recession poured cold water on the whole deal, used Ferrari F40s were going for six times their listed price, 959s three times, and 25th anniversary Countachs two times their list price. Osella Formula

One team sponsor Alberto Garnerone had a F40 and 959, with a 25th anniversary Countach and Cizeta supercar on order.

For years, American owners could only display their 959s. Porsche, bless its heart, didn't give in to the NHTSA's requirement of four cars being submitted for crash testing. What a waste that would have been! Dear 959, would you like to be subjected to the bureaucratic idiocy of the federal government? No, I would not, said the 959, as it quietly prepared for the Paris-Dakar Rally. Porsche made 292 examples during 1987-88, with a further eight cars assembled from NOS parts in 1992-93. The latter enterprise involved four red cars and four silver. These later cars were all in Komfort spec and carried a 747,500 Deutschmark price.

Those final 959s had the technical upgrade of speed-reading, adjustable shocks. The great 959 price increase probably reflected Zuffenhausen's dire financial straits. However, where did this madcap AWD bi-turbo plan start?! The genesis was a need to find the Porsche racer of the future, a car to take over from the 935. Briefly, the 944 and 928 were individually considered as project base coupés. Then Porsche – Helmuth Bott and Peter Schutz to be precise – settled on the 911.[112]

Consulting with Schutz in 1981, Bott made the case to explore the 911's limits, and use racing as the ultimate R&D test lab. All was agreed, and the target was the new Group B. However, the FIA was slowly changing its mind, and Group B became more rallying oriented than Porsche had bargained for. This limited the 959's applicability. Even so, rallying the 959 would go, specifically the Paris-Dakar Rally. After Porsche's 1984 triumph, 1985 was a let down. All three 959s expired, but 1986 saw a 959 1-2 finish on the event, and more that year from Le Mans.

The 959's track racing counterpart, the 961, had an outside chance at 1986's Le Mans, to put it mildly. *Motor's* Philip Turner put the question to a Porsche technician on test day: would the 961 make the top ten? The reply was, "Only if it snows." Well, it didn't snow at Le Mans that year, but the 961 came seventh overall, won its class, and made history by being the first all-wheel drive car to participate at Le Mans. The honors for Porsche were done by racers Rene Metge and Claude Ballot-Lena. The 959 also managed to flip the bird to the Ferrari 288 GTO a few times before its competition career closed. Group B ended in 1986, and the 959 made its belated road car debut in '87 MY. It was a racer without a reason. The road-going 959 appeared at the 1985 Frankfurt show,

Only 55 964 911 Carrera RS 3.8 road cars were built. Porsche believed in second chances, so the model continued with the 993. (Courtesy Porsche)

with a view to a 1986 release. However, production delays saw said release delayed for a year.

The 959 still managed to hold onto the World's Fastest Production Car title for three months. The terminal velocity of 317kph was good enough, until Enzo's present to himself, the F40, arrived in July 1987. Compared to the new, raw Italian go-kart, the Baur-built and Porsche-inspected 959 was a technological tour de force, with Komfort! If you like 911s, you will love the 959, but it did have its critics. F1 designer extraordinaire Gordon Murray for one: "The 959 is too boring, the F40 is too exhausting." Murray was a big fan of the Renault Espace.

In the November 1989 issue of *CAR*, Giancarlo Perini and Jose Rosinski tried the world's four fastest cars at the new Lambardore Circuit, north of Turin. The F40, 25th anniversary Countach, and new 540bhp Cizeta V16, met the 959. Compared to the Italian wedge crowd, the 959 was called a little German dumpling, with a dreary exhaust note. Certainly some hometown bias was afoot. Objective truth concerned the all-wheel drive trait of understeer, and 911 related high-speed wander. Turn in of an AWD car is never as sharp. However, compared to its Italian quasi rivals, the 959 offered a civility and refinement in a class above.

The 1987 959 was the same price as a Testarossa

and Countach combined. What did this get you? According to *Car and Driver*'s November 1987 issue, a 12-second flat quarter mile at 116mph for a 959 Komfort. Only 37 959 Sports were made. The remaining Komfort cars had power leather pews, and gizmos lifted from the 928S4. Optional for the Sport was the 959S' 515bhp. The factory would also up matters to 530 DIN bhp, but for most, the humble 450bhp at 6500rpm was elegant sufficiency. Torque was quoted at 360lb/ft at 5500rpm, weight at 3197lb, length, width and height at a respective 167.3in, 72.4in and 50in, with double wishbone suspension front and back.

The 959's 0.31Cd body involved aluminum, Kevlar and polyurethane. The motor had titanium connecting rods. The floor used Nomex, not steel, and the tech list was lengthy and innovative. The Mezger 2849cc flat-six had water-cooled heads, air cooling for the rest, and Bosch 2.1 Motronic. The engine had a vertically split case and seven main bearings. Two different-sized sequential KKK turbos tried to curb lag, their changeover occurred at 4300rpm, with a 7300rpm redline. The six-speed manual gearbox had an off-road gear ratio.

Front to rear power distribution was judged by spin detectors and micro processors. The center differential had a fluid coupling, and both it and the

Headlight visage and wide tail look mimicked the 959, but the price would be a more modest 200,000 Deutschmarks. Even so, the project didn't get off the ground. Engine cooling problems and Porsche's late '80s sales slide ended the dream. In December 1988, 15 of the 16 prototypes were destroyed. The remaining prototype hasn't been seen since.

More successful was the Porsche 962, the safety replacement for the 956. Crucial changes involved moving the front axle line ahead of the pedal box. In addition, a steel rollcage was integrated into the 962's new aluminum chassis. The latest sports car racer was the design work of Norbert Singer, and made its debut at the 24 Hours of Daytona. Porsche wanted a car that qualified for the World Sports Car Championship's Group C, and IMSA GTP. For the latter series, the safety mods and Type 935 2.8L air-cooled flat-six, with a single KKK K36 turbo, were necessary. In Europe, the 962Cs used twin K27 turbos for the familiar 2.65L flat-six with part water cooling. A heavier 3-liter unit also existed. By mid 1985, the US-raced IMSA GT 962 received the Andial-built 3.2L flat-six to improve the 962's competitiveness. This motor was banned in 1987. However, Porsche team protests concerning the dominance of factory Nissans in IMSA GTP saw twin turbo Porsche motors return in 1988, albeit with 36mm restrictors.

Could the 962C (Group C) allow Zuffenhausen to continue its winning ways at Le Mans? In 1985 a 962 set the lap record at three minutes and 25.1 seconds. There were seven 962s taking part in 1986's Le Mans 24 Hour race, and eight 956s. One factory 962 had the newfangled PDK electronic transmission, which increased weight to 900kg. Success was delivered by the 962. The factory 962C, driven by driver trio Bell/Stuck/Holbert, triumphed in 1986 and 1987 editions of the famous endurance race.

The 962 was successful, but did need some modification. Porsche built 91 962s between 1984-1991. Privateers got 75 of the 962s made. Those privateers, like Joest Racing, did bodywork and chassis mods. The stock aluminum chassis needed to be stiffer. Kremer Racing's 962CK6 replaced the aluminum tub with one made of carbon-fiber. Richard Lloyd Racing's GTI Engineering employed Peter Stevens and Nigel Stroud to do custom bodywork and the tub for the 962C GTi. This racer used an aluminum honeycomb tub, rather than a sheetmetal construction.

rear differential were lockable. PSK (Porsche Steuer Kupplung) AWD LSD could send 80 per cent of power to the rear wheels. A dash gage informed the driver of the power split. The computer controlled ride height was fixed on the 961. The 17in hollow spoke center lock aluminum rims, had the world's first tire pressure monitoring system. Naturally, it was developed by Porsche.

Dunlop ran the ad, "The 200mph Porsche 959. A pretty nippy set of wheels. The world's most advanced sports car is fitted with the world's most advanced tyres. Developed by Dunlop." The ad was referring to the special Dunlop Denloc bead tires, which went hand-in-hand with the aforementioned hollow spoke rims. Therein lay Porsche's distinction. Whereas the Italians had called it a day after the Miura, Porsche kept looking for the next high tech milestone. With the 959 it had found it, and so did Dr Wolfgang Porsche. The first 959 was delivered to Dr Porsche and kept at the Porsche family estate in Zell-am-See.

969 & 962

Porsche tried a humbler successor to the 959. Coded 969 and based on the upcoming 964, the 969 was intended to use an uprated version of the 911 Turbo's 3.3L motor, with around 380bhp.

Al Holbert's Holbert Racing did a special 962 HR-1. As with the 956, Porsche kept close tabs on the chassis it supplied to privateers. With the 962, Fabcar became a factory tub supplier of a stiffer, stronger design, with Porsche serial numbers attached.

In America, Holbert Racing became the source for US-produced 962s. Initially, meeting demand for affordable 962s for the IMSA GTP series saw some American privateers do their own panels and parts. Although not officially employed by Porsche in this capacity, Al Holbert was involved with the 962 program almost from the start.[113]

Holbert was one of the first to take delivery of a 962 for the IMSA Camel GT series. Al Holbert had helped Porsche with its SCCA D Production 924 and 924 Turbo Trans-Am programs. According to Holbert Racing crew chief Tom Seabolt, it was this assistance that led Porsche to give Holbert the official job of US 962 production. The result was the American-made 962 HR-1.

Holbert's 962s carried their own special serial numbers.

It was in the fall of 1984 that Al Holbert was made boss of Porsche's North American racing affairs. Holbert ran a fair operation; competitors didn't complain about conflict of interest. Holbert Racing's HR-1 featured stiffer alloys, fully machined front bulkhead, and improved shift linkage. It even had comfier seats! Holbert used the 962 HR-1 to win two IMSA driving titles. His debut solo victory with the car was at the Camel 300 in July 1985, in Portland, Oregon. Holbert Racing's 962 HR-1 103 won the Daytona 24 Hours twice.

In America and Europe, the non-factory creations of privateer concerns were offered to other privateers. If someone had a good idea, it was adopted. By the mid '90s, open cockpit 962s were around. There was the Kevin Jeanette-built Gunnar 966, and Kremer

On the street, Porsche fans were still digging the Carrera 3.2 flat six.
(Courtesy Porsche)

Racing CK7 and CK8. The Kremer Racing designs were very custom, with Porsche stuff limited to engine and some suspension parts. Indeed, it was a much modified 962C that won Le Mans in 1994.

Privateer Jochen Dauer got the 962C, reclassified as a road-legal GT1 car. The 1994 Le Mans-winning Dauer 962C was driven by a team of Dalmas/ Haywood/Baldi. The 962's winning ways included the 1985 and 1986 World Sports Car Championships, and 1985-88 IMSA GT Championships. Indeed, victory at Road America in 1993's IMSA GTP was the 962's final sprint race win in that series. The 962 also garnered the 1987-92 Interserie Championships.

If all of the above wasn't enough, some hadn't given up on the idea of owning a road-going racer, Count Rossi 917 style. Helping with this endeavor was the 962's thorough development and easy-going nature. In the words of Brian Redman, "The 962 was so civilized you felt you could drive it down to the local shopping centre."[114] So cameth the road-going 962s! The Koenig Specials C62 had amended bodywork and a 3.4-liter flat-six, with updated Bosch Motronic injection. DP Motorsports offered its 3.3L DP62, with three cars made. Former Le Mans winner Vern Schuppan enlisted the design services of future General Motors man Mike Simcoe to do the 1991 Schuppan 962CR for Japan. It had special bodywork, a custom chassis and a 3.3L blown flat-six. The Porsche factory helped Jochen Dauer with a road-going 962 GT1, and there was one Derek Bell very limited edition 962 road car. This last special used a 580bhp 993 GT2 flat-six.

The new 964 911 basked in Porsche's racing success. (Courtesy Porsche)

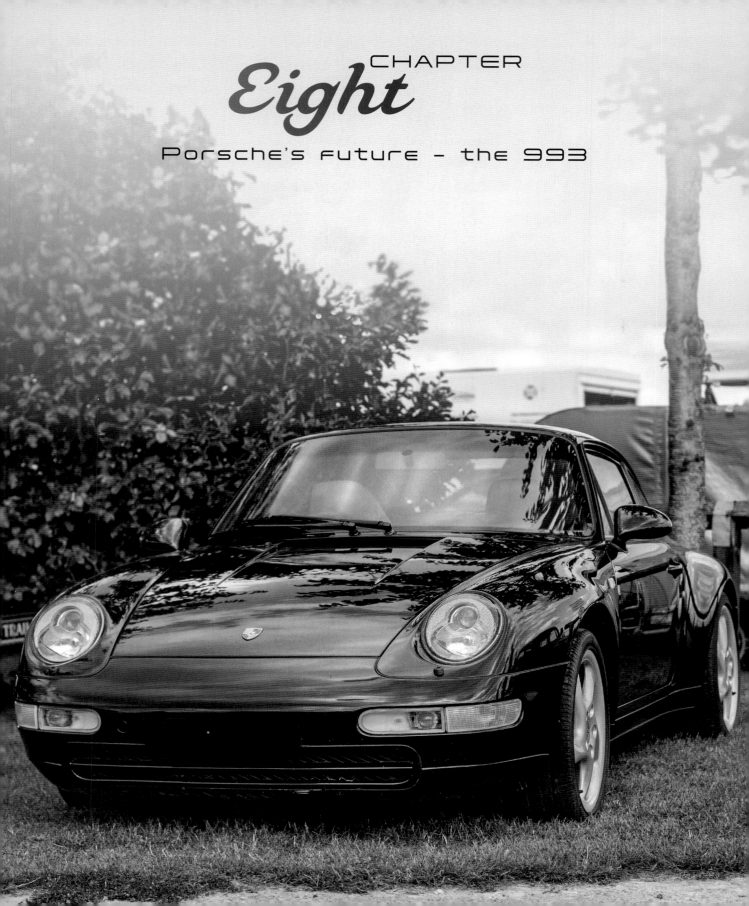

CHAPTER

Eight

Porsche's future – the 993

Losing traction in the sports car business

By early 1992 it seemed Porsche had reached its lowest ebb. The company's official statement said it all: "Reorientation of model policy is a reaction to changing customer attitudes in the top price and market segment." In plain speak, with the exception of the 911, what Porsche was making wasn't selling. The reaction to the 'new' 968 (944S3) had been lukewarm. There had also been a dramatic fall in orders for the 928.[115] *Classic & Sports Car*'s June 1999 Buyer's Guide said the 928 was the car Ferrari should have replaced the Daytona with. However, this engineering masterpiece had failed to woo the majority of Porsche fans away from the 911.

In his first era with Zuffenhausen, designer Harm Lagaay had major input in the Porsche 924's design. However, design boss Tony Lapine wasn't a fan. Lapine said the 924 looked like it was styled by someone who had always wanted a Ferrari but had never got one. It seemed styling didn't travel from Maranello to Zuffenhausen. Porsche faithful, and the world in general, saw Porsche through 911-tinted glasses. This explained Harm Lagaay's Porsche styling sermon. In 1989 the Dutch designer was invited back to Porsche, replacing Tony Lapine as design boss. The lesson now was, if a Porsche didn't look like a Porsche, people would be disappointed.

Chief designer of the 1993 Opel Corsa, Hideo Kodama, said you can't translate old shapes to new cars. Well, at Porsche you can and should. Harm Lagaay's crew were behind the 968, 986 and upcoming 993. Lagaay was happy with the poorly received Panamericana beach buggy show car, and the 989 four-door that never was. They showed that regardless of engine placement, or number of doors, a new car could be a Porsche if it had Porsche core design elements. Indeed, when he returned to Porsche, he underlined the importance of finding such elements and using them on future models, so that a Cayenne prospect wouldn't get that ol' 924 feelin' ... it doesn't look like a Porsche ... The plan worked, so well in fact that Porsche was able to get a diesel into the Cayenne and no one even noticed.

Future commercial success seemed a long way away in March 1992. Porsche stopped production for over two weeks to reduce stockpiles. All the while the company insisted that the controversial 989 four-door wasn't canceled, just postponed. As it turned out, the upcoming 996 was, at one stage, a development 989 twin. However, both went to the Porsche junkyard in February 1992. This included the associated first 996 silver clay buck. It seemed Porsche didn't want the media to figure out the pickle it was in.[116]

The importance of the 986 (Boxster) to Porsche, the media opinion of the marque, and the public's view of the company can't be overstated. In the words of Harm Lagaay: "Porsche needs to demonstrate that it is alive and kicking, that despite low sales we have not given up." From this point, the 996's development twin was the 986. Lagaay impressed upon Porsche the importance of concept cars. They energize the people working at a company, generate positive publicity and help sell existing models. German companies weren't aware of this, and had been reticent concerning revealing upcoming work.

At a projected 10k less than the slow-selling 968, the 986 was the entry-level coupe Porsche needed like yesterday. Porsche insiders favored the Boxster nameplate over the 986 development code. This was probably because American buyers favor nameplates. Indeed, in the modern era the 911 is the only regular production Porsche without a nameplate. Then again, so famous is the 911, such numbers are practically a nameplate. For the 986 all options were on the table. This included a V6 engine and using the upcoming Mercedes 190SLK as a platform buddy. Porsche's R&D boss Horst Marchart looked at the idea in detail. The two companies did have talks, but Porsche subsequently told the press it wasn't going to happen.

There was a major need for semi-affordable models. Harm Lagaay said the 989 was canned because Porsche didn't want yet another big buck car. Even after the Boxster's debut, there were rumors concerning a new sub Boxster VW-Porsche for 1999. A front drive, Golf MkIV based coupe with smart 'plus' front axle, available in VW and Porsche editions; similar to the 914's story. One VW sketch had inner headlamp grille vents like a Karmann Ghia. A two-liter flat-four, based on the 996's thought-to-exist 3.2-liter water-cooled flat-six, was on the cards. To satisfy future European Union noise and emissions rules, the future would be water-cooled. A strange development, given the amount of noise and hot air emanating from Brussels' bureaucrats.

In the meantime, most thoughts were on the 964's successor, the 993. When would it come out, how would it be funded? Early in 1993 the word was a debut at the 1993 Frankfurt car show. With funding, a special report from the Economist Intelligence Unit said Porsche had released a $450 million cash stockpile at the start of 1993 to help Zuffenhausen through hard times.

Developing the 993

Even in such bleak times, the 964 made *CAR*'s 1993 top ten list, with Gavin Green saying, "Driving a Porsche 911 hard is a little like bungee jumping. You do it for the thrill: for the kick of doing something risky in our sensible, sanitised world." The 911 was still great value. At £46,000 it could do 0-60mph in 5.5 seconds and reach 161mph, like the 964 Carrera 2. The £74,000 Ferrari 348tb had respective figures of 5.4 seconds and 170mph. In street cred, that prancing horse had no advantage, and the misfortune of being in the movie *Rocky V*.

In the early '90s, Porsche had managed to stave off takeover interest from various companies, including Toyota. However, new Porsche CEO Wendelin Wiedeking had learnt efficiency tricks from the Japanese giant. This allowed the 993 to be made more efficiently, using less resources at lower cost. The end result was a competitive price for the 993. It allowed Porsche to meet the price equivalency formula it was pursuing. Here, a new updated car would cost no more, adjusted for inflation, than the outgoing model.

That was certainly achieved in the 964 to 993 transition. According to L J K Setright, Toyota's 'just in time' inventory and lean production methods, led to Porsche's first profit in four years. The time taken

Top right: RUF Turbo R performance means 550bhp at 5700rpm and 700Nm at 4900rpm. So, the six-speed and AWD system are put to good use! (Courtesy www.ruf-automobile.de)
Right: Strosek could get more creative with its styling, thanks to smaller, projector lens headlights. They were applied to Strosek's 928s and 911s. (Courtesy *Euro Sport Car*)

to build a Porsche was cut 40%, factory space required was reduced 32% and the number of managers was reduced 31%. It was claimed defects per car were halved.[117] A case in point was the 993's die-cast Vacural alloy rear subframe. It had thin walls with a web structure for stiffness. Great, but the bottom line was that Porsche bought the unit in complete, from an outside supplier. At Zuffenhausen the bolt-in subframe saved time and money.

The 993's value and production efficiencies can be seen when comparing the UK prices of the 993 with the Ferrari F355. For '97 MY it was £61,000 for the 993 2+2, versus £93,000 for the only slightly faster Italian two-seater. More noticeable than value comparisons was the 993's new 911 styling. Harm Lagaay said work on the 993 started when he arrived at Porsche in 1989, and was wrapped up by 1991. Lagaay supervised English stylist Tony Hatter. Hatter created a shape reminiscent of the 959. Indeed, the 993 was like an affordable 959, in terms of looks and engineering, especially the 993 Turbo.

There were smoother bumpers front and rear, flatter ellipsoidal headlamps replaced the former upright lamps and associated 911 raised fender line, so famous since 1963. Production of the 993 commenced in January 1994. So, this latest 911 sold alongside the 968 and 928GTS. All three cars shared a smooth rounded front, with skyward facing headlamps. The 993 featured updated teardrop side mirrors, and a larger electronically speed-adjusted rear spoiler. The last item improved cool air supply to the engine, and increased downforce. A vented front air duct reduced drag, and an undertray brought mild ground effects. The use of said undertray pre-dated the Ferrari F355's use of the apparatus.

The flared arches were especially noticeable at the back. It was form following function, because the 993 came with a redesigned rear suspension. Dimensions of the new 993 2+2 coupe were: 167.7in length, 68.3in width, 51.6in height, all on an 89.45in wheelbase. The Carrera 2 was now officially just called Carrera. However,

In 1998, a RUF Turbo R won *Road & Track*'s Top Speed Shootout. This RUF Turbo R, represents a conversion on a 1996 993, performed in December 2003. (Courtesy www.ruf-automobile.de)

to distinguish the two-wheel drive Carrera from its AWD counterpart, fans still use the Carrera 2 moniker. That AWD 993 Carrera 4 arrived in Europe in 1995. The early 993 Carrera had orange turn signal lenses, and black Carrera rear deck script, plus base 16in rims. With optional 17in rims, the new 993 Carrera could register over 1.0 g on the skidpad.

Weight for the early Carrera was 3064lb. Ground clearance was 110mm for Europe, 120mm for North America and 90mm concerning the M030 sport option suspension 993s. The 993 was introduced in North America, in coupe and cabrio forms, in April 1994 as a '95 MY car. It would run into '98 MY, with 1998 being a truncated 993 production year. The latest 993 styling was a winner, and Porsche made a believable claim that 80% of the 993 was new. A big part of that 80%, was the rear suspension. Gone was the 911's familiar semi trailing arm rear suspension. In its place came the multi-link LSA (Lightweight Stable Agile) rear end, which Porsche said was "instrumental in finally putting an end to the capriciousness of the rear-engine-powered 911".

The 993's light alloy rear subframe was attached to the body via four rubber mounts. These mounts were flexible longitudinally, but rigid transversely. This helped improve ride comfort versus the 964, and improve handling. In ride/handling compromise, the 993 was widely judged an improvement. Transverse A arms and lower control links were complemented by two upper links that pivoted on the subframe. An 18mm rear swaybar joined the parade.

The acid test was a lap of Silverstone by McLaren F1 driver Martin Brundle. To show how state-of-the-art road cars compared to an F1 racing machine, *CAR* magazine teamed up with McLaren and its drivers to get some results. It was test driver Philippe Alliot in a Peugeot 306 S16 hot hatch, Brundle in the 993 Carrera and team-mate Mika Hakkinen in the Peugeot-powered McLaren MP4/9 F1 car.

For the 306 S16, 993 and MP4/9 the respective 0-60mph results were 8.1, 5.2 and 2.4 seconds. For 0-100mph it was 23.4, 12.9 and 3.9 seconds. By the time the F1 car had completed a lap of Silverstone, the 306 S16 did 60% lap distance and the 993 66%. Power-to-weight for the three cars was a respective: 132bhp per ton, 199bhp per ton and 1500bhp per ton. But about that 993 rear suspension … *CAR*'s Matt Bishop described the ease with which Martin Brundle drove the 993 around Silverstone: "He finds driving the doors off a 911 so easy that his banzai Porschemanship never interrupts his train of thought. Corner

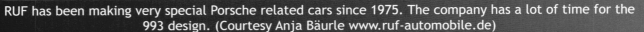

RUF has been making very special Porsche related cars since 1975. The company has a lot of time for the 993 design. (Courtesy Anja Bäurle www.ruf-automobile.de)

Happy to work on existing cars, and do special requests. The RUF Turbo R conversion done on this 993 was when it had 127,100km on the odometer. The interior was prepared for six-point seatbelts. (Courtesy www.ruf-automobile.de)

after corner, lap after lap he boots the 911's tail out – and holds it there, just for the fun of it – while answering my questions intelligently and reflectively, just as if he were sitting in his favourite armchair."[118]

Porsche was originally going to do a rear wheel steer axle for the 993. 911 project manager Friedrich Bezner was initially implementing this device when halfway through the 993's gestation, Porsche switched to the multi-link LSA. Reduced cost and complexity were probably the reasons. The LSA's 'Weissach Axle' principles of passive rear wheel steer, had originated with the Porsche 928. Such ideas were refined into the LSA seen on the defunct 989 four-door. Rather than let 150 million deutschmarks go to waste, Porsche put LSA into the 993!

Porsche's Bernd Kahnau adapted LSA to the 993. Kahnau said LSA was so good, the 911 no longer needed AWD to fix wild oversteer. Ulrich Bez was in charge of overall 993 engineering. Bez was searching for safer handling and a comfier ride than that possessed by the 964. Poor Porsche 964,

there seemed to be an historical 1990s parallel between the 964 and the, coincidentally similarly named, Nintendo 64. Both seemingly great at the start, but then a new technology came along. With the Nintendo 64 it was the changeover from cartridge to CD format.

Both the car and console were also similar in that their popularity rose in the years since, producing a cult following. The historical revision was anticipated by the *Daily Express 1997 World Car Guide*. The publication noted that the 993 was the easiest driving 911 to date. However, with such docility, the *Daily Express* noted some fans would be disappointed.

The 993 was the first 911 to get a six-speed manual gearbox. Ratios were 3.82 (first), 2.05 (second), 1.41 (third), 1.12 (fourth), 0.92 (fifth) and 0.78 (sixth). The final drive ratio was 3.44:1. Or one could have the Tiptronic four-speed torque converter automatic, as seen on the 964. The 993's Tiptronic could sense ascent and descent conditions for smarter shifting. 1995 would witness Tiptronic S, with buttons on the steering wheel. If one had to deal with heavy traffic on a regular basis, your clutch leg would thank you for ordering Tiptronic. However, with only four speeds, Tiptronic's ratio chasms were an enthusiast's black hole.

The Porsche 3.6-liter flat-six now made 272bhp at 6100rpm, and 243lb/ft at 5000rpm. According to Porsche the sprint to 60 took 5.4 seconds, with top speed being 168mph. Tiptronic cars were nearly one second tardier, and 3mph slower on top speed. The latest flat-six used hydraulic lifters, which eliminated valve adjustments and improved cold start emissions. This new 3.6L edition had lighter valves, valve springs and retainers. Pistons and connecting rods were lighter too.

With such weight savings, Porsche felt the engine's vibration damper was surplus to requirements. The new motor also boasted the efficiency of dual cats. For 1996 the 3.6L flat-six gained VarioRam. This device raised power output to 286bhp (a German fiscal cut-off point) and torque to 251lb/ft. VarioRam used different intake manifold tract lengths to maximize power and torque. VarioRam built upon the same theory used on the Porsche 928S3 and S4. In the 993's case, it was longer pipes for better low/medium rpm torque. A switch to shorter pipes up the rev scale made more power.

Concerning smaller 993 matters, the centrally located windshield wipers were mounted flush, and reduced wind noise. There was a new Bosch ABS 5 system, and Porsche claimed 60mph stops in 135 feet. The filtered ventilation system was handy in spring, and trunk volume was 20% higher. The standard seats had better support and flatter seams for more comfort. The opening North American Carrera list price, was $59,900. For seating, there was a choice of comfort, sport or racing buckets. Leather was standard, but optional soft ruffled leather was available for an extra £370 in the UK market.

For safer handling, the 964's rear track of 1374mm, had been raised to 1444mm with the 993's LSA. The new car also enjoyed a wider front track, up from the 964's 1379mm to 1405mm. For even more security, there was the AWD Carrera 4. Porsche had re-engineered the 911's AWD system, bringing it into line with the 959. In place of the 964's three differentials, there were two, and a 959-style center viscous coupling. The new system was lighter, and could send between five and 50% of power to the front wheels. More than this, the 993's ABD (Automatic Brake Differential) would brake the inner rear wheel going into a corner.

Cabrio, Targa & Speedster

According to factory figures, the Carrera 4 was quicker than the Carrera to 100kph, 5.3 versus 5.6 seconds. However, it fell back 6mph in top speed to 162mph. The AWD system brought a 110lb weight penalty, and Tiptronic added 55lb; you couldn't combine AWD and Tiptronic. However, unlike the 964, buyers could now select an AWD cabrio. That is, the 993 Carrera 4 Cabriolet. Like other Carrera 4s, this brought clear front and side indicator lenses, with red at the rear. The brake calipers and Carrera 4 tail script were in silver. The wheelcaps carried the Carrera 4 logo, not the Porsche shield.

Cabriolets featured a power operated, hand-stitched soft top with sheet metal reinforcements and automatic windblocker. The rear spoiler incorporated the 993's third brakelight. The whole shebang added 110lb to the 993, but a ton of style! The mechanically adventurous could sample the 993 Targa, available from '96 MY. This familiar 911 variant was cabrio-based. The targa now replaced the cabrio's fabric top with a glass panel. Said panel disappeared behind the 993's rear window at the push of a button.

In total, 4619 993 Targas were made. In its final '98 MY, 122 targas went to North America. 100 of these cars had Tiptronic, showing the sports luxo market's increasing predisposition towards automatic transmission, even with the 911. Targas featured special two-piece 17in rims, which could be optioned on other 993s if they didn't come with 18in rims as standard equipment. The glass-paneled targa, in spite of tinting, produced a hot interior. The system's weight and complexity didn't augur well for handling and reliability either.

March 1994 proved to be Porsche Cars North America's best sales month since May 1991. 457 cars were sold, and 53% of them were 911s. With such buoyant ordering of the new 993 coinciding with better economic times, it suggested that the entry-level 968 wasn't being bought not because of its high price, but because Porsche fans just didn't warm to it. On debut, *Autocar & Motor* called the 968 a fabulous handler and great value. In 1993, the same journal bestowed its Best Handling Car award on the 968CS, and noted its first class finish. Outside the 993RS, *Autocar & Motor* declared the 968CS the most fun and best value, but noted it looked pretty hideous!

The 993 was judged a well-built car of Porsche quality too. If the latest 911's price was an impediment, sports fans may have considered a model of the 993, rather than a real 968. The 911 is a tricky shape to render, but the 1994 Bburago 993 Cabriolet had accurate proportions and functional details: the trunk, soft top and doors opened; the steered wheels really swiveled, rear seats folded and the side mirrors reflected; molded door handles, a trunk with suitcases and headlamps with bulbs added detail; instrumentation graphics, and dashboard 'airbag' script were the icing on the cake. All this for a little over 30 bucks, and it didn't use any gas!

For something pricier, and more exclusive than a 911 Cabrio, try the 993 Speedster. A chopped roof and special interior were expected, but the source wasn't. With no official 993 Speedster, only two cars came from Porsche. A dark green Tiptronic S Speedster with 17in rims was produced for Ferdinand Alexander Porsche's 60th birthday in 1995. A 1998 Speedster was created by Porsche Exclusive for comedian Jerry Seinfeld. This latter example was a pre-existing 993 six-speed with 18in rims, sent to Porsche Exclusive for conversion work. A few more 993 Speedsters were cabrios converted by coachbuilders.

Carrera S, 4S & RS

911 connoisseurs seek out the Carrera S and 4S versions of the 993. Available from 1997, the enhanced two and four-wheel drive 993s represented the combination of wide body 993 Turbo, lowered suspension and 286bhp's worth of stock 3.6L flat-six. Porsche Exclusive did a few Carrera S Cabrios. In July 1998, a Carrera 4S had the honor of being the final air-cooled 911 to roll off the assembly line. The S variants harked back to the M491-optioned 911 Carrera 3.2s of the '80s. The 993 Carrera 4S was the safest and easiest to drive air-cooled 911 ever made. The extra wide rear rubber and AWD raised rear grip limits to an extremely high level. For all that, the S versions were no faster than normal 286 horse counterparts. According to Porsche they were good for 0-100 kph in 5.2 seconds and a 172mph top speed, in spite of a 66lb weight penalty.

The ultimate for naturally-aspirated, lightweight lovers was the 993 Carrera RS 3.8. It proffered the familiar 300bhp flat-six from 964 days, along with 993-specific fixed rear mega wing, small front spoiler flaps (like an '80s 956), and three-piece

18in alloys. Forget about rear seats, headlamp washers, most of the 993's sound deadening, and get used to snug racing buckets. For extreme individuals the Clubsport version supplied a rollcage and took the liberty of deep-sixing carpets, a/c, fast glass, in-car audio, and added an even bigger rear wing and deeper front spoiler. This 1995-96 Playstation Gran Turismo refugee wasn't available in North America unless you tried the gray market.

993 Turbo

The 911 Turbo returned in 993 form for '95 MY. It was an historic coupe for several reasons. It was the first 911 Turbo with twin turbos, and only the second production Porsche with this feature. The 993 Turbo was also the first AWD 911 Turbo, and last but not least, this would be the final air-cooled 911 Turbo. In total, 5978 993 Turbos were made, and, like the 1014 993 Carrera RS coupés, they are collectible classics of the highest order.

With twin turbos, viscous coupling AWD and hollow-spoke aluminum rims, the 959 kinship was very close. Air-to-air intercoolers, special cylinder heads and stronger internals permitted 408bhp and 398lb/ft. With 0-100kph in 4.5 seconds, the 993 Turbo was a leader of its era. It was the first volume production Porsche capable of 180mph. Front and rear track were a substantial 1411mm and 1504mm respectively. At 1795mm wide, the Turbo and Carrera S/4S were exactly 60mm wider than more plebeian 993s.

The 993 Turbo's wide body, with Turbo specific front and rear fascias, was very visible The four oxygen sensors and inaugural Porsche use of OBDII were less noticeable. If the 993 was the best 911, then many would nominate the 993 Turbo as the ultimate 993. However, Porsche was always on the move. For '97 MY stronger transmission input shafts and flashable ECU were upgrades. On a more mundane level, the passenger front airbag deactivated if a child seat was in play. Alarm system motion sensors were now placed in the map light.

1997 also saw a new top-level 993, in the form of the 430bhp Turbo S. More than this, a 450 pony upgrade package was available from the factory, and 183 cars were built. The torque level of the new Turbo S was still 398lb/ft, the 1500kg weight was also constant. However, it was faster, with 0-100kph in 4.3 seconds and 185mph top speed, but of course you want more. According to Zuffenhausen, the 450bhp edition was good for

186mph. It was the first time a regular Porsche hit 300kph!

Turbo S badges were on the color keyed brake calipers, on the rear deck, rocker panel strip, dashboard, fold-down seat back, and steering wheel. The Turbo S sat 30mm closer to terra firma than a normal 993, and 15mm lower than the outgoing Turbo. It had an extra oil cooler, reinforced suspension strut brace, revised front and rear airdams, extra air inlets for the front spoiler and rear fenders, larger diameter four-pipe exhaust system, plus interior carbon-fiber and aluminum trim. The six-speed manual gearbox and associated clutch were strengthened.

Back in its May 1, 1991 issue, *Autocar & Motor* tried the early 964 Turbo 3.3, with a mere 320bhp. 0-60 was 4.7 seconds and top speed was 167mph. Touring gas mileage for the 1460kg coupe was 21mpg. The final air-cooled 450bhp 911 Turbo, according to European Community testing standards, had improved to 22mpg. Unfortunately, its price had escalated from £72,294 to £129,950, and there were still options out there …

Beyond the 993 Turbo S was the manic two-wheel drive 993 GT2. Although formally called 911 GT, the GT2 was intended for GT2 racing, so that name stuck. The FIA's ban on all-wheel drive racers from Audi and Nissan meant Porsche's homologation special was basically a stripped 993 Turbo S, minus the AWD. The interior was Carrera RS minimalist. The exterior saw the 993 Turbo's fenders cut back and replaced with bolt-on plastic equivalents to save weight. The GT2 was certainly lighter: 1290kg versus the Turbo's 1500kg. It also had wider front and rear tracks at 1475mm and 1550mm respectively.

The same 430bhp and 398lb/ft meant the lighter 993 GT2 took a mere 4 seconds to hit 100kph. The extra aero addendum slowed top speed marginally to 184mph. However, it could have the optional 450bhp upgrade. In the racing GT1 series, an EVO edition boasted 600bhp. This version was eventually replaced by the also mid-engined, Le Mans-winning, 911 GT1-98.

All well and good, but to onlookers a 993 GT2 would be just a fast-moving blur. A better show was put on by the unofficial 993 Turbo Cabriolet. Predating the factory 993 Turbo, this blown ragtop was an 89,500 DM conversion job done on the 993 Cabrio. The recipe was a piece of Black Forest cake: just substitute the engine, five-speed, rear drive and rear spoiler from the 964 Turbo. Fourteen '95 MY 993 Turbo Cabriolets were so created.

993 and beyond

The 993 total saw 68,029 sports cars made. The 993 Carrera was the most popular at 46,923 units, and the Carrera 4 was next on 14,114. This was all just slightly more than the 964 over a similar time frame. Each 911 generation sold consistently well, even in bad times. There was never such a thing as a bad 911. The 1975 (a crunch year for pollution controls) North American 911 could be considered a low point. The heat-hating 2.7 motor was also in the mix. For all this, the 911 could still show a clean set of heels to its rivals. It was still lively thanks to the 911's low weight, and Dr Porsche's tradition of air-cooled VW and Porsche boxer motors that didn't mind low octane juice. *CAR* magazine pondered some possible 911 wrong turns. The leaky, squeaky targa, strange Sportomatic, less-than-pretty flachbau and in its words, "ridiculous Speedster." Well, you can't win 'em all. However, at the start of 1995 the journal considered the 993 Carrera 4 to be the pinnacle of 911 development.

As per the 964, there was a plethora of choices in the 993 game. In the UK, many items were still optional. Air-conditioning was £2375 and cabrio windblocker was £300. The latter had a frame of wire netting one foot behind the headrests. The 17in wheel package was a £1095 option that bought holy grail Pirelli P Zeros. ABD was a £1045 and £945 option, on manual and automatic 993s respectively. At 1995 prices the 993 Carrera started from £54,995, and the Carrera 4 was £58,245, with the cabrio at 5k extra. So, the 993 was pricier, and came with less standard stuff than in North America.

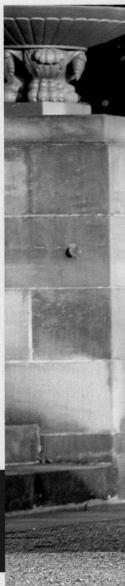

The ultimate development of Doctor Porsche's 1930s rear-engined, air-cooled thinking: the 1997 911 Turbo Coupe 3.6 with 408bhp at 5750rpm. This 993 chassis car could almost do 180mph! (Courtesy Porsche)

For all markets the stock standard 16in rims brought 205/55ZR tires at the front, and 245/45ZRs at the rear. The 17in rims changed things to 205/50ZR front and 255/40ZR rear. However, the universal consensus was that the standard 993 Carrera was more than fine. The cabrio brought a rigidity rarely seen in ragtops. The Tiptronic considered so many parameters, including transmission oil temperature, brake pedal use, lateral and longitudinal acceleration, etc, but the Carrera 4 earned great respect, and yet, as stated by Richard Bremner, "It's difficult to escape the notion that a pure 911, a real 911, is a pretty little fixed-head coupe powered by a flat-six driving the rear wheels via a manual gearbox."[119]

Normally, less is more, but there is never anything normal about a 911 Turbo, especially a 959-matching, 450 horse 993 Turbo S 3.6. *CAR*'s Jason Barlow confessed to nearly oversteering into a Cambridgeshire hedge in 1998 due to a slippery turn, second gear and sudden power. In keeping with Porsche tradition of excellent brakes, a system capable of reining in 1940bhp, or 100kph in 2.6 seconds; or "There are less effective brick walls."[120] As for quality, need you ask? For all cars up to 11 years old, a 1998 German TUV report said the Porsche 911 was the most reliable car surveyed. Take that, Lexus!

The 911 has also proven to be a wise investment for early birds. In 1999, *Autocar* noted few owners drive their 959s due to their ever-rising worth. The same thing is happening with air-cooled 911s today. UK prices in mid-1999 saw a 1975 911 2.7 with 147,000km (German market import) selling for £7,995. A 1984 911 Carrera 3.2 with a/c, full service history and 64,000 miles was £15,500. A 1997 993 C4 with 11,500 miles was £50,500, and a 1998 996 stick shift with 13,000 miles was £62,000. All cars were private sale entries.

15 years later and any reasonable condition air-cooled 911 started at £50,000. Interest in the 993 is ever rising, and the 996 became a bargain basement 911, sharing its budget location with the Boxster. How did this situation arise? An answer is hinted at in comments made at the time of the 993 to 996 transition. Such predictions turned out 100% accurate.

In judging the 993 against the new 996, most journals agreed. The new water-cooled 911 represented a larger, comfier car, with objectively measurable improvements in handling, ride comfort and performance, but … where was the love? In the words of *Autocar*, "there's something missing. A truly exceptional sports car has become a grand tourer." Using the magazine's figures for a 993 Carrera six-speed (23/3/94): 0-60mph in 5.2 seconds; 160mph; test/touring economy 19/33mpg; weight 1380kg. Equivalent figures for the 996 (1/10/97): 4.6 seconds; 173mph; 20/25mpg; 1320 kg.

Air-cooled VWs and Porsches have traditionally possessed excellent fuel economy. This probably dated back to the meeting between Adolf Hitler and Doctor Porsche at Berlin's Hotel Kaiserhof, in the May of 1934. Here, Hitler insisted the Beetle have excellent gas mileage of 7 liters per 100km. It set an historical precedent for fuel efficiency. In *CAR*'s opinion the 993 felt better built, more compact and was an even purer drive than the 996. The journal's 'against' section concerning the 996 stated: "New model's Boxster headlamps. Eastern-looking dash and creaky interior."

The sentiment was that the 996 was everything a late '90s 911 should be. That could be the problem: the 996 and subsequent 911s were cars of their time. The air-cooled 911 was a car for all time. *CAR*'s Georg Kacher tried a new 996 Cabrio, noticed the easier-to-persuade chassis, and still existing oversteer with little warning and noted, "While the shape of the 996 is undeniably more modern, many hardcore Porschephiles still prefer the 993. They always will, in all probability." The 996 went on to develop engine foibles, and interior quality left something to be desired. Such qualms, and the 996's styling, were largely addressed by the 2004 997.

For rivals, if it really had any, the 993 faced the new C5 Corvette. Note that when the four-wheel disk braked air-cooled 911 came out, it sort of faced the four-wheel drum braked C2 Vette! Now, as ever, the Corvette packed more all-alloy pushrod LS1 V8 power at a lower price, as Corvettes tend to do. The C5 got rave reviews at home, and conditioned praise overseas. It was judged a big improvement over the flex prone C4. However, the plastic coupe couldn't match the 911's interior quality, excellent build or fine road manners.

In the UK the Dodge Viper GTS was only slightly more expensive than the base 993, but packed 450 V10 horses and had that sexy look in red. However, the Viper was a musclecar bruiser, and not really a direct rival to even the relatively delicate Vette. De Tomaso's Pantera came out after the 911, but was now looking a little dated. That old Cleveland 351 V8 muscle had given way to a 248 horse Windsor V8. The Pantera was being phased out in favor of the new mid-engined Guara. The De Tomaso Guara had that Nikasil M60 BMW four-liter V8, and the Italian automaker hoped the new model would turn its fortunes around. It didn't.

The Honda NSX cost nearly £10,000 more than the '97 993 Carrera. At the time of the new '94 NSX Type R, North-American-delivered NSXs came with cupholders … saints preserve us. Honda's president said there would be no new NSX, due to the huge investment such sports cars require. The Mazda FD RX7 needed much less investment by consumers. It was a talented but fragile exotic, going for a bargain basement price. This left the new Ferrari F355, which mostly wiped out the sins, which were legion, of the 348.

The F355 had the world's first five-valve per cylinder motor in a production car. It drove and looked a lot better than the 348, but it cost 50% more than the 993, and it was debatable if it was even equally as good. Even with Fix It Again Tony's investment, it still wasn't too durable. *CAR* tried two automatics: a Porsche 996 and Ferrari F355. The 996 was rock solid, but Maranello's prancing steed creaked and groaned. Ferraris didn't have recalls, they just never left!

The Boxster was half the 993's price. If Zuffenhausen had called the budget Porsche the 986, as originally planned, it would have stopped *Top Gear*'s Jeremy Clarkson from bestowing an unkind sobriquet, the first syllable of which rhymed with 'sock.' The Boxster seemed to suffer from 924 syndrome: always trying to justify its worth in the immense shadow of the 911. The air-cooling quality of Zuffenhausen's famous sports car produced a kinship with Dr Porsche's early work. It was something in common with a Baja Bug, making its determined way through desert sand as fine as flour.

During 1998, the 993 Carrera 4S and Turbo S represented the last chance to get a new air-cooled 911, from Porsche at any rate. May 1998 saw the passing of Porsche's driving force, Ferry Porsche. He had lived to see the one millionth Porsche, a milestone achieved on July 15, 1996. The car, a 993 Carrera, was presented to the local autobahn police. Ferry Porsche also saw the arrival of the water-cooled 996. A managing director of Porsche for the majority of its history, it's unlikely Ferry Porsche would have sanctioned the attempted takeover of VW, which would cost Porsche AG its long-held independence.

There has now been over two decades of Boxsters, Porsche returned to Le Mans victorious, and the rear-engined 911 has continued even though Porsche has been under VW control for over a decade. In modern times most Porsche buyers want a prestige SUV, not a 911. However, a major reason buyers come to Porsche – and not one of its upscale SUV making rivals – is the 911's mystique. It explains why Porsche tries to make all its vehicles, SUV or otherwise, resemble the 911. That is, look like a Porsche. The fabled 911 eventually took on standard turbo and electric power steering for reduced fuel consumption and improved emissions performance. Some people would call that progress …probably the same ones that banned the grid girls from Formula One.

Strosek & RUF

In the old days, the styling house of Vittorio Strosek, Strosek Auto Design, based in Utting am Ammersee, would have been called a coachbuilder. However, in the extravagant 1980s such old-world terms seemed quaint. Strosek gained prominence for the bodykits it did in that decade for front-engined Porsches, especially the 928. With bold design examples suited to the power dressing '80s, Strosek certainly got noticed. Given the popularity

of the front-engined cars, there was a good sized market for custom conversion work. In Germany, there was value in setting your 944 apart from many other 944s on the road and bahn. Strosek's Design-Programm 944/Turbo achieved that goal.

The Strosek catalog was expensive, so too, the things contained therein. This included a 450bhp engine package for the 928's 4.7-liter V8. Two Roots-type superchargers were placed in the vee, and worked with the V8's Bosch K-Jetronic fuel-injection. With the right gearing, over 180mph was possible. With Strosek's engine upgrade, bodykit, special suspension and BBS rims, a 928SK conversion cost nearly 50 grand in the mid-'80s … not including the car! Strosek's restyling work was extensive, and the 928SK's flachbau meant no stock headlamps. Strosek's substitution of four spotlamps didn't really cut it: just not bright enough for a car of this speed potential at night.

Replacing the 928 V8's stock intake manifold with a pair of blowers, and rigging up the standard fuel-injection to feed said blowers with gas, was quite radical in the turbo era. Even more avant garde was Strosek's use of Bosch/PES-developed small projector-style headlamps by the 1990s. These units provided great styling freedom, and were applied to Porsche 944, 928 and eventually the 993. Now you could have that smaller, low hood look, with safe road illumination. More outlandish still was Strosek's 928 gullwing conversion called Ultra Wing.

Strosek did have a few agents outside Germany. Some were in America, like Anzianos of Santa Ana, California. However, the 29,000 DM Ultra Wing job, at 1993 prices, could only be done at Strosek's home facility in Germany. With the 1994 Carrera Cup, Strosek sponsored the Max Moritz Racing 928GTR. The bodykit and exhaust system came from Strosek. This semi works coupe was entered by the Porsche Club Schwaben. Porsche works drivers and Porsche styling boss Harm Lagaay raced this big 928GTR. It proved competitive against the series' 964s.

At the time of the 993's introduction, Strosek had a bodykit and associated package for the 964. It was 10 grand in its most basic form. New fenders, front air dam, rear valence and new side reversing mirrors were afoot. The Aera conversion was Strosek's take on the targa top. Its Mega 993 lived up to its name, by only keeping the stock doors and hood. Wider rear arches now accommodated seriously big rims. By now Strosek was using OZ rims, specially made.

As was usual for customizers, a chopped top was a given. The Speedster-style 964 windshield used was oftentimes sans exposed wipers, and was complemented by a low aero hardtop. In contrast, Strosek did very little to the 968. The stock swivel up headlamps stayed, and there were mild body add-ons as per the Strosek 944. Phone dial OZ rims completed the coupe, but Strosek also had packages for Porsche's ASC ragtops. They even offered a convertible conversion for the 928!

In America, Strosek gained publicity from one of its cars in vibrant lime green being featured in BFGoodrich ads. By stopping at the vehicle belt line, Strosek 911 conversions were doable on coupe, cabrio, targa and Speedsters. Strosek frequently updated its portfolio to reflect changing public tastes. By the 1990s the company even offered items for Ferraris and the 300ZX. With such a wide catalog choice, each Strosek car was practically unique.

Also unique are the very special Porsche related cars of RUF Automobile GmbH. Often working from a body-in-white base, RUF makes and fits its own design parts, has its own VIN serial numbers, and has long been recognized as a car maker by the German government. It all started in 1939 when Alois Ruf Sr opened a service station in Pfaffenhausen Germany. The operation soon branched out into vehicle design, and the successful creation of tour buses.

Left: The MMR 928GTR was a semi works entry, although formally entered by Porsche Club Schwaben. Porsche works drivers and head stylist Harm Lagaay, raced the big coupe. (www.strosek.de)

This automotive start influenced Alois Ruf Sr's son, Alois Ruf Jr, to start the service and repair of Porsches from his father's garage in 1960. When Alois Ruf Sr passed away in 1974, his son took control of the business. The focus was now special Porsches, especially the 911. The first Ruf-enhanced 911 came out in 1975, with the first complete RUF sports car arriving in 1977. This latter car was a 930 with a stroker motor. At 3.3-liters, RUF's 930 predated the factory's own 930 3.3L.

RUF also pipped Porsche to the post with its 3.2-liter 911SCR of 1978. This wonderful atmo 911 drew praise from *Auto Motor und Sport* in its #13 1978 issue. Concerning this improved 911SC, the journal enthusiastically declared, "Power,

everywhere you step!" At 217bhp strong, the RUF machine was handily more potent than the stock 180bhp 911SC. Progress witnessed the 1983-89 RUF BTR (Gruppe B Turbo RUF). Based on 1978-89 era 911s, the RUF BTR had a 3.4-liter turbo flat-six with 374bhp at six grand and 350lb/ft at 4800rpm.

The RUF BTR was the first RUF with its own VIN sequence, and by 1988 you could request a six-speed manual, seven years before Porsche offered one on the 911! The BTR made news in 1984, with the coupe winning *Road & Track*'s World's Fastest Cars challenge, registering 300kph in the journal's September 1984 issue. Using a narrow body car, *Auto Motor und Sport*'s 22/1984

Is it a bird, is it a plane? No, it's Strosek Ultra Wing! The gullwing 928 dreams were made of. Dreams weren't cheap, however – one needed 29,000DM and a 928, (a 928GTS in this case) for the gullwing experience. (Original pictures courtesy www.strosek.de)

The RUF SCR 4.0 made its formal debut at the 2018 Geneva Auto Show, after two years of research and development. The motor was a 4-liter, water cooled, flat-six, making 510bhp.
(Courtesy Anja Bäurle www.ruf-automobile.de)

issue, showed the BTR to have a new German 0-100kph record time of 4.6 seconds. 0-160kph was 9.6 seconds, with the quarter mile in 12.5 seconds at 112mph. You could have a wide body version, but it was 20kph slower on top speed due to drag. Around 25 BTRs were made from body-in-white, unmarked Porsche chassis. The rest were converted cars. The RUF BTR paved the way for the even more famous CTR (Gruppe C Turbo RUF), better known as the Yellowbird. The CTR was based on the '87 MY 911 Carrera 3.2, not the 911 Turbo. The atmo car's narrow body meant less weight and drag, plus RUF wasn't happy about using the 911 Turbo's four-speed. From this base, RUF seam welded the 911's body, put filler panels for the door pillars, shaved the rain gutters and used polyurethane front and rear bumpers. Aluminum doors, luggage compartment and

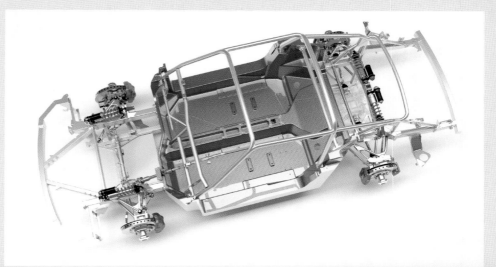

The SCR 4.0 has a 993 multilink rear, but the wheelbase is 70mm longer. The front axle is 50mm forward, and the rear axle line 20mm rearwards compared to a stock 993. However, the 993's overall length has been kept. (Courtesy Rafael Riethmüller www.ruf-automobile.de)

engine cover lids all contributed to a 441lb weight saving. Slightly flared rear arches accommodated Speedline rims.

Prototypes utilized NACA intercooler ducts on the rear fenders. However, these were dropped since a low pressure area formed causing air to

Above and opposite page: The 2018 RUF SCR 4.0 was a tribute to RUF's first formal model, the 1978 911SC based RUF 911SCR 3.2. The 2018 iteration first appeared at the 2016 Geneva auto show, as a display prototype. It appears 993 related, but RUF cars have become increasingly custom over the years. In this case, a 241lb carbon-fiber body, and integrated rollcage (IRC). (Courtesy Rafael Riethmüller www.ruf-automobile.de)

be forced out, not in. Rear bumper slots were incorporated to allow hot air to escape. The body possessed an integrated rollcage, and RUF pressed into service Porsche's 1972 fender-mounted oil filler, since it moved the dry sump forward to clear the engine's intercooler. The twin turbo 3.4L flat-six got its displacement by boring out with 98mm pistons. The motor used an uprated Bosch Motronic system, and ignition was set up in common with the Porsche 962.

The Yellowbird flew, with two turbos and two intercoolers, to 469bhp at 5950rpm and 408lb/ft at 5100rpm. The stock 911 five-speed couldn't be modified to suit, so a custom five-speed with special ratios was produced. RUF's 17in Speedlines, suspension package, 13in Brembo brakes and Porsche 959 type Dunlop Denloc tires kept the 2579lb $223,000 '88 MY missile safe. RUF built 29 cars from a body-in-white, Porsche-supplied starting point. Remaining Yellowbirds were converted 911s.

As published in its July issue, the RUF CTR won *Road & Track*'s '87 World's Fastest Cars contest. Taking 4 seconds from 0-60mph, it was slower out of the hole than a Ferrari F40 and Porsche 959. However, it creamed all comers concerning terminal velocity, which turned out to be 211mph. The quarter mile came in 11.7 seconds at 133.5mph. Paul Frère was moved to say, "This is faster than I've ever gone in my life!" Quite an admission from a Le Mans winner! There was a gray sky on test day, and the contrast with the CTR's bright yellow paint brought on the Yellowbird moniker from *Road & Track*'s staff. The turbo system's blow-off valve sounded bird-like as well. Over 200 grand was a small price to pay for the world's fastest production car and Nürburgring lap record holder for many a year.

The 1995 RUF CTR2 was capable of 217mph. This was better than the 213mph Jaguar XJ220, but slower than the much more expensive McLaren F1. The CTR2 was 993 Turbo-based, but came as a two-wheel drive coupe. AWD was optional with CTR2, maintaining RUF's tradition of being daring. A modified twin turbo 3.6L flat-six was used, based on the Le Mans 962C motor, making 520bhp and 505lb/ft. It was good for 0-60mph in 3.5 seconds, and the quarter mile in 11.4 seconds at 126mph. The CTR2 was subsequently improved to 580bhp.

Other CTR2 refinements included Recaro racing seats with Simpson five-point safety belts, larger brakes, integrated rollcage, and RUF custom coil overs. Not to mention the special integrated rear wings, to generate more downforce and channel

air to the intercoolers on either side of the flat-six. A Kevlar body and lightweight glass were utilized. The six-speed manual-only RUF CTR2 weighed 1358kg and cost at least $315,000. As the more potent CTR2 Sport, the latest Yellowbird, enjoyed success at 1997's Pikes Peak Hillclimb, Alois Ruf Jr organized the entry of two Yellowbirds driven by brothers Steve and David Beddor, and the cars were really driven.

Unlike trailered competitors, the CTR2 Sports were driven to and from the venue, as the street-legal road cars that they were. That said, they made exceptional power: 702bhp at 7300rpm and 580lb/ft at 5500rpm. It was enough for Steve Beddor to qualify first overall and finish second in the hillclimb. Brother David came fourth on the event. Concerning CTR2 build numbers, 16 regular cars were made, with 15 Sport versions done too.

As with Porsche, RUF never stood still. In April 2007, the RUF CTR3's debut coincided with the manufacturer opening its new Bahrain factory. The 2010 Geneva Motor Show witnessed the world's first production 911 with a V8: the RUF RGT-8. In light of the time and expense North Americans devoted to V8 swaps for their Porsches, RUF was making life easier and saving you R&D money!

In terms of wider media notoriety, RUF CTRs have been in the anime and games of the *Wangan Midnight* series. Character Tatsuya Shima drove a black CTR called Blackbird. RUF CTRs have also starred in other game franchises, like Playstation's *Gran Turismo*. In terms of legendary icons, it all started with that 1978 RUF 911SCR. Even back then, RUF's special engineering ran to a larger front spoiler, with round front brake cooling ducts, oil cooler and custom whaletail. For the new-age 2018 RUF SCR 4.0, the detail engineering of this SCR tribute coupe has gone to a new level in the realms of low volume, production car manufacture.

So many are the RUF changes, that one could say the SCR 4.0 is 993-inspired. The styling is faithful to the 993, it uses a modified form of the Weissach Axle, and the green color harks back to the 1978 special, but beyond this, its all clean sheet. A carbon-fiber monocoque chassis harnesses pushrod front and rear suspension. The wheelbase is 70mm longer than on a 993. The front axle has been moved 50mm forward, and the rear axle line 20mm rearward. However, the stock 993 length has been maintained.

The motor is a 4-liter naturally-aspirated, water-cooled flat-six making 510bhp. The 241lb carbon-fiber body, with integrated rollcage, contributes to the

SCR 4.0's low overall weight of under 2800lb. First shown at the 2016 Geneva show, two more years of R&D eventuated before the RUF SCR 4.0's debut at the 2018 Geneva show. Beyond this machine, the Blood Orange RUF SCR 4.2 has 525bhp at 8500rpm, weighs 2646lb, and also has a six-speed stick. The sticker shock started at $527,664! These aren't AWD coupés, and remain faithful to the rear-drive 911 ideal.

RUF had already created a tribute to the original 1987 CTR Yellowbird. The 2017 RUF CTR was that tribute car, and appeared at the 2017 Geneva show. This new Yellowbird was a personal dream of RUF boss Alois Ruf Jr, and had much in common with the 1987 Yellowbird. Much attention was given to body aerodynamics, a twin turbo air-cooled flat-six was used, and, most importantly, the new car was yellow! That said, the new version represented the first RUF completely designed and engineered in house. A custom rear drive, carbon-fiber monocoque chassis dealt with 710bhp and 649lb/ft.

Controlling such power was double wishbone suspension front and rear, and inner vented/perforated carbon ceramic disk brakes with six-piston calipers at the front and four-piston calipers rearwards. RUF's center locking, 19in forged rims wore 245/35ZR-19s at the front, 305/30ZR-19s at the back. This new Yellowbird had RUF's first carbon-fiber body and chassis. Safety came from an integrated rollcage, and a light, strong steel crumple zone at the front. Safety was key for a 225mph coupe using a six-speed manual, rear drive and LSD for control. Estonia Ruf promised an analog driving experience with the 2640 lb 2017 Yellowbird!

30 RUF new-age Yellowbirds were made, and one prototype, at RUF's Pfaffenhausen factory. RUF's victory in the famous 1987 *Road & Track* World's Fastest Car shootout happened at VW's Ehra-Lessien test track in West Germany. However, that year Alois Ruf Jr got approval from the NHTSA and EPA to sell RUF sports cars in America. So if cash was no problem, one could enjoy the Yellowbird's Alcantara upholstery, carbon-fiber seats and aluminum pedals, but hurry, RUFs sell out fast!

The 2016 RUF Turbo R Limited truly was limited, with only seven built! Even though they started at nearly 600 grand, they quickly sold out. The Turbo R used a 620bhp twin turbo air-cooled flat-six, with its engine block sourced from the hallowed 993 Turbo. It weighed 3175lb and could touch 212mph. An earlier RUF Turbo R had won a 1998 *Road & Track* top-speed shootout.

For the squeamish, RUF could make your car AWD. Or what about the RUF Ultimate? The Ultimate honored the 964's wheelbase length, had a carbon-fiber body and 590bhp worth of air-cooled 3.6L twin turbo flat-six. In spite of such custom cars, RUF has always been willing to convert existing Porsches into RUFs, or restore cars. In any case RUF's credo is to re-engineer everything, but stay understated.

WSC-95, 911GT1 & 919

Porsche continued its success in sports car racing after the 962. However, its next winner came from strange origins. The Porsche WSC-95, as it is sometimes called, started as a Porsche-modified Group C Jaguar XJR-14 intended for an IMSA series, under the World Sports Car (WSC) umbrella. This racer used a 3-liter version of Porsche's legendary Type 935 flat-six for super track economy. The sports car was going to be handled by Tom Walkinshaw Racing. Unfortunately, rulebook changes saw the project sidelined.

Long-time Porsche privateer outfit Joest Racing stepped in and told Porsche it would like to try out the prototype at Le Mans. Porsche said okay, and with Porsche knowledge and Joest Racing finance a second WSC-95 was constructed. The design was adapted to LMP1, with Le Mans victories for Joest Racing at Le Mans in 1996 and 1997. In 1996, the #7 WSC-95 driven by Davy Jones, Alexander Wurz and Manuel Reuter finished a lap ahead of the factory Porsche 911GT1. In 1997, it was former Ferrari F1 alumni Michele Alboreto and Stefan Johansson, plus a young Tom Kristensen, that won for Joest Racing.

The 911GT1 hadn't done well at Le Mans in 1997. Porsche thought it had better get hold of this fast WSC-95 for themselves! So, for 1998, Zuffenhausen redeveloped and renamed the WSC-95 to create the Porsche LMP1-98. Still campaigned by Joest Racing, the new LMP1-98 involved Porsche redoing the WSC-95 bodywork and aero, plus putting in a 911GT1-style 3.2 flat-six. Sadly, no dice; there was too much competition afoot. Porsche tried to improve its 911GT1 and the WSC-95 designs for 1998, but other automakers spoilt its party. Still, concerning the WSC-95 and Le Mans, as Meatloaf sang, "Two out of three ain't bad."

Porsche didn't give up on its 911GT1; that car didn't have much in common with the regular 911. The 911GT1 was designed by Porsche's legendary

Norbert Singer, and was intended for GT1 category sports car racing. However, Porsche had been creative with the ol' rulebook. Instead of creating a race car from a road car, Zuffenhausen did the race car and then worked backwards! So the Porsche 911 GT1 was a tube frame racer with carbon-fiber body, and double wishbone suspension front and rear.

Under the skin, the front half of the chassis was 993 related, whereas the rear part was 962 style. The 911 GT1 also took its water-cooled 3.2L flat-six, twin turbo, intercooled, four-valve per cylinder 600bhp motor from the 962. At the time, the rear-engined 993 GT2 had a mere two-valves per cylinder. No matter, winning is winning. The 911 GT1 garnered three victories in the 1996 BPR Global GT series at Brands Hatch, Spa and Zhuhai. It also came an honorable second at Le Mans that year. Unfortunately, the revised 911 GT1 Evo, with 996-style headlamps didn't do so well in the 1997 FIA GT Championship. Opposition was fierce in the new series.

Come 1998, Porsche had the newly designed, also mid-engined, 911 GT1-98.

The 2017 RUF CTR, represents the first car completely designed and engineered by RUF. Carbon-fiber trim inside and for the custom monocoque chassis.
A tribute to the famous 1987 CTR Yellowbird, the 2017 RUF CTR was unveiled at the Geneva Auto Show. It was a personal dream car project of Alois Ruf Jr.

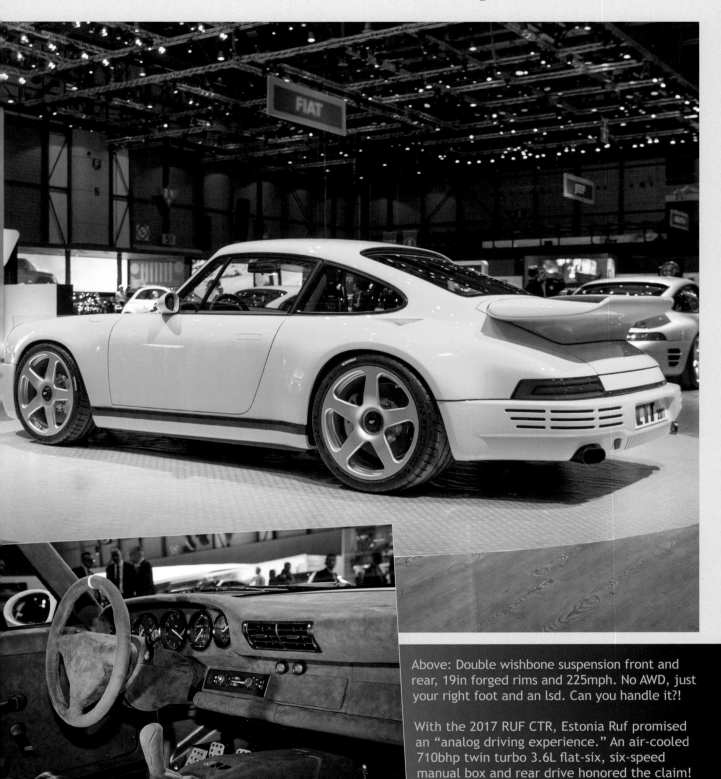

Above: Double wishbone suspension front and rear, 19in forged rims and 225mph. No AWD, just your right foot and an lsd. Can you handle it?!

With the 2017 RUF CTR, Estonia Ruf promised an "analog driving experience." An air-cooled 710bhp twin turbo 3.6L flat-six, six-speed manual box and rear drive honored the claim! (All pictures courtesy www.ruf-automobile.de)

A sequential gearbox was included, but problems came in the form of rulebook turbo motor air restrictors, uncompetitive Michelin tires, plus formidable rivalry from Mercedes, Toyota and BMW. However, even though Mercedes dominated the race series, the 911GT1-98 won 1998's Le Mans on reliability. If Toyota was the hare, Porsche was the tortoise, and we all know who won out that day! It was Porsche's 16th Le Mans victory, but with the GT1 class axed at the close of 1998, and newer rivals in the offing, Zuffenhausen's factory 911GT1 effort ended that year. However, what of the road car?

The powers that be said there had to be 25 road warriors for GT1 category entry. Well, Porsche made two cars with 993-style headlamps in 1996, 20 with 996-type headlamps in 1997, and one 911GT1-98 road car in 1998. Somehow, the authorities were cool with this – never look a gift horse in the mouth. *Auto Motor und Sport* tried one for size in 1997. It did 0-62mph in 3.9 seconds and over 190mph, which was fast in those days. The statistics said the street legal 3.2L twin turbo flat-six made 544bhp at 7200rpm and 443lb/ft at 4250rpm. Weight was 2535lb, and length, width and height dimensions were, respectively, 192.5in, 78.3in and 44.9in. It seemed some people always liked the concept of visiting the local shopping mall in a Le Mans winner!

Truly outside the air-cooled era, Porsche won three Le Mans in a row from 2015 to 2017. Zuffenhausen achieved this with its 919 Hybrid. The name drew a tenuous link with that one-time dominant sports car, the Porsche 917. However, the 21st century powerplant was a two-liter gasoline V4 turbo, combined with electric power. It got pole position at Le Mans in 2015 and won the race. Porsche unseated previously dominant and in-house rival Audi in the process. The class was now LMP1-H, the sports car an eco warrior. However, a victory is a victory, and a Porsche is a Porsche. Zuffenhausen ended its LMP1 program in 2017, with a view towards Formula E participation. 🐎

Previous pages: The Porsche 919 Hybrid narrowly lost Le Mans to Audi in 2014, but Zuffenhausen triumphed the following year. It was a successful return to La Sarthe. (Courtesy Porsche)

Opposite page, left: The 1998 Le Mans 24 Hour race winner, was this 911 GT1 driven by Laurent Aiello, Allan McNish and Stephane Ortelli. It provided Porsche with their sixteenth outright victory, at the French enduro. (Courtesy Porsche)

Below: The 1996 911GT1 at Weissach. Porsche's Weissach tech center, is like an uber "think and do tank" for Porsche and other companies, seeking Zuffenhausen expertise. (Courtesy Porsche)

A road-going 1996 911GT1. Count Rossi wouldn't have needed to ask the Alabama DMV to help license this Le Mans winner! (Original image courtesy Porsche)

BB-GT 196

Reference list

[1] L.J.K. Setright, "Great Engineers Part four." *CAR*, (February 1993): p115

[2] Christy Campbell, *The VW Beetle: A Celebration of the VW Bug*. (London: Hamlyn, 1990): p8

[3] *Porsche at 50 – Golden Anniversary Supplement, Classic & Sports Car*, April 1998, p109

[4] Campbell, op.cit. p10

[5] Jonathan Wood, "Classic Choice VW Beetle" *Thoroughbred & Classic Cars* (June 1992): p64

[6] Campbell, op.cit. p15

[7] *Porsche at 50 – Golden Anniversary Supplement*, op cit. p99

[8] Ibid. p108

[9] Jonathan Wood, *Great Marques Of Germany*. (London: Viscount Books, 1989): p154

[10] *Porsche at 50 – Golden Anniversary Supplement*, op cit. p91

[11] Wood, op cit. p158

[12] Pure Data, *GT Porsche*, (June 2015): p134

[13] Dennis Adler, "Nineteen Fifty Eight Sixteen Hundred Super Speedster – Porsche's "A" for effort" *European Car* (June 1994): p72

[14] Ibid. p73

[15] John Bentley (ed.), *All The World's Cars – 1954*. (New York: Cornell Publishing Corp, 1954): p80

[16] Ian Young, "Dream Machine" – *Thoroughbred & Classic Cars* (September 1994): p20

[17] Pat Braden, "Porsche Speedster 1600" *Euro Sport Car* (January 1995): p67

[18] Young, op cit. p21

[19] *Porsche at 50 – Golden Anniversary Supplement*, op cit. p115

[20] Wood, op cit. p174

[21] Malcolm McKay, "Sporting Stars." *Thoroughbred & Classic Cars* (August 1993): p48

[22] Andrew Bornhop, "Paul Frère: 50 Years At Le Mans." *Road & Track* (September 2001): p19

[22a] Dave Wallace, "Backstage Past Part 4: 1957." *Hot Rod Deluxe* (September 2018): p48

[23] Michael Sedgwick, *Classic Cars of the 1950s' and 1960s'*. (Twickenham: Tiger Books International, 1997): p184

[24] Brett Johnson, "1951 Porsche 356 Restoration Racer Part 5: Exorcising the rust devil." *European Car* (August 1994): p68

[25] Ibid. p69

[26] Jim Whipple (ed.) "All The 1964 Models." *Popular Mechanics CAR FACTS*. (New York: Popular Mechanics Company, 1963): p106

[27] "Greatest Sports Cars Of All Time." *Autocar* (2 June 1999): p113

[28] *Motorsport* (March 1985): p306

[29] Howard Walker, "Antiques Rodeo." *CAR* (April 1996): p99

[30] *Thoroughbred & Classic Cars* (November 1999): p195

[31] Andrew Frankel, "The Perfect Union." *GT Porsche* (June 2015): p17

[32] Sedgwick, op cit. p204

[33] Roy Kent, (ed.) *The Best Of CAR The '60s & '70s*. (London: Portico Books, 2007): p43

[34] Ibid. p44

[35] "Volkswagen Scirocco." *Road & Track* (February 1975): p34

[36] Graham Robson, T*he Illustrated Directory Of Classic Cars*. (London: Greenwich Editions, 2004): p392

[37] Peter Morgan, "Just Looking." *GT Porsche* (June 2015): p24

[38] "My Classic & I." *Classic & Sports Car* (July 1992): p210

[39] *Kent* (ed.), op cit. p44

[40] Ibid. p52

[41] Pure Data, *GT Porsche*, (June 2015): p135

[42] Marc Cranswick, *Porsche 928, 924, 944 And 968 The Front-Engined Sports Cars*. (Jefferson: McFarland Publishers, 2008): p6

[43] Mick Walsh, "Sugar Scoop." *Classic & Sports Car* (April 1998): p105

[44] Ibid. p107

[45] Wood, op.cit. p176

[46] Ibid. p176

[47] *Porsche at 50 – Golden Anniversary Supplement*, op cit. p99

[48] Randy Leffingwell, "Typ 911R." *European Car* (August 1994): p109

[49] Roy Kent (ed.), *The Best Of CAR The '60s & '70s*. (London: Portico Books, 2008): p96

[50] Graham Robson, *Classic & Sports Car A-Z Of Cars Of The 1970s*. (Devon: Bay View Books,1990):p177

[51] Ibid. p177

[52] *Autocar* (w/e 31 Aug 1974): p2

[53] *GT Porsche*, June 2015 p135

[54] Wood,op.cit. p166

[55] "Classic Choice." *Thoroughbred & Classic Cars* (September 1989): p49

[56] Kent (ed.),op.cit. p147

[57] Paul Walton, "Pushing The Limits Porsche 911 vs Alpine-Renault A310 V6." *Thoroughbred & Classic Cars* (November 2000): p72

[58] Jonathan Wood, "Classic Choice VW Beetle." *Thoroughbred & Classic Cars* (June 1992): p71

[59] Vic Elford, "The power of persuasion." *Motorsport* (June 2013): p61

[60] Pure Data, *GT Porsche*, (June 2015): p135

[61] Quentin Wilson, *Great Car.* (New York: Dorling Kindersley Publishing Inc, 2001): p450

[62] "Greatest Sports Cars Of All Time." *Autocar* (2 June 1999): p113

[63] Gavin Green, "Doing The Rounds." *CAR* (September 1985): p132

[64] Porsche at 50 – *Golden Anniversary Supplement*, op cit. p81

[65] Frank J.R. Incremona, "Remembered: Al Holbert – The friend behind the legend." *European* Car (June 1994): p64

[66] David Tremayne, "Lancashire hot shot." *Classic & Sports Car* (April 1998): p110

[67] Gavin Green, "63 Secondes du Mans." *CAR* (August 1998): p116

[68] Wood, op.cit. p183

[69] *Porsche at 50 – Golden Anniversary Supplement*, op cit. p88

[70] Ian Norris, "Le Mans." *Thoroughbred & Classic Cars* (June 1992): p98

[71] Gavin Green, "63 Secondes du Mans." *CAR* (August 1998): p116

[72] John Harvey, *Herbie Goes To Monte Carlo.* (London: New English Library / Times Mirror, 1978): p117

[73] Brian Palmer, "Test Match Seventies Coupés." *Thoroughbred & Classic Cars* (July 1992): p54

[74] James Sly, "Tech Porsche Procedure Up Front: 911, 912 and 914 anti-roll bar upgrade." *European Car* (August 1993): p70

[75] Jonathan Wood, "Classic Choice VW Beetle." *Thoroughbred & Classic Cars* (June 1992): p66

[76] Palmer, op cit. p60

[77] "Tech Letters." *European Car* (June 1994): p11

[78] Kent (ed.), op.cit. p159

[79] Graham Robson, *Classic & Sports Ca*r A-Z Of Cars Of The 1970s (Devon: Bay View Books,1990): p131

[80] Ibid. p132

[81] "World News." *European Car* (June 1994): p77

[82] Ray Hutton, "The Sport." *Autocar* (w/e 31 Aug 1974): p25

[83] Tony Dron, "White Heat." *Thoroughbred & Classic Cars* (June 1994): p36

[84] Ibid. p38

[85] Ibid. p38

[86] Jonathan Wood, *Great Marques Of Germany* (London: Viscount Books, 1989): p187

[87] Howard Walker, "Running Report Eleven Heaven." *Motor* (17 August 1985): p99

[88] Jay Jones, "911 Exhaust Upgrade." *European Car* (June 1994): p61

[89] *Popular Science*, Vol.227 No.2 (August 1985): p11

[90] Jerry Sloniger, "Ferry takes command again." *Motor* (16 May 1984): p24

[91] "Oracle." *CAR* (August 1984): p56

[92] "Screen Test." *Motor* (20 June 1981): p49

[93] Paul Guinness, "The Status Game: Think Of A Number." *Autocar* (6 February 1985): p36

[94] Michael Scarlett, "Scarlett's Selections." *Autocar* Road Test Yearbook 1986 (17/24 December 1986): p15

[95] Kieron Fennelly, "2.7 Carrera: An RS In Disguise." *Total 911* (issue no.166): p54

[96] John Simister, "Suffolk Punch." *Motor* (31 May 1986): p44

[97] "Alarm Call." *What Car?* (September 1987): p95

[98] "Timo Takes Them To Task." *Autocar* (5 June 1985): p17

[99] "Sport In Brief." *Autocar* (17/24 December 1986): p14

[100] "Porsche's '87 Stars." *Autocar* (3 September 1986): p6

[101] Dennis Adler, "Holbert 911" *European Car* (June 1994): p92

[102] Alex Forrest, "The Weekend West, West Wheels." *The West Australian* (22-23 November 2014): p92

[103] Tony Lewin, "Lifting The Lid." *What Car?* High-performance Special Supplement (June 1988): p18

[104] Peter Robinson, "The day the world changed…" *Wheels* (June 2012): p66

[105] Georg Kacher, "Geneva 88 Salon, and beyond." *CAR* (April 1988): p123

[106] James Ruppert, "Supercars For A Song." *CAR* (April 1993): p100

[107] Nigel Roebuck, "Thumbs Up." *CAR* (August 1994): p123

[108] Georg Kacher, "Waltzing Brunnhilde." *CAR* (March 1993): p83

[109] Jeff Hartman, "Begi Carrera 4 VATN Twin Turbo Porsche." *European Car* (August 1994): p100

[110] Chris Randall, "The Rarest Rennsport." *Total 911* (Issue 166): p32

[111] "Porsche to build the ultimate 4x4 road car." *Four Wheel Drive* (January 1985): p6

[112] Michael Stahl, "Awesome foursome." *Wheels* (June 2012): p160

[113] Bill Oursler, "Porsche 962 HR-1." *European Car* (June 1994): p69

[114] David Tremayne, "Lancashire hot shot." *Classic & Sports Car* (April 1998): p113

[115] "Small Porsche given top priority." *Autocar & Motor* (12 February 1992): p6

[116] "News Porsche's 911 plan." *CAR* (May 1993): p11

[117] L.J.K. Setright, "Any Other Business." *CAR* (April 1996): p105

[118] Matt Bishop, "Exactly How Fast…Are Formula One Cars?" *CAR* (September 1994): p50

[119] Richard Bremner, "Three steps to heaven." *CAR* (January 1995): p36

[120] Jason Barlow, "Pigs might fly." *CAR* (May 1998): p31

[121] Mike McCarthy, "Plastic Porsches." *Classic and Sports Car* (October 1993): p98

[122] Keith Seume, "Spawn of the Devin." *Thoroughbred & Classic Cars* (November 1999): p94

[123] *Frankel*, op cit. p22

[124] Pedr Davis & Tony Davis, *The Best Of Circles – Audi In Australia* (Blakehurst: Marque Publishing Co, 1992): p51

[125] Ben Oliver, "Every inch a Porsche." *CAR* (June 2017): p134

Bibliography

Adler, Dennis. "Holbert 911" *European Car*, June 1994.

Adler, Dennis. "Nineteen Fifty Eight Sixteen Hundred Super Speedster – Porsche's "A" for effort." *European Car*, June 1994.

"Alarm Call." *What Car?*, September 1987.

Autocar w/e 31 Aug 1974.

Bentley, John (ed.). *All The World's Cars – 1954*. New York: Cornell Publishing Corp, 1954

Bishop, Matt. "Exactly How Fast…Are Formula One Cars?" *CAR*, September 1994.

Bornhop, Andrew. "Paul Frère: 50 Years At Le Mans." *Road & Track*, September 2001.

Barlow, Jason. "Pigs might fly." *CAR*, May 1998.

Braden, Pat. "Porsche Speedster 1600." *Euro Sport Car*, January 1995.

Bremner, Richard. "Three steps to heaven." *CAR*, January 1995.

Campbell, Christy. *The VW Beetle: A Celebration of the VW Bug*. London: Hamlyn, 1990.

"Classic Choice." *Thoroughbred & Classic Cars*, September 1989.

Cranswick, Marc. *Porsche 928, 924, 944 And 968 The Front-Engined Sports Cars*. Jefferson: McFarland Publishers, 2008.

Davis, Pedr & Davis, Tony. *The Best Of Circles – Audi In Australia*. Blakehurst: Marque Publishing Co, 1992.

Dron, Tony. "White Heat." *Thoroughbred & Classic Cars*, June 1994.

Elford, Vic. "The power of persuasion." *Motorsport*, June 2013.

Fennelly, Kieron. "2.7 Carrera: An RS In Disguise." *Total 911* issue no.166.

Frankel, Andrew. "The Perfect Union." *GT Porsche*, June 2015.

Forrest, Alex. "The Weekend West, West Wheels." *The West Australian*, 22-23 November 2014.

"Greatest Sports Cars Of All Time." *Autocar*, 2 June 1999.

Green, Gavin. "Doing The Rounds." *CAR*, September 1985.

Green, Gavin. "63 Secondes du Mans." *CAR*, August 1998.

GT Porsche, June 2015.

Guinness, Paul. "The Status Game: Think Of A Number." *Autocar*, 6 February 1985.

Hartman, Jeff. "Begi Carrera 4 VATN Twin Turbo Porsche." *European Car*, August 1994.

Harvey, John. Herbie Goes To Monte Carlo. London: New English Library / *Times Mirror*, 1978.

Hutton, Ray. "The Sport." *Autocar*, w/e 31 Aug 1974.

Incremona, Frank J.R. "Remembered: Al Holbert – The friend behind the legend." *European Car*, June 1994.

Johnson, Brett. "1951 Porsche 356 Restoration Racer Part 5: Exorcising the rust devil." *European Car*, August 1994.

Jones, Jay. "911 Exhaust Upgrade." *European Car*, June 1994.

Kacher, Georg. "Geneva 88 Salon, and beyond." *CAR*, April 1988.

Kacher, Georg. "Waltzing Brunnhilde." *CAR*, March 1993.

Kent, Roy (ed.) *The Best Of CAR The '60s & '70s*. London: Portico Books, 2007.

Leffingwell, Randy. "Typ 911R." *European Car*, August 1994.

Lewin, Tony. "Lifting The Lid." *What Car? High-performance Special Supplement*, June 1988.

McCarthy, Mike. "Plastic Porsches." *Classic & Sports Car*, October 1993.

McKay, Malcolm. "Sporting Stars." *Thoroughbred & Classic Cars*, August 1993.

Morgan, Peter. "Just Looking." *GT Porsche*, June 2015.

Motorsport, March 1985.

"My Classic & I." *Classic & Sports Car*, July 1992.

"News Porsche's 911 plan." *CAR*, May 1993.

Norris, Ian. "Le Mans." *Thoroughbred & Classic Cars*, June 1992.

Oliver, Ben. "Every inch a Porsche." *CAR*, June 2017.

"Oracle." *CAR*, August 1984.

Oursler, Bill. "Porsche 962 HR-1." *European Car*, June 1994.

Palmer, Brian. "Test Match Seventies Coupés." *Thoroughbred & Classic Cars*, July 1992.

Popular Science, Vol.227 No.2 August 1985.

Porsche at 50 – Golden Anniversary Supplement, *Classic & Sports Car*, April 1998.

"Porsche to build the ultimate 4x4 road car." *Four Wheel Drive*, January 1985.

"Porsche's '87 Stars." *Autocar*, 3 September 1986.

Randall, Chris. "The Rarest Rennsport." *Total 911*, Issue 166.

Robinson, Peter. "The day the world changed…" *Wheels*, June 2012.

Robson, Graham. *Classic & Sports Car A-Z Of Cars Of The 1970s*. Devon: Bay View Books,1990.

Robson, Graham. *The Illustrated Directory Of Classic Cars*. London: Greenwich Editions, 2004.

Roebuck, Nigel. "Thumbs Up." *CAR*, August 1994.

Ruppert, James. "Supercars For A Song." *CAR*, April 1993.

Scarlett, Michael. "Scarlett's Selections." *Autocar* Road Test Yearbook 1986, 17/24 December 1986.

"Screen Test." *Motor*, 20 June 1981.

Sedgwick, Michael. *Classic Cars of the 1950s' and 1960s'*. Twickenham: Tiger Books International, 1997.

Setright, L.J.K. "Any Other Business." *CAR*, April 1996.

Setright, L.J.K. "Great Engineers Part four." *CAR*, February 1993.

Seume, Keith. "Spawn of the Devin." *Thoroughbred & Classic Cars*, November 1999.

Simister, John. "Suffolk Punch." *Motor*, 31 May 1986.

Sloniger, Jerry. "Ferry takes command again." *Motor*, 16 May 1984.

Sly, James. "Tech Porsche Procedure Up Front: 911, 912 and 914 anti-roll bar upgrade." *European Car*, August 1993.

"Small Porsche given top priority." *Autocar & Motor*, 12 February 1992.

"Sport In Brief." *Autocar*, 17/24 December 1986.

Stahl, Michael. "Awesome foursome." *Wheels*, June 2012.

"Tech Letters." *European Car*, June 1994.

Thoroughbred & Classic Cars, November 1999.

"Timo Takes Them To Task." *Autocar*, 5 June 1985.

Tremayne, David. "Lancashire hot shot." *Classic & Sports Car*, April 1998.

"Volkswagen Scirocco." *Road & Track*, February 1975.

Walker, Howard. "Antiques Rodeo." *CAR*, April 1996.

Walker, Howard. "Running Report Eleven Heaven." *Motor*, 17 August 1985.

Wallace, Dave. "Backstage Past Part 4: 1957." *Hot Rod Deluxe*, September 2018.

Walsh, Mick "Sugar Scoop." *Classic & Sports Car*, April 1998.

Walton, Paul. "Pushing The Limits Porsche 911 vs Alpine-Renault A310 V6." *Thoroughbred & Classic Cars*, November 2000.

Whipple, Jim (ed.) "All The 1964 Models." *Popular Mechanics CAR FACTS*. New York: Popular Mechanics Company, 1963.

Wilson, Quentin. *Great Car*. New York: Dorling Kindersley Publishing Inc, 2001.

Wood, Jonathan. "Classic Choice VW Beetle." *Thoroughbred & Classic Cars*, June 1992.

Wood, Jonathan. *Great Marques Of Germany*. London: Viscount Books, 1989.

"World News." *European Car*, June 1994.

Young, Ian. "Dream Machine." *Thoroughbred & Classic Cars*, September 1994.

Appendix A
Porsche quartet specifications

1953 Porsche 356 1500 Super Coupe

Price: $4584

Engine: Flat-four OHV 1488cc, light alloy heads & crankcase, 8.2:1 CR, 2 x Solex 40 PBIC carbs, 70bhp @ 5000rpm, 80lb/ft @ 3600rpm

Dimensions: Length: 155.5in, width: 65.4in, height: 51.2in

Weight: 1784lb

Gearbox: four-speed all synchro (Porsche patented baulk ring synchromesh), 0.82 overdrive fourth, 4.38 final drive.

Suspension: Front: independent – trailing arms, transverse torsion bars, telescopic dampers, swaybar.
Rear: independent – swinging half axles, transverse torsion bars, telescopic dampers.

Rims & tires: 16x3.25in & 16x5.00in tires

Brakes: 4x11in (280mm) drums

Top speed: 108mph

0-62mph: 13.5 seconds

Fuel economy: 29mpg overall (US gallon, 13.7-gallon tank)

(*Performance/economy data: manufacturer figures*)

The 356 was the first car to bear the Porsche moniker. The 1500 was the first 356 to break 100mph.

It was all the realization of Dr Porsche and Ferry's sports car dream. The 356 maintained American sports car interest, was a classic in its lifetime, and notched up a 76,302 production total!

1978 Porsche 930

Price: $34,000

Engine: Flat-six SOHC 3299cc, light alloy heads & crankcase, 7.0:1 CR, Bosch K-jetronic fuel-injection, KKK Turbo (11.8psi max boost), air-to-air intercooler, 261bhp @ 5500rpm, 291lb/ft @ 4000rpm

Dimensions: Length: 168.9in, width: 63.4in, height: 52.3in

Weight: 2844lb

Gearbox: four-speed all synchro, 0.62 fourth, 4.22 final drive.

Suspension: Front: independent – MacPherson struts, parallel torsion bars, lower wishbones, tube shocks, swaybar. Rear: independent – semi trailing arms, transverse torsion bars, tube shocks, swaybar.

Rims & tires: 16x7in (front) 16x8in (rear); 205/55VR-16 (front) 225/50VR-16 (rear)

Brakes: 4x12in vented disks

Top speed: 165mph

0-60mph: 4.9 seconds

Fuel economy: 15.25mpg overall

(*Data: Car and Driver, April 1978*)

When the 3-liter 930 first hit America in 1976, it had 228 horses and no intercooler.

Now, it had an upgraded motor, more performance, but only slightly less turbo lag. With only 350 imported, exclusivity was assured, leaving onlookers to wonder which was bigger, the owner's bank account or ego?!

1986 Porsche 911 Cabriolet

Price: $36,450

Engine: Flat-six SOHC 3164cc, light alloy heads & crankcase, 9.5:1 CR, Bosch LE-jetronic fuel-injection, 200bhp @ 5900rpm, 185lb/ft @ 4800rpm

Dimensions: Length: 168.9in, width: 65in, height: 51.6in

Weight: 2750lb

Gearbox: five-speed overdrive (915) all synchro 0.79 fifth, 3.86 final drive.

Suspension: Front: independent – MacPherson struts, parallel torsion bars, lower wishbones, tube shocks, swaybar. Rear: independent – semi trailing arms, transverse torsion bars, tube shocks, swaybar.

Rims & tires: cast alloy 16x6in (front) 16x7in (rear); 205/55VR-16 (front) 225/50VR-16 (rear)

Brakes: 4 x vented disks – 11.1in (front) 11.4in (rear)

Top speed: 130mph+ (estimated)

0-60mph: 5.7 seconds

Fuel economy: 18.6mpg overall

(Data: Road & Track, January 1986)

Your favorite 911 ragtop was back, with a smog-law-friendly 3.2-liter flat-six called Carrera, which gave up little to its Euro counterpart.
　　The price was high, but so were the driving thrills and owner cachet pleasure. Possibly the ultimate '80s pose machine, but beware, that ultimate oversteer could still knock your Ray Bans off!

1995 Porsche 911 Carrera

Price: $59,900

Engine: Flat-six SOHC 3600cc, light alloy heads & crankcase,11.3:1 CR, Bosch Motronic M52 fuel-injection, 270bhp @ 6100rpm, 243lb/ft @ 5000rpm

Dimensions: Length: 167.7in, width: 68.3in, height: 51.8in

Weight: 3064lb

Gearbox: six-speed all synchro, 0.92 fifth, 0.78 sixth 3.44 final drive.

Suspension: Front: independent – MacPherson struts, parallel torsion bars, lower wishbones, tube shocks, swaybar. Rear: independent – Cast alloy multilink LSA, transverse arms, lower toe control links (928 Weissach axle), tube shocks, swaybar.

Rims & tires: 16x7in (front), 16x9in (rear); 205/55ZR-16 (front) 245/45ZR-16 (rear)

Brakes: fixed four-piston vented & cross drilled disks 11.97in (front) 11.77in (rear)

Top speed: 168mph

0-60mph: 5.4 seconds

Fuel economy: 15mpg city, 23mpg highway, 18mpg overall (EPA) *(Data: Porsche/EPA)*

Final manifestation of the air-cooled wonder that started as the 1963 901. Still with SOHC flat-six, but minus the pontoon fenders, plus the 928's rear wheel-steer Weissach Axle. The 911's positives always outweighed the negatives. Autocrossers could option the 17in wheel/tires for over 1.0g on the skidpad. City slickers could specify the Tiptronic automatic. Truly a car for all reasons.

Appendix B
VW/Porsche specials – Apal & Devin

The Apal of Pery's eye & Devilish Devin
Frankfurt's Walter Glockler wasn't the only one concocting interesting machines. Go beyond West Germany to Belgium and a gentleman called Edmond Pery would help you out. As ever, all plans were aided by Dr Porsche's Type 1 Bug pan frame design. Just add a body, and you were good to go! In this case, it was the fiberglass Apal body on a VW Beetle base. Like Porsche, Apal was located near the parts source. Being in close proximity to the German border got one Wolfsburg building blocks. Pery was good friends with Belgium's Beetle importer. So from 1962, Apal was commercially solid.

Using its high quality body, an effective monocoque was created. Top, bottom and interior sections equaled a stiff structure. Using the hi po Okrasa 1300 flat-four and low weight, Apals were fast. It didn't stop there: that Belgian importer had Porsche contacts too. The next Apal seed was planted on a Porsche 356 base, and utilized a Porsche Super 90 engine. Of course, a 356 weighed 2100lb. This was portly next to Apal's 1430lb. Little wonder the Apal was the 1964 Belgian Rally Championship winner.

To drive the longer wheelbase of the Bug platform made for more secure handling and less twitchy oversteer than a Porsche. This car drove like a Beetle and 356 cross, according to *Classic and Sports Car's* Mike McCarthy. Looks wise, the Apal resembled a 356 and 911 blend that was stretched. Apals were well made and a commercial success: 150 cars with 50 having Porsche power. Unfortunately, a fire destroyed the factory in 1965. Edmond Pery turned to Formula Vee, and then very successfully to VW-based beach buggies. Pery was running a winning bath and jacuzzi business by the early 1990s. Is there anything fiberglass can't do?! However, he still got the occasional visit from an owner seeking a service for their beloved Apal.[121]

The experience of Bill Devin, shows how hard it can be to produce a sports car dream. Located mostly in El Monte California between 1955-64, Devin Enterprises made high quality fiberglass bodies, and sold them as kits. In the portfolio were also auto accessories and parts to help complete a custom sports car project. Devin Enterprises even made turn key completed cars. It all started when Bill Devin sold his Ferrari 250MM and took a Deutsch-Bonnet (DB) Le Mans Barquette as part payment.

The DB acquisition inspired Devin to combine his own-design ladder frame chassis, custom body and a Panhard engine/front-drive transaxle to create the Devin Panhard. Through his ingenuity this may have been one of the first toothed timing belt applications in the world. It probably was in North America. From this starting point, Devin became famous for his fiberglass bodies. For a start he used fiberglass cloth on the outside for a superb finish. For another, his different sized mold combinations were adaptable to variably sized base cars, from small imports to large domestics.

Soon, Devin Enterprises was the world's biggest aftermarket fiberglass body maker. His kits were sold worldwide. Notable car illuminaries used his Devin bodies to create their custom specials, but Devin had a Porsche connection. He also had a view to production sports cars, not unlike Dr Porsche himself.

Actor Richard Boone owned a Porsche Speedster, customized by Bill Devin. Boone wrote about this car in the May 1958 issue of *Motor Trend.* Sadly, the car was subsequently fire damaged, and suspected lost from the actor's home, while he was away filming.

Bill Devin's Devin D was a new 1958 model that combined his own fiberglass body design and chassis, with VW and Porsche hardware. On this 82in chassis was modified VW front suspension of transverse torsion bars and trailing links, with single coilover dampers and trailing arms out back. It was all similar to an early '60s Formula Vee open wheeler, and handling was just like that. Devin Ds were built to take a VW four-speed, and it didn't matter if one used a VW or Porsche flat-four. Today, any Porsche hardware used, especially the presence of a Porsche motor, makes a Devin D collectible and valuable.

The basic Devin D kit body and frame retailed for $895. A more complete example, with laminated safety glass windshield, folding soft top, side curtains, full carpeting, chromed bumpers/brake & fuel lines, and operational headlights/tail lights/parking lights/ turn signals, cost $1495. A fully assembled turnkey VW-powered Devin D cost $2950, with the 1582cc Porsche version at $3350. This was big money by late '50s standards, but commensurate with Devin's high quality, and there was a lot of Porsche stuff within.

46 Devin Ds were produced, a popular model for Devin Enterprises. In November 1999, *Thoroughbred & Classic Cars* featured a restored Porsche-engined Devin D. In the article written by VW guru Keith

Seume, the extent of Porsche-included hardware was described. There were Porsche pre-356A dashboard gages, warning lights, and 356A brakes, plus bell-crank throttle linkage. The steering column and box were 356 in origin. The steering column was custom extended to suit the Devin's lower and further back driving position. After all, the Devin D was a pure two-seater.

There was also a pre-356A reversing mirror, mounted on a Devin made bracket. As part of the subject car's restoration during the mid to late '90s, the genuine Les Leston steering wheel came from Mr Devin … from his workshop shelf! The car's period-correct Mobil Pegasus logo strikes a chord with vintage Porsche hot rodders.

The feature car was completed in February 1998, and participated in the Monterey Classics at Laguna Seca. Owner Steve Herron got a class award for performance and presentation, winning a watch. The restored car had 356A aluminum drums all around, but stronger 356B front spindles, and 5.5J 356 steel rims, along with Dunlop racing tires. It made good use of this hardware when racing at the 1998

Edmond Pery's early '60s Apal was a low volume, fiberglass-bodied Belgian sports car. In this case, it used a Porsche 356 chassis and Super 90 1600 flat-four. (Courtesy Thesupermat)

Monterey Show. The field sported 14 or 15 Porsche 550 Spyders, 550 RSKs and Brian Redman in a two-liter flat-eight RS61. In spite of such star power, Steve Herron's Devin D finished mid-field.[122]

Also pretty much his own car was the ready to go Devin SS (Super Sport). Long before anyone said DeLorean DMC-12, the Devin SS commenced in Northern Ireland. Two textile engineers, who happened to be racing enthusiasts, also had a dream of building their own sports car. Noel Hillis owned the Belfast business Devonshire Engineering, and his employee Malcolm MacGregor designed the chassis. They both called upon Bill Devin for advice.

Devin came to Belfast to look over the plan in 1957. The three guys struck a deal: the MacGregor chassis would be used by the new 1959 Devin SS. To productionize the proposal, some ladder frame chassis changes were made, and a Chevy 283 V8/ BW T10 four-speed replaced the prototype's Jag XK I6/Moss four-speed. The Irish-built rolling chassis was shipped to El Monte, California where the completed car sold for the kingly sum of $5950. Sales distribution was by Evans Industries.

The concept and performance predated the AC Cobra. Britain's *Motor* magazine tested both in 1959; the Devin SS's top speed, 0-60mph, and quarter mile stats were 131mph, 5.7 seconds, and 14 seconds respectively. The same journal got 140mph, 5.5 seconds, and 13.9 seconds out of a '65 Cobra 289.

Unfortunately, Chevrolet didn't get behind the Devin like Ford did with the Cobra. The reason was the Chebby boys already had their plastic two-seater: the Corvette.

Problems with the Irish-supplied chassis situation led to Devin Enterprises using its own design replacement. The big problem was the prices charged by component suppliers. The ten grand 1960 Devin SS priced out the same as a specialized Jaguar D-Type! So, sadly, the Devin SS ended in 1960. Devin then tried his Devin C. This was a Corvair-engined version of the Devin D. As the Corvair motor and options improved, so did the Devin C. Devin Enterprises used a similar sales arrangement to its Devin D.

The Devin C's success led to plans for the more refined Devin GT. One car was built and shown at the 1964 New York Auto Show. However, Devin lacked the funds to build the 60 cars ordered by Imported Cars of Greenwich Connecticut, so the plan stopped there along with Devin Enterprises. The Devin example shows there was an American demand for a custom, bespoke sports car upscale of an MG, Triumph or Corvette, but below a Ferrari or Maserati. The revived Avanti II comes to mind. However, a company has to produce, distribute and sell such cars. This requires great design and good business, which probably explains why Porsche and Ferry succeeded in '50s America while others did not.

American Bill Devin offered his Porsche-like Devin sports car that used Porsche 356A parts, a Porsche flat-four... or Chevy 283 V8! (Marc Cranswick)

Appendix C
Porsche + Audi – a century of association

A Formula One introduction

Geographically, Porsche of Stuttgart and Audi of Ingolstadt aren't that far from each other. However, during the last century the two companies have been even closer than that, on occasion. Today, they have never been closer, but it all started in 1934, in the fast and furious world of Grand Prix racing. With concerns over how fast the Formula One cars were getting, the powers that be considered a 750kg maximum weight limit an excellent idea. The constructors wouldn't get up to too much mischief with that. However, it was the only rule set, and inventive minds soon circumvented the 'go slow' plan.

With a view to restoring national pride, rebuilding the country from the economic depths of the 1920s, Chancellor Adolf Hitler offered a prize to the German company that could come up with a World Championship-winning car. It was thought Mercedes would be a shoe-in, but they hadn't considered the genius of Dr Porsche or his recently formed design consultancy. Dr Porsche thought a mid-engined V16 would have many advantages. Traction would be excellent, and weight would be less due to no driveshaft. There would be better aero from a smaller frontal area, plus a lower polar moment of inertia would make the racer more agile. Weight distribution would be less affected by a changing fuel load.

Many of these good points would show up later on Porsche road cars and racers. In the meantime, Dr Porsche took his idea to Auto Union. Auto Union was much smaller than Mercedes, but had

a luxury car portfolio and that four interlocking rings logo. Horch, Wanderer, DKW and Audi had banded together for economic survival due to the Depression. Then, just prior to the formation of Auto Union, one of the first jobs done by the Porsche design consultancy was the Type 8 Wanderer. Porsche came up with a large 3.5-liter, straight-eight luxury car design, with fastback styling for the Wanderer. However, in the Auto Union family the big car role was given to Horch, so the Type 8 never went into series production. That said, Dr Porsche did use the Type 8 prototype as personal transport for a spell.

Hitler also heard about Porsche's racing car proposal for a radical mid-engined, supercharged V16, all-independent suspension racer with five-speed gearbox. The result would be a split prize of 300,000 Reichmarks each, to encourage competition between Auto Union and Daimler-Benz. In the 1934 Grand Prix season, Hans Stuck dominated with his 4.4-liter V16 Auto Union. Mercedes won out in 1935, its car also coming from a Porsche design. 1936 saw Bernd Rosemeyer super dominant in his Auto Union Type C, with 600bhp V16 motor. He won every championship race except Monaco, and more besides; a supremely talented racer, capable of taming a powerful, oversteer-prone wild beast. Rosemeyer died trying to break a speed record on the autobahn. In 1938, Tazio Nuvolari took Rosemeyer's place at the wheel of the relatively more sedate 3-liter Auto Union Type D V12. The 'D' stood for the racer's de Dion rear suspension; Dr Porsche was weary of the swing axle even back then! The Type D's designer, Robert Eberan von Eberhorst, had a hand in the V1 flying bomb. After the war, he did the Aston Martin DB3, and had an influence on the Porsche 356.[123]

Selling Porsche 914s & Audi 100s
The next time Porsche crossed paths with Auto Union, or Audi as it was now called, was 1970s America. VW had bought the sole postwar survivor of Auto Union, DKW, from Mercedes in 1964. VW got Audi's intellectual property and a new DKW family car design called F102. Wolfsburg combined both to create the winning 1965 Audi 60, giving VW a luxury brand it has used ever since. Eventually, related to this, was the joint venture concern VW-Porsche VG GmbH, starting in April 1969 to handle sales and distribution of the Porsche 914 and 911 worldwide.

On October 1, 1969, the Porsche-Audi dealer network was also established. Prior to this, VW dealers had also tended to sell Porsches. Now, VW wanted to formalize things in an upscale manner, with separate Porsche-Audi dealers in North America.

A VW dealer had to choose between staying just a VW dealer, or spending $250,000 on a special Porsche-Audi showroom. The latter would sell Porsche 911s, 914s and the also new 1970 MY Audi 100.

In Can-Am racing, the 917PA (Porsche-Audi) 917 Spyder was raced by Jo Siffert with limited success. The 917PA did help inspire the safer-handling 917K, and was tested with a 750 horse 6.6-liter flat-sixteen!

VW wanted upscale Audi, in order to battle further upscale, using the Porsche shield. Historically, Ferry Porsche had tested the 1930s Auto Union mid-engined machine at the Nürburgring. He came up with an LSD to help the racer handle. The Porsche-Audi arrangement would continue through to the end of 1984. Audi was making the snazzy 100S Coupe at the time, and hoped to sell another eye-candy coupe off of the joint dealership.

The car in question was project EA-425, which became the Porsche 924. Originally, the 924 was going to be an Audi, taking over from the Karmann Ghia and complementing the 914. VW knew about the Super Porsche 928 that Zuffenhausen was working on. Wolfsburg wanted a smaller, cheaper version of that V8 dream car. Ferry's nephew, Ferdinand Piëch, was at VW-Audi at this time. Piëch

had left his Porsche post of technical director in 1971, after making Porsche a sports car racing 'King of the Track.' He thought VW-Audi parts and Porsche sports car design know-how would make the new Audi a winner. It was a commercial winner, just not for Audi.

An exchange of ideas & parts
Even though VW's new boss, the pipe-favoring Toni Schmucker, canned the planned Audi, the new 924 was built at the Audi-NSU Neckarsulm factory. So was the 924's successor, the 944. At least until the end of 1990 MY, when Porsche took over production. This was the plant that built the NSU Ro80, and would go on to make the Audi R8 sports car. Porsche was forced for 2 years to use VW-Audi parts for the 924 and 944, even after the two-year agreement VW contractual condition. Initially, Porsche had to follow this to get its own 924 design back! From '80 MY, regular 924s and 944s used the overdrive five-speed Audi box, and automatic versions before and after that date used Audi slush boxes too.

During development of the original Audi Quattro, a Porsche 928 was on hand, as was ex-Porsche engineer Jorg Bensinger. It was at Hockenheim in April 1978 that Bensinger and Walter Treser took turns to push the 240 horse 928 and non-intercooled 170bhp Quattro, using an Audi 200 Turbo motor, around the track. In the dry, the 928 had a slight lap time edge.[124]

It also shouldn't be forgotten that the Tiptronic name, and separate sequential shift gate design used by Audi from the mid '90s, originated on the 1990 964 Porsche 911. Porsche knew stuff about active autos – remember the Sportomatic? It seemed many couldn't ignore the high-performance knowledge of Zuffenhausen. Spanish automaker Seat needed efficient four-cylinder engines for the '80s Ibiza and Malaga. Mercedes entrusted Porsche to build its high-performance W124 500E in the 1990s. It was just too specialized for Mercedes, who didn't have AMG in-house at the time.

The other Audi that Porsche built – Audi 80 RS2
Similarly, for the swansong to the Audi 80 range, and start of the marque's RS (Renn Sport – Racing Sport) sub brand, Ingolstadt turned to Zuffenhausen. In fact, in the early '80s the original Audi 80 Quattro was developed at the Porsche Weissach tech center. The super high-performance 1994 Audi 80 RS2 Avant was a hotter version of the

Dr Porsche speaking to Bernd Rosemeyer, seated in the 1937 Auto Union Type C V16 Streamliner.
(Courtesy Porsche)

in-house 80 S2 cars. It took Porsche to go all the way. Porsche took the turbo inline five-cylinder 20-valver from 230bhp to 315bhp. Porsche fitted a bigger KKK turbo-making 20psi, better injectors/intercooler, sportier cams, special intake and exhaust manifolds and custom did the car's Bosch ECU. The motor was built at the VW Salzgitter plant, where a Porsche script cam cover was added, and rightly so.

More than engine work, Porsche added 993 911 side mirrors, front indicators and fog lights, plus 17in rims and tires from the respected Porsche 968 Clubsport. If that wasn't enough, Porsche built this Audi too! The figures were 0-62mph in 5.4 seconds, and an unlimited top speed of 275kph. 0-50kph took 1.5 seconds, faster than a McLaren F1. The fastest wagon in the world? No wonder Porsche added its Brembo 322mm brakes, with white Porsche script on red calipers … sweet!

The madness of King Wendelin
In the January 1968 issue of *Motor Trend*, concerning the 'European Hotline' section, the journal mistakenly said VW owned Porsche! This caused O Erich Filius, the Executive VP of Porsche of America Corp (Teaneck, NJ) to write to the magazine, and state that Porsche was still independent. *Motor Trend* misinterpreted a R&D contract bestowed upon Porsche by VW. The journal's editors were rather embarrassed, and printed the retraction: "Porsche still carries its own banner." (*Motor Trend,* March 1968, Interchange – the last word, p98). Then again, perhaps *Motor Trend* had a premonition.

Above: The Porsche+Audi arrangement was already visible in the promotion of these 1971 2.2-liter 911s. It was part of VW's plan to give Audi an upscale image. (Courtesy Porsche)

Right/above right: Hidemi Aoki with the 1997 Audi A6 2.8 30v. This car, and the Porsche 924/944, were all built at the Audi-NSU Neckarsulm factory. Porsche's 924 contract saved Neckarsulm from closure. (Both courtesy www.nepoeht.com)

The Porsche+Audi North American dealer network lasted from 1970 to the end of 1984.
(Courtesy Ms Reiko Takao)

Since the VW buyout of Porsche, Audi has become an in-house Porsche rival, the Q5 and Macan are brothers under the skin. Hidemi Aoki is posing with the VW Golf R's twin, the Audi RS3.
(Courtesy www.nepoeht.com &
www.audicentreperth.com.au)

Through all of the above, VW and Porsche were independent companies, but this was about to change. On September 26, 2005, Porsche planned to increase its stake in VW from 5% to 20%. This was to prevent a hostile takeover of VW that would have disrupted Porsche's development partner and parts supply deals. Remember when Porsche had to pay more for 914 bodies?

Well, the 914 was long gone, so too the 924 and its descendants, but the Porsche Cayenne was afoot. This SUV had put Porsche back in the black. It was done with VW help, and used over 25% VW parts. If only Porsche had stopped at this point. Unfortunately, Ferry's youngest son and then current Porsche CEO, Wendelin Wiedeking, had a plan. Wolfgang Porsche was Porsche chairman at the time, and Wiedeking had been CEO since 1993. The latter had guided Porsche from near bankruptcy and an attempted Toyota buyout, and through the much needed Boxster to the profit land of SUVs in the 2000s. Wolfgang and Wendelin felt Ferdinand Piëch was wasting VW money by pursuing the luxury angle with the Phaeton and Bentley brand. They wanted to buy out VW and run it right. To do this they purchased VW shares, which needed money, so they got Porsche into hock up to its eyeballs. Come the global financial crisis of 2008 and things turned sour. Some of Porsche's investment bets hadn't paid off.

As The Guardian's Gwyn Topham said, "the Beetle's maker will swallow up the Spyders." That's what happened when Wolfgang and Wendelin fell short. Porsche was now 10 billion Euros in debt, and still failed to reach the 75% shareholder majority required for a corporate takeover. Porsche's October 2008 buyout attempt failed. VW happened to have the amount Porsche was in the hole for, so bought them out! At this hour, VW bought 49.9% of Porsche, and purchased the remaining 50.1% on Thursday July 5, 2012. Installment number two cost 4.46 billion. You have to sell a few diesels to get that much foldin' fun! CEO Wiedeking had appealed to Qatari investors to get Porsche over the 75% line, but no dice. Ferdinand Piëch promised the Qataris Bugatti Veyron discounts, so they invested in VW instead. Wendelin stepped down from the CEO position in 2009, and Wolfgang moved on too. Golden parachutes for one and all. Crafty Ferdinand Piëch had done it again! He then went on to dodge 'Dieselgate' and *CAR*'s Gavin Green reckoned he might yet step back into the fray to save VW's bacon one more time.

The long-term consequence of Porsche being a sub brand, along with Bentley, Audi, et al, was hinted at by *CAR*'s Ben Oliver. The upcoming launch of the VW-built Porsche Macan saw Porsche people say how many changes they had to make to the Audi Q5, to create the Macan SUV. Audi boss Rupert Stadler contacted Porsche CEO Matthias Muller to stop the anti Audi talk.[125] It is hard to imagine VW's Professor Heinz Nordhoff telling this to his friend Ferry Porsche, but then again, that was the era of the gentlemen's agreement.

Below: The Porsche connection lifted Audi's North American profile. (Courtesy Porsche)

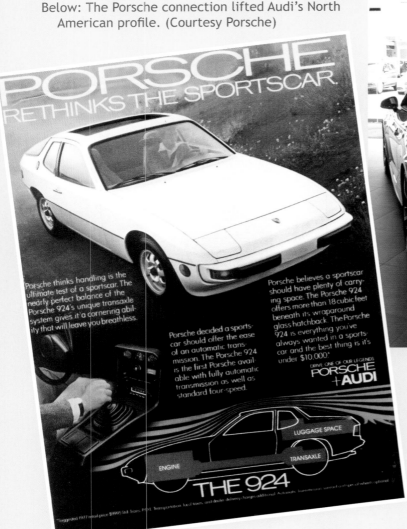

Dr Porsche designed the 1930s Auto Union grand prix racer, a famous flyer with Audi's four ringed logo. Today, at a stretch, the Audi RS5 could be a Cayman alternative. (Courtesy www.nepoeht.com & www.audicentreperth.com.au)

Appendix D

The grand experiment – front-engined Porsches 1975-1995

Porsche 924 – a 1970s 356

In February 1976, *Road Test* magazine said how much positive interest there was in the new red 924 they were driving. In Porsche-popular California, there was usually an escort of five 911s, with their drivers checking out the new set of wheels. The faithful knew a cheaper version of the long promised V8 supercar was in the works. However, they didn't think the 924 would come out before the 928.

The fuel crisis and ensuing recession being what it was, meant temporary freezes on the Porsche 928, Mercedes 450SEL 6.9 and BMW e23 7 series. The price-leader 924 was more appropriate, and the first in more ways than one. At the September 1975 Frankfurt International Auto Show, the 924 was the first front-engined, water-cooled Porsche … ever! Like Volkswagen, Porsche was answering the call of different times. A need for interior space efficiency, proposed federal safety tests, noise pollution regulations, comfort and Japanese competition. Yes, like VW, the rear-engined, air-cooled ways didn't seem relevant to the 1970s, but Porsche was in for a surprise.

The Porsche-designed 924 came with 911 sourced buckets. This '78 924 has the optional 911 close ratio five-speed. (Courtesy Benny Proot)

Until the 1982 944 arrived, the 924 was judged Porsche's best handler. (Courtesy John Gacioch)

Whereas VW was congratulated on its move into modernity, with ensuing commercial and critical kudos, Porsche AG was not. Sure, the new cars were competent, well engineered and built, efficient and superb handlers, but, well, they weren't very Porsche. They didn't look or sound like a Porsche because by 1975 many folks had an idea on what a Porsche was or should be. That is, a rear-engined, air-cooled wundercar with 200 or more horses, and just one name ... 911.

Porsche was its own worst enemy. Although Doctor Porsche and his design consultancy had done all kinds of things, when the public thought Porsche, they thought 911. However, there were many things about the newbies that were very Porsche. For a start, Porsche designed all the cars. These weren't badge-engineered SUVs in drag. Even Project EA-425, which became the 924, had much in common with the Porsche 356. Like that revered ride, the 924 made great use of VW parts to get going, including Beetle parts!

The 924's Porsche connection list was lengthy: rear transaxle, console oil temp gage, anti clockwise tach, 911 seats, optional dogleg five-speeder, Super Beetle semi trailing arm rear suspension, optional 911 leather clad 3 spoke steering wheel, Le Mans racing success, Carrera variants, and Porsche-designed engine (924S). But you know what? It didn't look like a Porsche ...

With VW's early '70s corporate problems, Rudolf Leiding's successor Toni Schmucker said no thanks to EA-425. The new VW Scirocco would do just fine, thank you kindly. So Porsche bought back its own work – with conditions. For two years Porsche had to buy parts for the 924 from VW. Poor thing, it needed the money! From that point, Porsche would be free to substitute more of its stuff, and they did. To make the whole project cost effective, in economies of scale, the 924 was built at Audi-NSU's Neckarsulm plant. However, somehow Porsche quality was maintained.

The Bermuda Triangle of quality control
NSU Ro80s weren't the most reliable cars, and '70s Audis gave North American owners some headaches too. In a Dasher/Fox February 1976 survey, *Road & Track* mentioned the reliability shortfall and poor

Whether it was the SCCA's GT-2 & GT-3 or Le Mans, the 944 had perfect balance. (Courtesy John Gacioch)

reported service that Audi owners received. This was odd, because in North America Porsche-Audi dealers involved one set of mechanics servicing Porsches and Audis. The 911/914 owners almost always reported good service. It seemed this high quality carried through to the Neckarsulm factory. Even though Porsche 924s were being made alongside Audi 100s, the 924s always had a solid reputation. The Porsche coupe did well in ADAC German motoring organization durability surveys.

Perhaps respect for the Porsche shield made the assembly workers more careful? Maybe Porsche secured the good VW/Audi parts for the 924? Whatever the reason, the results spoke for themselves. *Road & Track* drove 100,000 miles in a VW Rabbit diesel. After three and a quarter years, ending in 1981, many things had gone wrong on the Rabbit, beyond normal wear and tear. The UK's *Motor* magazine observed a 100,000-mile Porsche 924 in 1987. Admittedly this was a careful one-owner car, with seven years needed to reach 100,000 miles. However, little went wrong beyond fuel pump related problems. The journal tested this

seven-year-old for 0-60mph and top speed. It did 9.3 seconds and 121.8mph respectively. When the same magazine tested a brand new 924 in 1979, it achieved 9.3 seconds and 121.3mph; very consistent, very Porsche.

The VW/Audi two-liter may have had the aural qualities of an under sink garbage disposal unit, but it was tough. With turbocharger it could also be powerful. Just three years post launch, Zuffenhausen had a 924 Turbo ready. In Porsche tradition it was thoroughly developed and *Autocar*'s figures for 0-60mph, top speed and fuel economy for the 170bhp 924 Turbo, 180bhp 911SC and 240bhp 928 showed little brother to be a bargain. All three coupés had Porsche's dogleg five-speed and achieved respective stats of: 6.9 seconds, 142mph, and 19.8mpg; 6.5 seconds, 141mph, 17.9mpg; and 7.5 seconds, 142mph, and 17.1mpg. The 911SC was approximately three quarters of the 928's price, and the 924 Turbo just two thirds, or 15 per cent cheaper than a 911SC and cheaper to run.

With Pasha upholstery, anti-clockwise tach and 911 seats, steering wheel and five-speed, the blown

In the guise of the 924 GTP, the Porsche 944-came seventh outright at 1981's Le Mans 24 Hour Race.
(Courtesy John Gacioch)

924 was a hoot! Porsche added an intercooler and more refinements to create the 1980 210 horse 924 Carrera GT homologation special. With FIA rules being rewritten towards production car based racers, the new Carrera typified the traditional thinking of race what you make. Not forgetting win on Sunday, sell on Monday.

Porsche's Helmuth Bott and CEO Peter Schutz were both pro 911, but also believed in keeping a link between race and road cars. So it was that the 924 Carrera GT came sixth, 12th and 13th outright at the 1980 Le Mans 24-Hour race. In the June 20 issue of *Motor*, Jerry Sloniger said that in West Germany people were lining up to pay the equivalent of £23,000, to get one of the 50 homologation requirement 924 GTS racers. The new coupe, with 930 vented and cross drilled disk brakes, was intended to take over from the 934 in Group 4.

Porsche had achieved dominance in IMSA, but hadn't looked at the SCCA production car side of things until the end of the '70s. This omission was quickly corrected when the Porsche 924 elbowed out British and Japanese machinery in 1980. Doc Bundy was racing co-ordinator for Al Holbert's Porsche-Audi-VW dealership. He won the 1980 SCCA D-Production title, and came second to 924 driver Tom Brennan in 1981, third place went to Donald Istook in a Porsche 911T!

944 – a worthy addition

1981's 924 GTP, with 2.5-liter 16-valve DOHC inline four-cylinder, managed seventh outright at Le Mans in 1981, when driven by Jurgen Barth and Walter Rohrl. This was a curtain raiser to 924 version 2.0, or Porsche 944. This new machine was basically the 924 Carrera's flared body in steel, plus that car's chassis and brakes, along with half the 928's V8. 137mph on just 163bhp was very efficient, and very Porsche. The critics generally liked the 924, but really liked the 944. The twin counter rotating balancer shaft 2.5-liter inline four, replete with Porsche script cam cover, was Porsche enough for them. In the wake of the second fuel crisis, this flared arch car with Fuchs, and smooth economical four banger, did 0-60mph in under 7.5 seconds sans turbo.

If the Jag XJ-S V12 was the wrong car for the times, the 944 was the right ride. It built on the sales success of the 924, which had reached 100,000 units by 1981. However, the 944 still wasn't a 911, and comments were made by press and public alike. As with *Autocar*'s 944 used car survey 'Novelty Value' from June 24, 1987, "Porsche purists probably wouldn't dream of owning a front-engined coupe …" They went on to admit the 944 was great value, very popular and well liked.

Then there was *Motor Trend*'s December 1984 944 owner survey, where one participant said, "My fiancée left me and I wanted to console myself with a Porsche; the 944 was all I could afford." And surely some Boxster owners buy their cars because they can't afford a 911. Even so, the Boxster and 944 can and should be enjoyed in their own right. A 1982 944 with Pasha, Fuchs, anti-clockwise tach and brawny 2.5L four-pot, had its own charm. Gripping the 911-sourced three-spoker was fun, and one needn't fear sudden oversteer.

Such fine balance, such great basis for higher performance. Porsche CEO Peter Schutz was behind 1985's 944 Turbo, subsequent convertible and more variants, like the collectible Silver Rose. The 944 even gave its 2.5 atmo motor to the 924, creating the 924S. Where the 944 got into trouble was matching the 911. The 944 Turbo and 911 Carrera 3.2 had the same performance and price. The head said 944 Turbo, the heart 911 Carrera and Porsche is an enthusiasts car, so ...

Porsche 968 – The most polished four-cylinder diamond

The 1987 Wall Street Crash and ensuing shaky economic times, with early '90s recession, showed many Porsche customers were now 'greed is good' financial sector high flyers. Production of the 944 scaled down as Porsche sold off excess 944 stocks, and concentrated on upscale versions. By 1991, Porsche was making the 944 itself at Zuffenhausen, and would also do so with the car's successor, the 1993 968. This Porsche 944 MkII had a VarioCam-enhanced version of the 944 S2's 3-liter DOHC I4, and 993 like visage.

Harm Lagaay had returned to Porsche, this time as styling boss. In the '70s, he had worked on the 924 under Tony Lapine. Now, as Papa Boxster, he gave the 911 look to everything in sight, for commercial and aesthetic reasons. In the early 1990s recession, the 968's high price created glacial sales, but the stripped 968 Clubsport became a mid '90s

The 1983 928S was the fastest production car sold in America. It was also a gift for the 1983 *Playboy* 'Playmate of the Year,' Marianne Gravatte. (Courtesy Porsche Cars North America)

performance icon. A real athlete, a real sports car, a real … Porsche! It showed the BMW e36 M3 for the sports sedan it was, and prowess over Japanese high tech rivals. The 1986 Mazda RX7 was an admitted homage to the 944, and even now in the '90s, the 968's rear drive, large 3-liter atmo motor and six-speed stick were proof positive Porsche was sports car king.

There was a blown 3-liter 968 Turbo S, to homologate the 337bhp Turbo RS for the German ADAC GT Cup. However, rulebook changes left the 968 Turbo RS high and dry. These were increasingly SUV rather than sports car times. When one considers that the 2018 Porsche Cayenne is a Slovenian made SUV, related to the VW Touareg, and with a diesel variant too, the front-engined Porsche's credentials become highlighted indeed.

Big Bruder 928

The European Car of the Year title is usually won by a run of the mill, practical family car. The judges weigh such values as being very important in reaching their verdict. As a result, exotic dream cars didn't win … until now. In 1978, the Porsche 928 became the first sports car to win the European Car of the Year title. It achieved this because, being a Porsche, it was so well thought out it could do mundane and marvelous equally well. It was a 'practical supercar,' which happened to be the title of *Autocar*'s April 9, 1977 introductory story by Jeffrey Daniels. Porsche even gave the 928 a low compression ratio so it could survive in the Golden State – how thoughtful.

The trouble was, Porsche CEO Dr Ernst Fuhrmann, although a great engineer, didn't know diddly squat about demographics. Porsche has never admitted it, but it saw all those Corvette sales and thought, if we build something like that, North Americans will really flip over it! Unfortunately, domestic car buyers and import car buyers are two different tribes. So the people that wanted a car like the Corvette, bought a Corvette. The people that wanted a Porsche, bought a … 911.

Ferry got a new 300 horse 928S for his 70th

birthday. However, by 1981 the 928 wasn't traveling well on 5000 annual sales. Zuffenhausen had expected 10,000. In this recessionary time after the second gas crunch, the 911 was on 10,000 sales, with the 924/944 on 17,000. Persistent Porsche kept improving the 928, and in 1983 it was a headline grabber, in more ways than one. It was the fastest production car one could buy in America. It was a cinema darling in two hit movies *Risky Business* and *Scarface*, starring Tom Cruise and Al Pacino respectively. If that wasn't enough, the 1983 Playboy Playmate of the Year Marianne Gravatte received a red Porsche 928S. Playboy had stopped gifting pink cars to the Playmates, because that's sexist!

Even with such achievements, the 928 was still struggling. TV's *MotorWeek* took a new 928S and Chevy Camaro Z/28 to Summit Point raceway in 1983. Here, the proletariat's coupe outlapped the 928S, albeit with a lot less finesse. Indeed, some oversteer outtakes made the Chebby worthy of TV's

America's Funniest Home Videos. Then there was the general sentiment that the 928 was the perfect Porsche for people that didn't like Porsches (911).

In April 1983, *Car and Driver* took the 928S, 911SC and Audi Quattro to Sears Point and let former Formula One champion Phil Hill try them out. *C&D* folks tried them too. Hill lapped faster in the 928S than the 911SC, a 1:10.20 versus 1:10.35, and the 928 had a precise threading through the eye of a needle response, lacking in the 911. Although Hill reckoned the 928 to be a big car with a meaty shift, he liked it and thought it was the most fun of the three. Hill also said the 928's great competence showed it came from excellent Porsche racing stock. Ferry Porsche was still around when all the front-engined Porsches were current. He wouldn't have wanted the Porsche honor sullied by average cars. The front-engined Porsches, were Porsches.

As it stood, the 928 was often bought by celebrities and rich folk. Mainly because it was

Opposite and below: Mild bodykit and Smurf Blue paint job aside, Strosek didn't play too much with Harm Lagaay's 968. (www.strosek.de)

an expensive status symbol and it was a Porsche. Charlie Sheen had one. Regardless of all this, the 928S became the 928S2, S3, S4, GT and finally the 350bhp 5.4-liter 928 GTS. In Porsche's own words, that final edition represented Zuffenhausen "polishing the diamond," or making it as good as it can be. There was even the nifty, stripped 928S4 Clubsport. So focused, it was the only 928 road car delivered, with a lightweight a/c system. You need to save weight with the condenser, electrical wiring harness, etc. Racers that they were, Porsche understood this!

In 1971, Porsche started working on the 928 as the 911's eventual replacement. The 924 started as a junior version of the 928, as requested by VW.

Eventually, Porsche 928 GTS and 968 production fell to a respective two and four cars per day by 1995. This, and the fact that under 3000 968s were produced in entirety, matters not a whit. Both cars represented the ultimate in front-engined Porsche evolution. They were well-made, competent sports cars that reversed Porsche's reputation for sudden tail happy handling. A Porsche could have neutral handling, but it could never compromise. The front-engined cars never did.

Hidemi Aoki with a Porsche 928. This Hong Kong market car has a Gemballa bodykit.

(Pictures courtesy www.facebook.com/pg/swissmotorsau & www.nepoeht.com)

Appendix E
The art of Porsche

Many of the great cars of the world have been judged automotive works of art. So, it's little surprise that such cars often inspire artists to create works of art in a more traditional sense.

Tanja Stadnic

Tanja Stadnic is closely associated with the world of Porsche in this respect. With artistic passion from a young age, she went on to study formally, and is now known for vibrant acrylic interpretations of Zuffenhausen's four-wheeled creations, her working medium being linen canvas. Tanja does commissioned works of people's dream cars, and sometimes uses exotic materials to do so.

Dave 'Big' Deal

Cars and cartoons both start with the same three letters. VWs and Porsches have certainly figured prominently in the latter. To this day, the logo of custom car designer and illustrator Dave 'Big' Deal, has a black and white cartoon of Mr Deal holding a Porsche 911 under his right arm. Deal is also resting on an oversize fountain pen with his left hand. Dave Deal drew many VW Beetles, Buses and Porsches. Bob C Hardin has also done iconic illustrations depicting the work of Dr Porsche.

Above: In the history of racing, the 356 and Mille Miglia are natural partners. Tanja loves her Porsches!

Above right: Tanja Stadnic using a linen canvas, acrylic paint and real gold to capture the 911 Turbo S. (Pictures courtesy www.tanjastadnic.com)

Artist Dave 'Big' Deal, did many a VW and Porsche caricature. (Courtesy Porsche Salvage)

Bob C Hardin

Hardin has spent decades in the traditional and computer software mediums of commercial illustration. Comic books, children's books, and the rising vogue of the graphic novel. He has also provided his services to a number of well-known entities.

Bob C Hardin was a frequent contributor to *CARtoons magazine*. His famous 911SC Cabrio fantasy cartoon, is from 1983. (Courtesy Bob C Hardin)

The 911 had survived, against all odds, Jeff Bridges drove one in the like-named 1984 movie. (www.facebook.com/bob.c.hardin)

With its crazy caricatures, and car customizers Krass & Bernie, *CARtoons* has been an institution since the '50s. Marc Methot revived the publication in 2015. (www.facebook.com/MarcMethotCARtoons/)

These include rock band ZZ Top, NASCAR Team Red Bull and the US Army. The latter concerned inking in its training journal *PS* magazine. However, if you grew up in the '70s, you would recognise Bob's work from seminal cartoon caricature publication *CARtoons* magazine. It's for this publication that Hardin created his memorable Porsche 911SC Cabrio fantasy cartoon. Like the car, it's a classic!

Manu Campa
Manu Campa does ultra realistic paintings of classic cars, motorbikes and bicycles. A fine arts college graduate, he loves the effect of body panel reflections and chrome finishes. This is why he leans towards air-cooled 356s and 911s. His interest runs to all air-cooled works of the good doctor, so naturally the immortal Beetle figures prominently.

Manu also has a great love of photography, and a photograph is the starting point for his work. With clean images and amazing use of light, and using acrylics and oils, his completed works are hard to distinguish from ultra clear photographs, or even the real thing. Own a Manu Campa painting, and you are virtually a Porsche owner!

Left: The starting point for Manu's work is a photograph. He also has a great background in photography. (Courtesy manucampa.com)

Manu Campa 2016

Manu is well known for ultra realistic Porsche paintings, and is a fan of all Dr Porsche's air-cooled masterpieces. That includes the VW Beetle, naturally! (Courtesy manucampa.com)

Appendix F

The 'frontdated' 912E

Car restorers and customizers are artists too. They use certain models as a blank canvas to show their ideas. Jeremy Brooks, owner of Vancouver, Washington VW specialist Loose Nuts, is just such a fellow. With a lifelong interest in air-cooled Vee Dubs, he has also always dreamed of owning a Porsche. The start of his project involved a Porsche 912E. In the last ten years, backdated Porsches have become big news. That is, taking a younger Porsche 911, and making it look like an earlier model using trim pieces, decals, altered color schemes, early 911 accessories, etc. Why do they do this? Some like the look of older 911s, but prefer the practicality of a newer air-cooled edition. Especially if they are going racing. Perhaps, because they will never be able to afford a genuine '73 911 Carrera RS 2.7? Then again, maybe they just like backdating for the hell of it!

A customizing trend that has been going on even longer is upgrading an early 911 with the visual and mechanical refinements of later model 911s. A 3.2-liter conversion for a two-liter 911? 964 power seats in a '74 G series? Retrofitting all-wheel drive and ABS, on a chrome bumper 911 might prove a challenge. However, if you have the time, budget and skill, it's doable. Backdating and 'frontdating' between the O series 911 and 993 is possible, due to the tremendous constancy of the air-cooled 911 design. This means there is interchangeability between parts from the various eras. Whereas other companies went clean sheet every few years, Dr Porsche's Beetle, 356 and 911 believed in evolution. This historical fact helps customizers.

Jeremy's 912E was involved in an auto accident, prior to his ownership, in the early 2000s. The coupe was then dry stored, with its motor, gearbox and rear section of the wiring harness going to another 912E that had caught fire. Jeremy sent his dry stored 912E body to the body shop Body Worx in Eugene, Oregon, to get the tub straightened out. Early parts amassed for the project were Euro headlights, VW Type 4 motor and 901 gearbox. Powerwise, this was done with a view to utilize Weber 44 carbs, already at the Loose Nuts workshop. There were also genuine Fuchs and a NOS backlight.

Removing the rear body sections facilitated measuring and careful checking before cutting. With everything lined up, a patch panel was used to fix the upper corner of the rear window. Making sure the roof section squared up with the rear quarters was key. This was followed by welding new metal sections to complete the bodyshell.

Jeremy then had a change of heart and decided to build a 964 style 911 – he has always liked that generation – so it was time to sell the early era Fuchs, and get 964 front and rear fascias and side rocker panels, along with the rear 964 bumper and back 964 decklid. Many body parts were just initially placed, without secure attachment, to judge final fit. Dents and dings had to be repaired, and housings/brackets for body parts made.

Paul Lozzio helped work out the offsets for custom wheels. These were sized 18x7in front and 18x9.5in out back. Intermediate plans for a Subie motor swap were axed. In its place came a 911 flat-six, a 2.2-liter mill with 40mm Zenith carbs. The unit was disassembled and cleaned. Carrera hydro chain tensioners and 930 valve covers were upgrades.

Opposite: Jeremy Brooks' Porsche project started with an accident-damaged 912E. A proprietor of VW specialist Loose Nuts, Jesse had a long time dream of owning a Porsche.

As a 964 fan, Jeremy chose this version as the frontdated 912E target. Body Worx of Oregon straightened out the 912E body.

Engine choices went from a VW Type 4 with dual Weber 44s, to a Subaru swap, before finishing with a 2.2-liter 911 flat-six, with Zenith carbs.

1980s 911 Carrera hydraulic chain tensioners, 930 valve covers and 18in custom alloy rims were some of the upgrades (Pictures all courtesy www.vwloosenuts.com)

Appendix G
Carrera RX –
the Rallycross 911

This page and overleaf, top: This is the Carrera RX built to compete in the SCCA Detroit Region Rallycross
series. It dominated the 2013 and 2014 racing seasons, winning the series two years in a row.
(Courtesy www.teamilluminata.com/Scott Banes)

Below and opposite, top: In the Rallycross series, the Carrera RX was up against a couple of Porsche 944s. As part of the rules, the Carrera RX's use of BRAID Wheels' rims took the coupe out of the stock class. The original a/c compressor had to be installed also. (Courtesy www.BRAIDUSA.com)

Below and next page, top: Carrera RX is influenced by the Rothmans livery of the 1980s Porsche 911 and 959 rally cars. However, some colors come from Team Illuminata and sponsor BRAID Wheels USA. Carrera RX has a gray stripe, and uses yellow instead of gold. (Courtesy www.teamilluminata.com)

Right and opposite, top: The Carrera RX project started with a 1984 911 Carrera with 100,000 miles on the odometer. In racing, Paul Eddleston shared the car with a professional racer, but did get the edge on him a couple of times. Today, Carrera RX is semi retired, being taken out occasionally for fun. (Courtesy www.BRAIDUSA.com)

It's the 1987 Porsche line-up, from ever so humble 924S to very mighty 959! (Courtesy Porsche)

Appendix H
Porsche-Audi & VW items of interest

ruf-automobile.de

Since the mid 1970s, Alois Ruf Jr has been making the Porsches of dreams. The original 1978 911 SCR and '80s Yellowbird have become legends. Today's RUFs represent highly individual interpretations of the Porsche 911 concept.

www.strosek.de

Starting in the early 1980s with resculpted exteriors and wild horsepower for his Porsche 928, Vittorio Strosek has gone on to carry out extravagant reworkings of the 964 and 993 911s.

www.gemballa.com

Gemballa GmbH was founded in 1981 by engineer Uwe Gemballa, starting out by modifying Porsches. By the mid '80s Gemballa's Avalanche, Cyrrus and Mirage represented complete 911-based cars. The firm has continued as a car maker ever since.

www.urbanoutlawshop.com

Avant garde Porsche interpreter Magnus Walker's love and interest in matters 911 started at the 1977 Earl's Court Motor Show in Britain. Today, he is known to have stockpiled several 924 Turbos!

https://rwb.jp

RAUH-Welt BEGRIFF, or RWB, sounds German, but happens to be a Japanese Porsche tuning house. Started by Akira Nakai, the company was a small countryside bodyshop in Chiba Prefecture, and now does extreme body-in-white 911 projects.

www.audicentreperth.com.au

The Audi Centre Perth is your first stop for Ingolstadt's finest in Perth, Western Australia, the state's only authorized Audi dealer!

www.vwloosenuts.com

Vancouver, Washington-based air-cooled VW specialist Loose Nuts does unique things to Dr Porsche's early work, such as Safari window kits for Type 1 and Type 3 Squarebacks. Loose Nuts owner Jeremy Brooks also knows his way around a Porsche 911.

"*Beauty is in the eye of the beholder*" Margaret Wolfe Hungerford, *Molly Bawn*, 1878

Steve McQueen, Sean Connery, Janis Joplin and James Dean have all famously owned a Porsche 356, arguably one of the world's most stunning car designs of all time. An undoubted classic, often copied, but never equalled.

Veloce proudly presents *The Ultimate Book of the Porsche 356*. A new, individually numbered, luxury leatherbound and slip-cased limited edition comprising just 356 copies. The definitive and fascinating account of the Porsche 356, and all the racing and rallying cars that sprang from it, told in breathtaking detail by marque expert Brian Long.

Stunning colour and historic photographs, colour and trim options, range details, engine specifications, chassis numbers, and production figures from the Gmünd cars to the very last production models, make this exclusive edition an historical reference to treasure. Truly a Catalogue Raisonné for the world's most discerning Porsche 356 enthusiasts.

www.ultimate356.veloce.co.uk

At Veloce, we've produced *just a few* Porsche books over the years ...

As an automotive publisher of some standing, we at Veloce have come to know and represent many marques over the years. Porsche is one of those much-loved marques and one that has an incredibly comprehensive history both on and off the track. Veloce has had the honour of producing many books by well-known expert

... and, just like Porsches, it would be wrong not to want them all, wouldn't it?

authors about all aspects of the continually unfolding Porsche story, and there will be more to come in the future.

Look online and find your next favourite Porsche book, or, at a substantial saving on the cost of a real Porsche, buy one as a gift for a loved one.

VELOCE.CO.UK

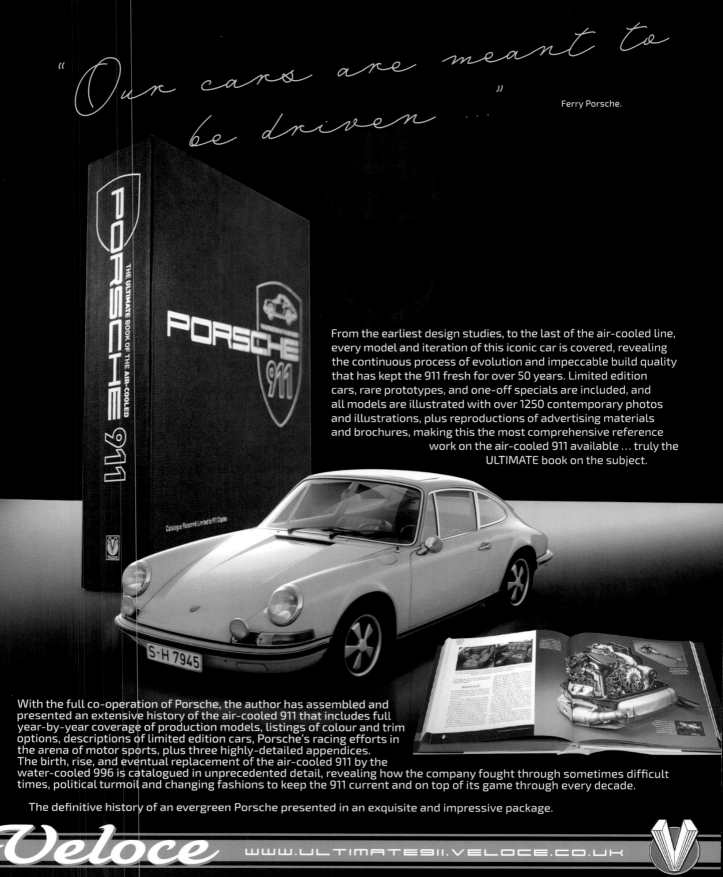

"Our cars are meant to be driven ..."

Ferry Porsche.

THE ULTIMATE BOOK OF THE AIR-COOLED

PORSCHE 911

Catalogue Raisonné Limited to 911 Copies

From the earliest design studies, to the last of the air-cooled line, every model and iteration of this iconic car is covered, revealing the continuous process of evolution and impeccable build quality that has kept the 911 fresh for over 50 years. Limited edition cars, rare prototypes, and one-off specials are included, and all models are illustrated with over 1250 contemporary photos and illustrations, plus reproductions of advertising materials and brochures, making this the most comprehensive reference work on the air-cooled 911 available ... truly the ULTIMATE book on the subject.

With the full co-operation of Porsche, the author has assembled and presented an extensive history of the air-cooled 911 that includes full year-by-year coverage of production models, listings of colour and trim options, descriptions of limited edition cars, Porsche's racing efforts in the arena of motor sports, plus three highly-detailed appendices. The birth, rise, and eventual replacement of the air-cooled 911 by the water-cooled 996 is catalogued in unprecedented detail, revealing how the company fought through sometimes difficult times, political turmoil and changing fashions to keep the 911 current and on top of its game through every decade.

The definitive history of an evergreen Porsche presented in an exquisite and impressive package.

Veloce

WWW.ULTIMATE911.VELOCE.CO.UK

Index